THE MUSIC

ADDRESS BOOK

THE MUSIC

ADDRESS BOOK

2ND EDITION

HOW TO REACH ANYONE

WHO'S ANYONE IN MUSIC

MICHAEL LEVINE

HarperPerennial

A Division of HarperCollins*Publishers*

HarperCollins books may be purchased for educational, business, or sales promotional use. For information please write: Special Markets Department, HarperCollins Publishers, Inc., 10 East 53rd Street, New York, NY 10022.

FIRST EDITION

Designed by George J. McKeon

Library of Congress Cataloging-in-Publication Data
Levine, Michael, 1954–
  The music address book : how to reach anyone who's anyone in music / Michael
Levine. — 2nd ed.
    p. cm.
  ISBN 0-06-273257-9
  1. Popular music—Directories. I. Title.
ML12.L48 1994
781.64'025—dc20   93-21463
                                                       MN

94 95 96 97 98 ❖/HC 10 9 8 7 6 5 4 3 2 1

CONTENTS

ACKNOWLEDGMENTS

With lovers and friends, I still can recall.
Some are dead and some are living.
In my life, I've loved them all.

Saying thank you to my friends and family somehow seems so inadequate. It's what I say to people who hold the elevator door open for me.

So, to the following loyal friends and family I send my love and deepest appreciation through these words.

Special thanks to Craig Nelson, who inspired me to write this book in the first place.

My brilliant literary agent and friend, Alice Martell, and her assistant.

My encouraging friends at HarperCollins: Nancy Peske, Lisa Berkowitz, Maureen O'Neill, Bill Shinker and Susan Moldow.

My dedicated father Arthur O. Levine, stepmother Marilyn, and sister Patty.

My special friends: Tina Abas, Keith Atkinson, Rana Bendixon and Sorrell, Ken Bostic, Bill Calkins, Susan Gauthier, Bill Hooper, Richard Imprescia, Bette Geller Jackson, Lori and Lisa Kleinman, Bonnie Larson, Richard Lawson, Karen L'Heureux, Nancy Mager, John McKillop, Dennis Prager, Joshua Trabulus, Michael and Deborah Viner and Earlene White.

My wonderful business partners Mitchell Schneider and Monique Moss.

My office family Victoria Archer, Kristine Ashton, Todd Brodginski, Amanda Cagan, Roxanna Castillo, Tracie Collins, Naomi Goldman, Jeff Golenberg, Rob Hazelton, Kim Kaiman, Kathy Koehler, Kevin Koffler, Matt Labov, Howard Lorey, Julie Nathanson, Robert Pietranton, Tresa Redburn-Cody, Marcee Rondan, Beth Seligman, Jane Singer, Melissa Spraul, Samantha Wright, Lesley Zimmerman and Tami Zummallen.

My business associates Charles Sussman, Patty Grabowski, Laura Herlovich, Mark Kaplan, Joy Sapieka, and Terrie Williams.

Endless gratitude to Kathleen Conner for her hard work in helping bring this book to life.

HOW TO USE THIS BOOK

The world of popular music is an enormously large one. There are artists in rock, country, jazz, R&B, pop, blues, gospel, ethnic, big band, middle-of-the-road, and folk, plus newer genres such as rap, heavy metal, adult contemporary, and new age. Behind the scenes are record producers, songwriters, record company executives, journalists, disc jockeys, music video directors, and on and on. I have attempted to include as many of the most important people as possible, ranging over as many musical styles as there are, all in this one volume.

It was often difficult deciding whether someone should be included. To those inadvertently left out, my apologies. To those who were considered but did not make the final cut, maybe you will next time.

For fans, here's your opportunity to write to your favorite artists. For musicians, here are the people who can help you get ahead in the music industry. For both, remember that as in any entertainment field people tend to move and change addresses frequently—as do agents, managers, record companies, and so on. I have included the latest and most reliable addresses anywhere. Even if a person is no longer there by the time you mail a letter, it's a start in tracking that person to his or her current business address. I strongly urge you not to show up in person to those included here, but rather to send a letter. It's professional and it's courteous.

For behind-the-scenes talent, I've identified what they're largely known for, such as record production or songwriting. However, I haven't separated or identified performers with a particular musical style. The way I look at it, music is *music*, not *labels*. Diversity and new horizons are what music is about—and, in its own way, what this book is about too. Enjoy!

IF YOU ARE A MUSICIAN...
GETTING YOUR MUSIC HEARD

Everyone in the music business is looking for that tremendously talented artist and that Number One hit. But no record company executive, music publisher, agent, manager, or producer knows who that artist is or what that song sounds like—until he or she hears it. That's why they are on a never-ending talent search. But while some may attend live performances, most spend the majority of their time listening to demo tapes. Each and every day they listen to dozens of tapes, trying to find an undiscovered but gifted songwriter or musician.

Many of these tapes reach them via mail or are delivered to their offices. Some come recommended, others are unsolicited. If yours is in the latter category, being heard, and heard promptly, will be tougher but by no means impossible. If your song is good, it doesn't make any difference who you are. They will want you.

So, how do you get your music heard? You've already taken an important step by having this book in your hands. You now have the names and direct addresses of many of the people who can help you with your career. Write or call them and ask if they are accepting new material. Never send a demo to the A&R (Artist & Repertoire) department of a record company without specifying an individual's name. If you do, your music may end up in the circular file.

The following are some of the most commonly asked questions about breaking into the music business and hopefully some helpful answers:

Q. What is a demo?
A. In the music business, people want to hear your work, not read it. Sometimes you'll get the chance to play it for a producer or record company executive in person. But more often than not, you'll need to deliver your work to them, and that's done in the form of an audio tape. A demonstration tape, or demo, is a simply but professionally produced four-song audio cassette, engineered in a recording studio.

Q.*How do I mail or deliver my demo?*
A.Use a padded envelope or small box to present your demo. If it's coming ""over the transom" (i.e., you're sending it to a stranger), give it the best chance for success by using a printed or typed return address on the envelope, preferably using a business name. Sloppily written and illegible addressing will hardly show a stranger that you're a serious, professional artist. You can send your demo first-class, but if you're doing a mass mailing and need to save money, there is also a less expensive class of mail specifically for audio recordings. Tell the counter person at your local post office that enclosed is an audio cassette. If there is also a letter enclosed, tell the postal employee that too. You'll be charged the going rate for a first-class letter, but the rest of the weight will be at the lower fee.

Q.*What do I say in the cover letter?*
A.Every demo should include a cover letter. If not, it will be tossed away. If you have an agent, manager, otherwise-important-person, or friend of the addressee who can make sure that you'll be paid attention to, have them write the letter, on their letterhead.

In the cover letter, briefly explain who you are (a photo might be useful, too). Ask for the addressee's comments, suggestions, etc. Be friendly and creative but also get to the point. There's no need to go on about how "this is the next Number One record." Music industry professionals know it's not that easy. It will signal to them that you're new to the business, and that means more work for them.

Q.*What else should I include in the envelope?*
A.Make certain your name, address, and telephone number are written on the tape. Also, include a list of the songs in the order they're heard on the tape and a typed lyric sheet for each song, again with your name, address, telephone number, and the copyright notice on each. Just as important (if you want a response or want the tape returned), include a self-addressed, stamped envelope.

Q.*I'm worried about someone stealing my song. How can I protect my rights when I send a tape of my music?*
A.Once you write a song, it's yours, you own it. But it's best if you *register* that copyright with the government. Registration makes it much easier in a court of law if there is ever a problem. You can do this by registering your copyright with the U.S. Library of Congress Copyright Office. You will need either Form PA (for music sheets or song lyrics) or Form SR (for

sound recordings). Form SR covers the recording itself as well as the music and lyrics that have been recorded. So if you use Form SR, you don't need to use Form PA. You can get the necessary forms by writing the Copyright Office, Library of Congress, Washington, D.C. 20559; or by calling the 24-hour hotline number (202) 287-9100 and telling the message machine which forms you need. You can also pick up forms at any U.S. Government Printing Office.

When you complete and return the forms, you will also need to include one non-returnable copy of the work, whether a song or lyric sheet, or a tape cassette. Copyright registration costs $10 for each separate work. However, if you are registering many songs and want to save a few dollars, simply send all your songs on one cassette. For the $10 fee, they will all be copyrighted at once, provided you give the collection a single title. Even something as simple as "The Works of Jane Smith" will do. If you want the individual titles listed too, file Form CA with another $10 fee.

After filing, you will receive a certification. You may then print a copyright notice on your work. The notice should read: Copyright (Year) by (Your Name). Copyright protection lasts for 50 years after the death of the last surviving writer of the song.

If you need further information, call the Copyright Office at (202) 287-8700, or write to the Information and Publications Section, LM-455, Copyright Office, Library of Congress, Washington, D.C. 20559.

AVOIDING RIPOFFS

Here are some professional tips (from interviews with leaders within the music industry) for avoiding ripoffs.

•Never pay a company to connect you with a collaborator. If you need a collaborator, try searching for organizations that offer collaboration services to their members.

•Don't pay to have your lyrics or poems set to music. For a fee, "music mills" might use the same tune for hundreds of lyrics and poems, whether it sounds good or not. Publishers will identify one of these melodies as soon as they hear it.

•Don't pay to have your songs published. An established company interested in your songs will assume the responsibility *and* the cost of promoting your work. That company invests in your song because it anticipates a profit once the song is recorded and released.

•Never sell your songs unconditionally. It's dishonest for anyone to offer you such a deal.

•Don't pay to have your material "reviewed" by a company that may be interested in recording, producing, or publishing it. Distinguished companies review material free of charge as a means of searching for hits for their artists or recording projects. Of course, consultation and critique by another songwriter, or by someone not in search of original material, is a different matter.

•Read all contracts carefully before signing. Never sign any contract you're in doubt about or don't understand. Never assume that any contract is better than no contract at all. Remember it's well worth paying an attorney to review a contract before you sign it, thus avoiding a bad situation later that may cost you thousands of dollars in royalties if your song becomes a hit.

ARE YOU ANYONE?

The Music Address Book is updated frequently, and you can take an active role in this procedure. If you are notable in any field (or know someone who is), send your name, mailing address, and some documentation of your notability (newspaper clippings are effective) for possible inclusion in our next edition.

Also, we are very interested in learning of any success stories that may have resulted from *The Music Address Book*.

Write to:

Michael Levine, Author
The Music Address Book
8730 Sunset Blvd., Sixth Floor
Los Angeles, CA 90069

If you have found *The Music Address Book: How to Reach Anyone Who's Anyone in Music* to be useful, you may also find its predecessors, *The Address Book: How to Reach Anyone Who's Anyone* (Perigee) and *The Kid's Address Book* (Perigee), of assistance.

THE ADDRESSES

A

Music is well said to be the speech of angels.
—THOMAS CARLYLE

A & M Records, Inc.
1416 N. LaBrea Ave.
Hollywood, CA 90028
record company

A & M Records, Inc.
New York
595 Madison Ave.
New York, NY 10022

A & R Records
900 19th Ave. S, #207
Nashville, TN 37212
Ruthie Steele, Owner
independent record label

A Good Old Summer Time
State Office Bldg.
207 Genessee St.
Utica, NY 13501
music festival

A La Mode
8489 West 3rd St.
Los Angeles, CA 90048
hairstylist/makeup rep

'A' Train Management & Consulting
P.O. Box 29242
Oakland, CA 94604
Al Evers, President

A°Vision Entertainment
75 Rockefeller Plaza
New York, NY 10019
Diane Zabawski, GM

a-ha
c/o Warner Bros.
3300 Warner Blvd.
Burbank, CA 91510
group

A-WY Entertainment/Hype Productions
6619 Leland Way, #212
Hollywood, CA 90028
Bill Wyatt
artist management

A.C. Entertainment Inc.
52 Carmine St., #12
New York, NY 10014
Anthony Countey
artist management

A.R.M.
792 29th Ave. SE
Minneapolis, MN 55414
artist management

Aaron & LeDuc
Video Production
2002 21st St., #A
Santa Monica, CA 90404
Greg LeDuc
music video production company

Abacus Pictures
9336 Washington Blvd.
Culver City, CA 90230
Elizabeth Ward, President
music video production company

Abba
P.O. Box 26072 S-100 41
Stockholm, Sweden
group

Abbado, Claudio
c/o Columbia Artists Management
165 West 57th St.
New York, NY 10019
conductor

Abdul, Paula
12424 Wilshire Blvd., #770
Los Angeles, CA 90024
singer.

ABKCo Records
1700 Bradway, 41st Fl.
New York, NY 10019
independent record label

Abnak Records
P.O. Box 5807
Englewood, NJ 07631
Philip Kurnit, Agent
independent record label

Abono, Debbie
1674 Matheson Rd.
Concord, CA 94521
artist management

Abrams, Muhal Richard
P.O. Box 612 Times Square Station
New York, NY 10108
pianist, composer

Abramson, Rochelle Susan
c/o L.A. Philharmonic
135 N. Grand Ave.
Los Angeles, CA 90012
violinist

Abravanel, Maurice
123 S. 7th S.
Salt Lake City, UT 84102
musical director

Absolut Management Group
1203 Preservation Park Way, #300
Oakland, CA 94612
Mark A. Hooker, CEO
artist management

Absolute Pitch
3378 W. Harvard
Santa Ana, CA 92704
Bill Laster
independent record label

Absolute-A-Go-Go
P.O. Box 187
Oakland, NJ 07436
Brad Morrison
independent record label

AC/DC
11 Leonminster Road, Morden
Surrey SM4 U.K.
group

Acacia Records
14150 Fielding St.
Detroit, MI 48233
Kelli Hand, CEO
independent record label

Academy Film Productions, Inc.
210 W. 29th St.
Baltimore, MD 21211
video production company

Academy of Country Music
6255 Sunset Blvd., #923
Hollywood, CA 90028
Fran Boyd,
Executive Director

**Academy of Country Music
Awards Programs**
Entertainment Media Corp.
P.O. Box 2772
Palm Springs, CA 92263
published lists

**Academy of Motion Picture
Arts and Sciences**
8949 Wilshire Blvd.
Beverly Hills, CA 90211
Karl Malden, President
OSCAR's parents

**Academy of Television Arts
and Sciences**
3500 W. Olive Ave., #700
Burbank, CA 91505
James L. Loper,
Executive Director
Emmy's parents

**Accordion Federation of North
America**
11438 Elmcrest St.
El Monte, CA 91732

Accurate Records
P.O. Box 390115
Cambridge, MA 02139
Russ Gershon
independent record label

Ace
P.O. Box 11201
Shawnee Mission, KS 66207
magazine for people interested
in underground and pirate radio
stations

Ace Beat Records
6 Blossom Ct.
Daly City, CA 94014
Alex Aquino
independent record label

Acid Ceiling Records
913 Walnut Ave.
Huntington Beach, CA 92648
Craig O'Keefe
independent record label

Acoustic Alchemy
c/o GRP
555 W. 57th St.
New York, NY 10019
group

Acoustic Guitar
The String Letter Corporation
412 Red Hill Ave., #15
San Anselmo, CA 94960
David A. Lusterman,
Publisher magazine

Acousticats, The
c/o Carlin
411 Ferry St., #4
Martinez, CA 94533
group

Act of Balance
B Dunollie Rd., Kentish Town
London, NW5 3AA U.K.
Phil Rapier
video production company

Act One Entertainment
P.O. Box 1079
New Haven, CT 06504
Johnny Parris,
President/Owner
artist management

Adamany, Ken Associates
315 W. Gorham St.
Madison, WI 53703
artist management

Adams, Bryan
1416 N. LaBrea Ave.
Hollywood, CA 90028
singer

Adams, Stanley
c/o ASCAP
1 Lincoln Plaza
New York, NY 10023
lyricist

ADC Band
17397 Santa Barbara
Detroit, MI 48221
group

Addis/Wechsler & Associates
955 S. Carillo Dr., 3rd Fl.
Los Angeles, CA 90048
Danny Heaps
artist management

Adelphi Records Inc.
P.O. Box 7688
Silver Spring, MD 20907
Jon Curlin, VP/A&R
independent record label

Adirondack Festival of American Music
P.O. Box 562
Saranac Lake, NY 12983

Adler, Richard
8 E. 83rd St.
New York, NY 10028
composer, lyricist

Adler, Samuel Hans
26 Gibbs St.
Rochester, NY 14604
conductor, composer

Adobe Records
P.O. Box W
Shallowater, TX 79363
Tom Woodruff, President
independent record label

Adoration Inc.
6750 W. 75th St., #2-A
Overland Park, KS 66204
Jim Tatom, President
artist management

Advance Entertainment
5 Locust Place
Livingston, NJ 07039
Ed Pudliesi
artist management

Adventure Discs
P.O. Box 14581
Alburquerque, NM 87191
Craig Evans
independent record label

Adwater & Stir Inc.
9000 Sunset Blvd., #405
Los Angeles, CA 90069
Andrew Frances, President
artist management

Aegis Entertainment
1370 6th Ave., 26th Fl.
New York, NY 10019
independent record label

Aerosmith
c/o Fan Club
P.O. Box 4668
San Francisco, CA 94101
rock group

Affirmative Action
c/o Rainforest
225 N. New Hampshire Ave.
Los Angeles, CA 90004
Ed Davis
group

Aftershock
c/o Virgin
1790 Broadway, 20th Fl.
New York, NY 10019
group

AFTRA
(American Federation of TV
and Radio Artists)
260 Madison Ave.
New York, NY 10016
John C. Hall, Jr.,
Executive Secretary

Agency, The
41 Britain St., #200
Toronto, Ontario M5A 1R7
Canada
artist management

**AGF Entertainment/Shelter
Island Sound**
30 W. 21st St., 7th Fl.
New York, NY 10010
Ron Fierstein
artist management

Agitpop
c/o Twin/Tone
2541 Nicollet Ave.
Minneapolis, MN 55404
group

AGM Management
1680 N. Vine St., #1101
Hollywood, CA 90028
Tony Meilandt
artist management

AGVA
American Guild of Variety Artists
184 5th Ave.
New York, NY 10010

Ahimsa Management
34 W. 76th St., #1
New York, NY 10023
video production

AIE Records
3441 Cahuenga Blvd. W
Hollywood, CA 90068
Ryan Sangha
independent record label

Aigyle Music
6 Danielie Dr. Malahide Rd.
Dublin EIR 5 Ireland
video production

Air Supply
1990 S. Bundy Dr., #590
Los Angeles, CA 90025
group

Air Supply Fan Club
14755 Ventura Blvd., #1-710
Sherman Oaks, CA 91403

Air Tight Management
P.O. Box 113
Winchester Center, CT 06094
Jack Forchette
artist management

Akiyama, Kuzuyoshi
411 Montgomery St.
Syracuse, NY 13202
conductor

AKO Productions
20531 Plummer St.
Chatsworth, CA 91311
A.E. Sullivan
artist management

Akos, Francis
220 S. Michigan Ave.
Chicago, IL 60604
violinist

Alabama
P.O. Box 529
Ft. Payne, AL 35967
country music group

Alabama Fan Club
207 Gault Ave.
Ft. Payne, AL 35967

Alabanese, Licia
Nathan Hale Dr.
Wilson Point, S. Norwalk, CT 06854
operatic soprano

Alaska Video Productions
P.O. Box 80545
Fairbanks, AK 99708

Albert, Stephen Joel
P.O. Box 343
Newtonville, MA 02160
composer

Alcantara, Theo
711 Penn Ave. 8th Fl.
Pittsburgh, PA 15222
conductor

Alcazar Records
P.O. Box 429/Demerritt Pl.
Waterbury, VT 05676
Murray Krugman, CEO
independent record label

Alert Management
41 Britain St., #305
Toronto, Ontario M5A 1R7
Canada
Kathy Meisler
artist management

Alexas Music Productions
3365 W. Millerberg Way
West Jordan, UT 84084
Pat Melfi, Managing Partner
artist management

Alfred University Summer Chamber Music Institute
c/o Alfred University Summer
School
P.O. Box 826
Alfred, NY 14802

Alias Records
374 Brannan St.
San Francisco, CA 94107
Lorry Fleming
independent record label

Alifera, Greg Management
3406 N. Ocean Blvd.
Fort Lauderdale, FL 33308
artist management

Aliso Creek Productions Inc.
P.O. Box 8174
Van Nuys, CA 91409
William Williams, President
independent record label

Alive Enterprises Inc.
8912 Burton Way
Beverly Hills, CA 90211
Shep Gordon, Personal
Manager
artist management

**All American Association of
Contest Judges**
1627 Lay Blvd.
Kalamazoo, MI 49001
judges of High School music:
bands, chorus, etc.

Allegro Artists
33555 Lenox Rd. NE, #750
Atlanta, GA 30326
Tom Barfield
artist management

Allegro Productions
1000 Clint Moore Rd., #211
Boca Raton, FL 33487
video production company

Allen, Betty
Harlem School of Arts
645 St. Nicholas Ave.
New York, NY 10030
mezzo-soprano

Allen, Bruce Talent
406-68 Water St.
Vancouver BC V6B 1A4 Canada
Bruce Allen, President
artist management

Allers, Franz
c/o Columbia Artists
165 W. 57th St.
New York, NY 10019
conductor

Alliance Artists Ltd.
3423 Piedmont Rd. NE, #220
Atlanta, GA 30305
Charlie Brusco, President
artist management, promotions

Alligator Artist Management
P.O. Box 60234
Chicago, IL 60660
Bruce Iglauer, President
artist management

Alligator Records
P.O. Box 60234
Chicago, IL 60660
Bruce Iglauer, President
independent record label

Allison Productions
1833 Kalakaua Ave., #404
Honolulu, HI 96815
video production company

Allisongs Inc.
1603 Horton Ave.
Nashville, TN 37212
Jim Allison,
President/Producer
independent record label

Allistro Film Corporation
616 Royal Oaks Place
Nashville, TN 37205
video production company

Allman Brothers Band, Inc.
18 Tamworth Road
Waban, MA 02168
group

Allman, Greg
1801 Century Park W.
Los Angeles, CA 90067
musician

Almara, Lucine
Metropolitan Opera House
New York, NY 10023
opera and concert singer

Almighty, The
825 8th Ave.
New York, NY 10019
group

Alpert Entertainment
1065 Maitland Commons,
#104
Maitland, FL 32751
Jeff Alpert
artist management

Alpert, Herb
Rondor Publications
360 N. La Cienega Blvd.
Los Angeles, CA 90048
music publishing company executive,
musician

Alpha International Records
1080 N. Delaware Ave.
Philadelphia, PA 19125
Rick Winward, VP/A&R
independent record label

Alshire International Inc.
1015 Isabel St., P.O. Box 7107
Burbank, CA 91510
Al Sherman, President
independent record label

Alston Management
250 W. 57th St., #603
New York, NY 10019
artist management

Alt and the Lost Civilization
c/o Atlantic
75 Rockefeller Plaza
New York, NY 10019
group

Alter, Rick Management Inc.
P.O. Box 150973
Nashville, TN 37215
artist management

Altern 8
c/o Virgin
1790 Broadway, 20th Fl.
New York, NY 10019
group

Alternative Music Hotline
10 Center St.
Califon, NJ 78301
newsletter

Alternative Tentacles
P.O. Box 424756
San Francisco, CA 94142
Greg Werckman
independent record label

Alternative Visions
2102 Ashwood Ave.
Nashville, TN 37212
Peter Lippman
video production company

Alvin and the Chipmunks
4400 Coldwater Canyon, #300
Studio City, CA 91604
group

Amadeus Music Productions
256 S. Robertson Blvd., #111
Beverly Hills, Ca 90211
Wolfgang Aichholz, President
independent record label

Amanita Artists
8 Cloisters Ct. 77 Cromwell A
London, N6 5XG Les Mills U.K.
artist management

**Amateur Organists and Keyboard
Association International**
6436 Penn Ave. S.
Richfield, MN 55423

Ambitious Lovers
c/o Elektra
345 Maple Dr., #123
Beverly Hills, CA 90210
group

America
8730 Sunset Blvd., Penthouse
Los Angeles, CA 90069
group

American Accordion Musicological Society
334 S. Broadway
Pitman, NJ 08071
Stanley Darrow, Secretary

American Bach Foundation
1211 Potomac St., NW
Washington, DC 20007
Raizza Tselentis Chadwell, President

American Bandmasters Association
110 Wyanoke Dr.
San Antonio, TX 78209
Dr. Richard E. Thurston,
Secretary/Treasurer

American Bands Management Inc.
P.O. Box 840607
Houston, TX 77084
John Blomstrom, President
artist management

American Banjo Fraternity
271 McKinley St.
Pittsburgh, PA 15221
Norman W. Azinger, Executive Secretary

American Beethoven Society
c/o Center for Beethoven Studies
San Jose State University
1 Washington Sq.
San Jose, CA 95192
Dr. William Meredith, Director and Editor

American Berlin Opera Foundation
666 5th Ave., 21st Fl.
New York, NY 10103
Christa Drechsler, Executive Director

American Choral Directors Association
P.O. Box 6310
Lawton, OK 73506
Dr. Gene Brooks, Executive Director

American Choral Foundation
c/o Chorus America
2111 Sansom St.
Philadelphia, PA 19103
Kenneth Garner, Executive Director

American Composers Alliance
170 W. 74th St.
New York, NY 10023
Rosalie Calabrese, Executive Director

American Federation of Musicians of the U.S. and Canada
Paramount Building
1501 Broadway, #600
New York, NY 10036

American Federation of Pueri Cantores
(Children in Roman Catholic Church Choirs)
5445 11th Ave., N
St. Petersburg, FL 33710
William Tapp, Executive Officer

American Festival of Microtonal Music
c/o Johnny Reinhard
318 E. 70th St., #5FW
New York, NY 10021

American Folk Music & Folklore Recordings
American Folklife Center
Library of Congress
Washington, DC 20540
annual list

American Gramaphone Records
9130 Mormon Bridge Rd.
Omaha, NE 68152
Michael Delich, National Sales Dir.
independent record label

American Guild of English Hand-bell Ringers
1055 E. Centerville Station
Dayton, OH 45459
Vic Kostenko, Executive Director

American Guild of Music
5354 Washington St.
Downers Grover, IL 60515
Elmer Herrick, Executive Director

American Guild Of Music Artists
1727 Broadway
New York, NY 10036

American Guild of Organists
475 Riverside Dr., #1260
New York, NY 10115
David Nelson Coburn II, Executive
Director

American Harp Society
6331 Quebec Dr.
Hollywood, CA 90068
Dorothy Remsen, Executive Secretary

American Institute for Verdi Studies
New York University Department of
Music
Faculty of Arts and Science
24 Waverly Pl., #268
New York, NY 10003
Dr. Martin Chusid, Director

American Institute of Musicology
Hanssler-Verlag
Bismarckstrasse 4
Postfach 1220
W-7303, Neuhausen, Germany
Dr. Carapetyan, Contact

American Israel Opera Foundation
185 Madison Ave.
New York, NY 10016
Efraim Margolin, President

American Liszt Society
c/o Fernando Laires
210 Devonshire Dr.
Rochester, NY 14625

American Lithuanian Musicians Alliance
c/o Anthony P. Gedratis
7310 S. California Ave.
Chicago, IL 60629

American Music Center
(U.S. Information Center for American Music)
30 W. 26th St., #1001
New York, NY 10010
Nancy Clarke, Executive Director

American Music Conference
303 E. Wacker Dr., #1214
Chicago, IL 60601
Paul Bjorneberg, Director
sponsors school and church music

American Music Festival
c/o National Gallery of Art
6th St. and Constitution Ave. NW
Washington, DC 20565

American Music Festival Association
2323 W. Lincoln Ave., #225
Anaheim, CA 92801
W. Harrison Wusinack, Executive
Director

American Music Scholarship Association
1826 Carew Tower
Cincinnati, OH 45202
Gloria Ackerman, Executive Director

American Music Teacher
Music Teachers National Association,
Inc.
617 Vine St.
Cincinnati, OH 45202
magazine

American Musical Instrument Society
c/o The Shrine to Music Museum
414 E. Clark St.
Vermillion, SD 57069
Margaret Downie Banks, Registrar

American Musicians Union
c/o Joe Garry
393 Tenafly Rd.
Englewood, NJ 07631

American Musicological Society
University of Pennsylvania
201 E. 34th St.
Philadelphia, PA 19104
Alvin H. Johnson, Executive Director

American Orff-Schulwerk Associa-tion
P.O. Box 391089
Cleveland, OH 44139
Cindi Wobig, Executive Secretary
music for children

American Outlines Management
1313 W. Cronelia Ave.
Chicago, IL 60657
Mindy Giles
artist management

American Radio Association
26 Journal Square, #1501
Jersey City, NJ 07306

American Record Guide
Salem Research
R.D. 1, Box 183
Stoddard Hollow Rd.
Delancey, NY 13752
magazine

American Recorder Society
580 Broadway, #1107
New York, NY 10012
Alan G. Moore, Executive Director

American Society for Jewish Music
129 W. 67th St.
New York, NY 10023
Jack Gottlieb, President

American Society of Composers, Authors and Publishers
ASCAP
1 Lincoln Plaza
New York, NY 10023

American Society of Music Arrangers and Composers
P.O. Box 11
Hollywood, CA 90078
Bonnie Janofsky, Executive
Secretary

American Songwriter Magazine
42 Music Square W.
Nashville, TN 37203
Jim Sharp, Publisher

American Symphony Orchestra League
777 14th St. NW, #500
Washington, DC 20005
Catherine French, CEO

American Theatre Organ Society
P.O. Box 417490
Sacramento, CA 95841
Douglas Fisk, Executive Director

American Union of Swedish Singers
c/o Martin Ahlm
333 N. Michigan Ave., #712
Chicago, IL 60601

American Videogram
12020 W. Pico Blvd.
Los Angeles, CA 90064
John Berzner, President/Producer
video production company

American Viola Society
c/o Alan de Veritch
24883 Sage Crest Rd.
Newhall, PA 91321

American Women Composers
1690 36th St. N.W.
Washington, DC 20007

**America's Boychoir
Federation**
120 S. 3rd St.
Connellsville, PA 15425
Rodolfo Torres, President

America's Most Wanted
151 El Camino
Beverly Hills, CA 90212
group

**Ames International Orchestra
Festival**
Ames International Orchestra
Festival Association
P.O. Box 1243
Ames, IA 50011

Amethyst Group Ltd.
273 Chippewa Dr.
Columbia, SC 29210
Ron Sparks, A&R
independent record label

AMG International
1220 E. West Highway, #118
Silver Spring, MD 20910
Edward C. Arrendell III
artist management

Amherst Records Inc.
1800 Main St.
Buffalo, NY 14208
David E. Parker, VP/GM
independent record label

Amoeba Records
5337 La Cresta Court
Los Angeles, CA 90038
Keith Holland
independent record label

Amos, Tori
c/o Atlantic
75 Rockefeller Plaza
New York, NY 10019
singer

Amphetamine Reptile
2541 Nicollet Ave. S
Minneapolis, MN 55404
Tom Hazelmyer
independent record label

AMU Quarternote
American Musicians Union
8 Tobin Ct.
Dumont, NJ 07628
union publication

Amuse America
599 Broadway, 5th Fl.
New York, NY 10012
artist management

An Emotional Fish
c/o Atlantic
75 Rockefeller Plaza
New York, NY 10019
group

And All That Jazz
New Orleans Jazz Club
P.O. Box 1225
Kerrville, TX 78029
magazine

And Why Not?
c/o Island
8920 Sunset Blvd., 2nd Fl.
Los Angeles, CA 90069
group

Anderson, Don Inc.
840 Malcolm Rd., #170
Burlingame, CA 94010
artist management

Anderson, Donna Kay
262 Music
SUNY Cortland
Cortland, NY 13045
musicologist

Anderson, June
c/o Columbia Artists
165 W. 57th St.
New York, NY 10019
soprano

Anderson, Lynne (Rene)
c/o Buddy Lee Attractions
38 Music Sq. E.
Nashville, TN 37203
singer

Anderson, Marian
40 W. 57th St.
New York, NY 10019
contralto

Anderson, Ray
Entertainment Inc.
626 Las Lomas Ave.
Pacific Palisades, CA 90272
artist management

Anderson, Robert Theodore
Music Division
Southern Methodist University
School of Arts
Dallas, TX 75275
organist, educator

Anderson, Scott David
1441 Kapiolani Blvd.
Honolulu, HI 96814
clarinetist

Anderson, Thomas Jefferson Jr.
Tufts University Department of Music
Medford, MA 02155
composer

Andon Artists Inc.
130 W. 57th St., #5A
New York, NY 10019
artist management

Andrews, Julie
P.O. Box 666
Beverly Hills, CA 90213
singer

Angel City Productions
7000 Romanine St.
Los Angeles, CA 90038
video production company

Angelus Entertainment
9016 Wilshire Blvd., #346
Beverly Hills, CA 90211
Pete Angelus, President
artist management

Animal Logic
c/o IRS
3939 Lankershim Blvd.
Studio City, CA 91604
group

Anka, Paul
P.O. Box 100
Carmel, CA 93921
singer

Ann Arbor May Festival
University Musical Society
Burton Memorial Tower
Ann Arbor, MI 48109

Ann Arbor Summer Festival
P.O. Box 4070
Ann Arbor, MI 48106
music festival

Ann-Margret (Olsson)
151 El Camino
Beverly Hills, CA 90212
singer

Anne Murray Fan Club
c/o Leonard T. Rambeau
4881 Yonge St., #412
Toronto, Ontario M2N 5X3 Canada

Annette Funicello Fan Club
P.O. Box 134
Nestleton, Ontario L0B 1LO Canada
Mary Lou Fitton, President

Annie Productions
P.O. Box 1294
Brighton, MI 48116
Annette Oxner, Owner
artist management

Annihilator
c/o Roadrunner
225 Lafayette, #709
New York, NY 10012
group

Annual Festival of the Arts
City of Richmond
Department of Recreation and
Parks
Richmond, VA 23219
music festival

Another Off the Wall Production
13203 Agarita Lane
Houston, TX 77083
Gene Wall
video production company

ANS International Video
91 5th Ave.
New York, NY 10003
music video production company

Ansbacher, Charles Alexander
P.O. Box 1692
Colorado Springs, CO 80901
conductor

Ant Banks
c/o Jive
6777 Hollywood Blvd., 9th Fl.
Hollywood, CA 90028
group

Ant, Adam
P.O. Box 866
London SE1 3AP U.K.
musician

Antenna
c/o Mammoth
Carr Mill, 2nd Fl.
Carrboro, NC 27510
group

Anthem Records Inc.
189 Carlton St.
Toronto, Ontario M5A 2K7 Canada
Ray Daniels, President
independent record label

Anthrax
c/o Island
8920 Sunset Blvd.
Los Angeles, CA 90069
group

Antilles Records
825 8th Ave., 26th Fl.
New York, NY 10019
independent record label

Antithesis Records
273 Chippewa Dr.
Columbia, SC 29210
Jojo St. Mitchell, GM
independent record label

Anton Management, Inc.
1431 Washington Blvd., #716
Detroit, MI 48226
Douglas Clay Anton, President
artist management

Antone's Records
609-B W. 6th St.
Austin, TX 78701
Susan Piver, GM
independent record label

Apache
c/o Warner Bros.
3300 Warner Blvd.
Burbank, CA 91510
group

Apexton Records
1650 Broadway, #607
New York, NY 10019
M. Busacca
independent record label

Apollonia (aka Patty Kotero)
P.O. Box 480356
Los Angeles, CA 90048
Prince collaborator, singer

Apostles
151 El Camino
Beverly Hills, CA 90212
group

Applause
132 Liverpool Rd.
London N1 1LA U.K.
magazine

Apple Hill Center for Chamber Music
Apple Hill Chamber Players
c/o Eric Stumacher
Apple Hill Rd.
East Sullivan, NH 03445

Aquarius Records
200-1445 Lambert Closse, #200
Montreal Quebec H3H 1Z5 Canada
Mark Lazare, A&R
independent record label

Araiza, Francisco (Jose Francisco Araiza Andrade)
Kurisdem Mgmt.
Kurfurstenstr 8
D-8000 Munich 40 Germany
opera singer

ARC Entertainment
426 East 9th St., #4A
New York, NY 10009
Abi Reid
artist management

Arcady Music Festival
c/o Arcady Music Society
P.O. Box 780
Bar Harbor, ME 04609

Archive of Contemporary Music
110 Chambers St.
New York, NY 10007
Robert George, Director

Ardoin, John Louis
Communications Center
Dallas, TX 75265
music editor, critic

Arf!Arf!
P.O. Box 860
East Dennis, MA 02641
Erik Lindgren, President
independent record label

Argus Records
625 Main St., #844
New York, NY 10044
Johnny Jones, President
independent record label

Arhoolie Records
10341 San Pablo Ave.
El Cerrito, CA 94530
Chris Strachwitz
independent record label

Arista Records, Inc.
6 W. 57th St.
New York, NY 10019
Clive Davis, President
record label

Arista Records, Inc.
Los Angeles
8370 Wilshire Blvd.
Beverly Hills, CA 90211

Arista Records, Inc.
Nashville
1 Music Circle N., #300
Nashville, TN 37203

Armstrong, Pat Associates
5104 N. Orange Blossom Trail, #205
Orlando, FL 32810
artist management

Armstrong, Vanessa Bell
c/o Jive
6777 Hollywood Blvd., 6th Fl.
Hollywood, CA 90028
singer

Arnold & Associates
280 S. Beverly Dr., #206
Beverly Hills, CA 90212
Larkin Arnold
artist management

Arnold's Archives
1106 Eastwood, S.E.
East Grand Rapids, MI 49506
Arnold Jacobsen, Archivist
rare Broadway show, musical comedy
records and memorabilia

Arnold, Eddy
2110 E. 51st St.
New York, NY 10022
singer

Arnold, Linda
c/o A&M
1416 N. LaBrea Ave.
Hollywood, CA 90028
singer

Arrey Management
1973 Cheremoya Ave.
Hollywood, CA 90068
Lesa Arrey, Personal Manager
artist management

Arron, Judith Hagerty
Carnegie Hall Corp.
881 7th Ave.
New York, NY 10019
concert hall exec.

Arsenal
c/o Touch & Go
P.O. Box 25520
Chicago, IL 60625
group

Arslanian & Associates
6671 Sunset Blvd., #1502
Hollywood, CA 90028
Oscar Arslanian
artist management

Art of Dance Records
19145 W. Hine Mile
Southfield, MI 48075
Kenny Larkin
independent record label

Arterberry, Benita
c/o SBK
810 7th Ave., 8th Fl.
New York, NY 10019
singer

Artichoke Productions
4114 Linden St.
Oakland, CA 94608
Paul Kalbach, Producer/Director
video production company

Artifex Records
604 Overview Lane
Franklin, TN 37064
Peter Miller, President
independent record label

Artist Direction Agency
P.O. Box 50
Nashville, TN 37202
Fay Shedd, President
artist management

Artist Investment & Management
590 Centerville Rd., #164
Lancaster, PA 17601
Nick Gianoulis, President
artist management

Artist Issue
Schwann Publications
21625 Prairie St.
Chatsworth, CA 91311
annual guide to classical recordings

Artist Operations
1204 DeFoor Ct.
Atlanta, GA 30318
Andy Oblander
artist management

Artist Representation & Management Inc.
729 29th Ave. SE
Minneapolis, MN 55414
John Domagall, President
artist management

Artist Services
130 W. 57th St., #12B
New York, NY 10019
Dave Loncao
artist management

Artistic Distractions
2265 W. Saint Paul, 3rd Fl.
Chicago, IL 60647
Mark Steiner
independent record label

Artists and Athletes International
10866 Wilshire Blvd., 10th Fl.
Los Angeles, CA 90024
Chip Oliver
artist management

Artists International Representatives Inc.
285 W. Broadway, #300
New York, NY 10013
Jane Friedmand, President
artist management

Artists Only Management
152-18 Union Turnpike, #12-R
Flushing, NY 11367
artist management

Artists Services Inc.
666 11th St. NW, #1010
Washington, DC 20001
Ed Yoe
artist management

Artists/Alexander Ltd.
8831 Sunset Blvd., PHW
Los Angeles, CA 90069
Morey Alexander, President
independent record label

Ascona Records
3301 Barham Blvd., #300
Los Angeles, CA 90068
Michael Fuchs, A&R
independent record label

Asgard Mgm't
125 Park Way
London NW1 7PS U.K.
Paul Charles
artist management

Asher, Peter Management
644 N. Doheny Dr.
Los Angeles, CA 90069
Peter Asher, Personal Manager

Asherton Fine Arts Corporation
1888 Century Park E., #1900
Los Angeles, CA 90067
Rockwell D. Sheraton, President
independent record label

Ashkenazy, Vladimir Davidovich
Royal Philharmonic Orchestra
16 Clerkenwell Green
London EC1R ODP U.K.
concert pianist, conductor

Ask a Silly Question
P.O. Box 1950
Hollywood, CA 90078
Kathleen Conner, President
music research

Asleep at the Wheel
c/o Buddy Lee
38 Music Sq. E, #300
Nashville, TN 37203
group

Asociacion Pro Zarzuela en America
P.O. Box 7500, FDR Station
New York, NY 10150
Carmen Bejarno, Artistic Director
spanish operatic form

Aspen Music Festival
P.O. Box AA
Aspen, CO 81612

Asphalt Ballet
c/o Virgin
338 N. Foothill Rd.
Beverly Hills, CA 90210
group

Associated Entertainment
205 Raintree Trail
Lafayette, LA 70507
Michael Hebert
artist management

Associated Male Choruses of America
P.O. Box 771
Brainerd, MI 56401
Forbes H. Martinson, Executive Secretary

Association
c/o Variety Artists International
15490 Ventura Blvd., #210
Sherman Oaks, CA 91403
group

Association for the Advancement of Creative Musicians
7058 S. Chappel Ave.
Chicago, IL 60649
Douglas Ewart, President

Association of Concert Bands
3020 E. Majestic Ridge
Las Cruces, NM 88001
Dr. Donald M. Hardisty, Executive
Administrator

Aston Magna Festival
P.O. Box 28
Great Barrington, MA 01230
music festival

Atco Enterprises
1312 Vandalis
Collinsville, IL 62234
Lori Cummings
artist management

Atco/East West America
75 Rockefeller Plaza
New York, NY 10019
Sylvia Rhone, Chairperson/CEO
record label

Atco/East West America
Los Angeles
9229 Sunset Blvd.
Los Angeles, CA 90069

Atencio, Tom & Associates
5517 Green Oak Dr.
Los Angeles, CA 90068
artist management

Atkins, Chet
CGP Entertainment
1013 17th Ave. S
Nashville, TN 37212
record company exec., guitarist

Atlanta Rhythm Section
c/o Variety Artists
15490 Ventura Blvd., #210
Sherman Oaks, CA 91403
group

Atlantic Records
75 Rockefeller Plaza
New York, NY 10019
Ahmet M. Ertegun, Chairman/CEO
record company

Atlantic Records
Los Angeles
9229 Sunset Blvd., #900
Los Angeles, CA 90069

Atlantic Records
Nashville
1812 Broadway
Nashville, TN 37203

Atomic Communications Group
9724 Washington Blvd., #200
Culver City, CA 90232
Gabriel Leconte, President
artist management

Atomic Records
1813 Locust St., #2
Milwaukee, WI 53211
Rick Menning
independent record label

ATS Management
8306 Appalachian Dr.
Austin, TX 78759
Carlyne Majer, Owner/Manager
artist management

Attaway, Murray
c/o Geffen
9130 Sunset Blvd.
Los Angeles, CA 90069
musician

Attic Music Group
102 Atlantic Ave.
Toronto, Ontario M6K 1X9 Canada
Alexander Mair, President
independent record label

Attitude Records
2071 Emerson St., Unit 16
Jacksonville, FL 32207
Jeff Cohen, Owner
independent record label

Aucourant Records
P.O. Box 672902
Marietta, GA 30067
Dr. Robert Scott Thompson
independent record label

**Audio Arts Recording/
Johnny Q Records**
6241 Highway 290 W
Austin, TX 78735
Jeff Moeller, Owner
independent record label

Audio Plus Management
41 Britain St., #203
Toronto, Ontario M5A 1R7
Canada
Floyd Chan
artist management

Audio Pro Management
2 Park Ave., #1E
Eastchester, NY 10707
Sasha Mullins
artist management

Audio Two
c/o Atlantic
75 Rockefeller Plaza
New York, NY 10019
group

Audiopost
27 E. 21st St., 9th Fl.
New York, NY 10010
Ed Steinberg
video production company

Auerbach, Erik
14 Cumberland, #2
San Francisco, CA 95110
artist management

August Records
P.O. Box 7041
Watchung, NJ 07060
Meg Poltorak, Exec. VP
independent record label

Aural Gratification
P.O. Box 8658, Academy Station
Albany, NY 12208
independent record label

Austin, Patti
c/o APA
9000 Sunset Blvd., #1200
Los Angeles, CA 90069
singer

Auto & Cherokee
c/o Morgan Creek
1875 Century Park E, #600
Los Angeles, CA 90067
musicians

**Automatic Musical Instrument
Collectors Assoc.**
AMICA
919 Lantern Glow Trail
Dayton, OH 45431
paper roll instrument assoc.

Autonomy Productions
4720 Lincoln Blvd., #250
Marina del Rey, CA 90292
video production company

Autumn Cathedral
c/o Epithet
P.O. Box 6367
Stanford, CA 94309
group

Avalanche Recording
10650 Irma Dr., #27
Northglenn, CO 80233
Linda Warman, Manager
video production company

Avalon Entertainment Group
1025 16th Avenue, S #401
Nashville, TN 37212
Greg Janese, President
artist management

Avalon Entertainment Management
3 Newells Meadow Lane
Derry, NH 03038
Paul W. Gasparolo
artist management

Avalon, Frankie
5513 S. Rim St.
Westlake Village, CA 91362
singer

AVC Entertainment Inc
6201 Susnet Blvd., #200
Los Angeles, CA 90028
Jim Warsinske, President
independent record label

Aversion
c/o Restless
1616 Vista Del Mar
Hollywood, CA 90028
group

Avid Productions
235 E. Third Ave., #300
San Mateo, CA 94401
Chris Craig, Producer
video production company

Ax, Emanuel
173 Riverside Dr., #12G
New York, NY 10024
pianist

Axbar Records
5230 San Pedro
San Antonio, TX 78212
Joe Scates, GM
independent record label

Axton, Hoyt
Jeremiah Records Inc.
P.O. Box 1077
Hendersonville, TN 37077
singer, composer

Aznavour, Charles
4 Avenue De Lieulee
78, Galluis, France
singer

Azra International
P.O. Box 459
Maywood, CA 90270
D.T. Richards, President
independent record label

Aztlan Records
P.O. Box 5672
Buena Park, CA 90622
Carmen Ortiz
independent record label

Music is the universal language of mankind.
—HENRY WADSWORTH LONGFELLOW

B Angie B
c/o Bust It Productions
80 Swan Way, #130
Oakland, CA 94612
group

B Side
P.O. Box 1860
Burlington, NJ 08016
magazine

B-52's Addicts Anonymous
P.O. Box 506, Canal Street
Station
New York, NY 10013
fan club

B-52's, The
P.O. Box 506 Canal Street
Station
New York, NY 10013
rock group

B-Rated Records
533 1/2 Howard Ave., #B
Covina, CA 91723
Roy Nystrom, Owner
independent record label

B.B.
532 Burgundy St.
New Orleans, LA 70112
artist management

B.R. Entertainment
315 Bainbridge St., #2
Brooklyn, NY 11233
Regina Lawrence, CEO
independent record label

B.T.R. Entertainment
11915 Riverside Dr., #405
N. Hollywood, CA 91607
W.L. Bohannon
artist management

Baby Faze Records & Tapes
45 Pearl St.
San Francisco, CA 94103
G. Miller Marlin
independent record label

Baby Sue
P.O. Box 1111
Decatur, GA 30031
Don W. Seven, President
independent record label

Babylon Minstrels
c/o Hollywood Records
500 S. Buena Vista, Animation Bldg.
Burbank, CA 91505
group

Babylon Post
901 N. Seward St.
Hollywood, CA 90038
Robin Fellows, Owner
video production

Bach Aria Festival and Institute at Stonybrook
P.O. Box 997
Stony Brook, NY 11790

Bach Society of Kalamazoo
Kalamazoo College
1200 Academy St.
Kalamazoo, MI 49007

Bacharach, Burt
1875 Century Park E.
Los Angeles, CA 90067
composer, conductor

Back Porch Blues
P.O. Box 14953
Portland, OR 97214
Jeffrey Dawkins, Manager
independent record label

Backroom Associates
1450 N. Cleveland Ave., 3rd Fl.
Chicago, IL 60610
Gordon Kennerly
artist management

Bad 4 Good
c/o Atlantic
9229 Sunset Blvd., #900
Los Angeles, CA 90069
group

Bad Brains
151 El Camino
Beverly Hills, CA 90212
group

Bad Company
c/o Atco
9229 Sunset Blvd.
Los Angeles, CA 90069
group

BAD II
c/o Columbia
2100 Colorado Blvd.
Santa Monica, CA 90404
group

Bad Religion
c/o Epitaph
6201 Sunset Blvd., #111
Hollywood, CA 90028
group

Badea, Christian
Columbus Symphony Orchestra
55 E. State St.
Columbus, OH 43215
conductor, music director

Badfinger
c/o Nationwide Entertainment Services
7770 Regents Rd., #113-905
San Diego, CA 92122
group

Badfinger Fan Club
5126 Creekbend Circle
Cleveland, TN 37311

Badlees, The
c/o Media Five Entertainment
400 Northampton St., #600
Easton, PA 18042
group

Badura-Skoda, Paul (Ludwig)
5802 Julia St.
Madison, WI 53705
pianist

Baerwald, David
151 El Camino
Beverly Hills, CA 90212
singer

Baez, Joan Chandos
P.O. Box 818
Menlo Park, CA 94026
folk singer

Bagwell, Wendy
c/o Word
3319 W. End Ave., #200
Nashville, TN 37203
singer

Baha Men
c/o Atlantic
75 Rockefeller Plaza
New York, NY 10019
group

Bahia Records
1133 Ave. of the Americas, 9th Fl.
New York, NY 10036
independent record label

Bailey, Philip
c/o Columbia
2100 Colorado Blvd.
Santa Monica, CA 90404
singer

Bailey, Robert C.
Portland Opera Association Inc.
1516 SW Alder St.
Portland, OR 97205
opera company exec.

Bainbridge Records
P.O. Box 8248
Van Nuys, CA 91409
Harlene Marshall, President
independent record label

Bait String Music
1219 Kerlin Ave.
Brewton, AL 36426
Shannon Edwards, A&R
independent record label

Bajus Film Corp.
3414 Zenith Ave., S
Minneapolis, MN 55416
video production

**Baker's Biographical
Dictionary of Musicians**
Schirmer Books
666 Third Ave.
New York, NY 10022

Baker, Anita
All Baker's Music
804 N. Crescent Dr.
Beverly Hills, CA 90210
singer

Baker, Ginger
c/o Axiom/Island
8920 Sunset Blvd., 2nd Fl.
Los Angeles, CA 90069
musician

Baker, Robert Hart
Asheville Symphony Orchestra
P.O. Box 2852
Asheville, NC 28802
conductor, composer

Balada, Leonardo
Music Department
Carnegie Mellon University
Pittsburgh, PA 15213
composer, educator

**Balalaika and Domra
Association of America**
2225 Madison Sq.
Philadelphia, PA 19146
Stephen M. Wolownik,
Executive Director

Baldwin, Bob
c/o Atlantic
75 Rockefeller Plaza
New York, NY 10019
musician

**Balin, Marty (Martyn Jerel Buch-
wald)**
P.O. Box 347008
San Francisco, CA 94134
founder of Jefferson Airplane

Balin, Trace
c/o Word
5221 N. O'Connor Blvd., #1000
Irving, TX 75039
singer

Ballard, Louis Wayne
P.O. Box 4552
Santa Fe, NM 87502
Native American composer

BALLS
c/o Original Sound Records
7120 Sunset Blvd.
Hollywood, CA 90046
group

Balmur Ltd.
4950 Yonge St., #2400
Toronto, Ontario M2N 6KI Canada
Leonard T. Rambeau, President
artist management

Balmur Music
818 18th Ave. S., #200
Nashville, TN 37203
Tinti Moffat, GM
artist management

Balter, Alan
Memphis Symphony Orchestra
3100 Walnut Grove Rd., #402
Memphis, TN 38111
conductor, music director

Bananarama
c/o London Records
825 8th Ave., 24th Fl.
New York, NY 10019
group

Band AKA, The
151 El Camino
Beverly Hills, CA 90212
group

Band Associates
7325 1/2 Reseda Ave., #659
Reseda, CA 91335
Don Martin, President
artist management

Band of Susans
c/o Restless
1616 Vista Del Mar
Hollywood, CA 90028
group

Banderas
c/o London
825 8th Ave., 24th Fl.
New York, NY 10019
group

Bandier, Martin
SBK Entertainment
1290 Ave. of the Americas
New York, NY 10104
record company executive

Bands of America
P.O. Box 665
Arlington Heights, IL 60006
L. Scott McCormick, Executive Director
school band association

Banff Festival of the Arts, The
The Banff Centre School of Fine Arts
P.O. Box 1020
Banff, AB T0L 0C0 Canada
music festival

Bang Communications
177 Prince St., #4B
New York, NY 10012
Scott Mehno, President
artist management

Bang on a Can Festival
c/o Lynn Garon Mgmt.
1199 Park Ave.
New York, NY 10128

Bangon Productions
402 W. Pender St., #214
Vancouver, BC V6B IT6 Canada
Bruce Payne, President
independent record label

Banton, Pato
c/o I.R.S.
3939 Lankershim Blvd.
Studio City, CA 91604
musician

Banx, Robyn
c/o Wingate
P.O. Box 10895
Pleasanton, CA 94588
singer

Bar Harbor Festival
c/o Bar Harbor Festival Corporation
36 Mount Desert St.
Bar Harbor, ME 04609
music festival

Bar/None Records
P.O. Box 1704
Hoboken, NJ 07030
Glenn Morrow, Creative Director
independent record label

Barber, Patricia
c/o Antilles
825 8th Ave., 26th Fl.
New York, NY 10019
singer

Bardens, Pete
c/o Cinema
812 W. Darby Rd.
Havertown, PA 19083
singer

Bare Bones Productions
285 Rose St.
San Francisco, CA 94102
Andrew Burton
artist management

Bare, Bobby (Robert Joseph)
P.O. Box 2422
Hendersonville, TN 37077
singer, songwriter

Barenboim, Daniel
Chicago Symphony Orchestra
220 S. Michigan Ave.
Chicago, IL 60604
conductor, pianist

Bargemusic
Fulton Ferry Landing
Brooklyn, NY 11201
music festival

Barker, Dave
91 Highbury New Park
London N5 U.K.
artist management

Barker, Edwin Bogue
Boston Symphony
251 Huntington Ave.
Boston, MA 02115
bassist

Barking Pumpkin Records
P.O. Box 5265
N. Hollywood, CA 91616
Dottie Flynn
independent record label

Baron, Samuel
Department of Music
SUNY Stony Brook
Stony Brook, NY 11794
flutist

Barrington Management Corp.
P.O. Box 852
Barrington, IL 60011
Ron Ranke, Management Director
manages Eastern European recording
artists

Barry All the Time
521 Pulaski Blvd.
Bellingham, MA 02019
Barry Manilow Fan Club

Barry Gibb Record
99 Tindall Rd.
Middletown, NJ 07748
fan club

Barshai, Rudolf Borisovich
Allied Artists
42 Montepelier Sq.
London, SW 1J2 U.K.
conductor

Bartoletti, Bruno
Lyric Opera of Chicago
20 N. Wacker Dr.
Chicago, IL 60606
conductor

Baruck/Consolo Management
15003 Greenleaf St.
Sherman Oaks, CA 91403
John Baruck
artist management

Bas Noir
c/o Atlantic
75 Rockefeller Plaza
New York, NY 10019
group

Basement Music
1841 Broadway, #701
New York, NY 10023
John Telper
artist management

Basilean Films
P.O. Box 50111
Chicago, IL 60650
video production

Bass-O-Matic
c/o Virgin
338 N. Foothill Rd.
Beverly Hills, CA 90210
group

Bassment Records
234-C Columbus Dr.
Jersey City, NJ 07302
Craig Bevan
independent record label

Batish Music
1310 Mission St.
Santa Cruz, CA 95060
Ashwin Batish
independent record label

Bats, Judy
151 El Camino
Beverly Hills, CA 90212
singer

Battle, Kathleen
165 W. 57th St.
New York, NY 10019
soprano

Baustian, Robert Frederich
424 Abeyta St.
Santa Fe, NM 87501
conductor

Bay Chamber Concerts
Rockport Opera House
P.O. Box 191
Camden, ME 04843

Bay Cities Inc.
9336 Washington Blvd.
Culver City, CA 90232
Bruce Kimmel, President
independent record label

Bay City Rollers
31 St. Leonards Rd.
Bexhill-on-Sea, East Sussex
TN40 1HP U.K.
group

Bay, Peter
Rochester Philharmonic Orchestra
108 East Ave.
Rochester, NY 14604
conductor

Baylor, Helen
c/o Word
3319 W. End Ave., #200
Nashville, TN 37203
singer

BCM
9200 Olympic Blvd.
Beverly Hills, CA 90212
Sam Lauren, Manager
independent record label

Beach Boys
101 Mesa Lane
Santa Barbara, CA 93109
perennial pop group

Beach Boys Fan Club
P.O. Box 84282
Los Angeles, CA 90073

Beachwood Recordings, Inc.
6253 Hollywood Blvd., #810
Hollywood, CA 90028
James Lee Stanley, President
independent record label

Beacon Records
P.O. Box 3129
Peabody, MA 01961
Tony Ritchie
independent record label

Bearden, Victoria
P.O. Box 672902
Marietta, GA 30067
singer

Bearsville Records
P.O. Box 135, Wittenburg Rd.
Bearsville, NY 12409
Sally Grossman, President
independent record label

Beastie Boys, The
1750 N. Vine St.
Hollywood, CA 90028
rappers

Beat Fantastic, The
17 Gosfield St.
London W1P 7HE U.K.
group

Beat Farmers
15490 Ventura Blvd., #210
Sherman Oaks, CA 91403
group

Beatles Fan Club: Good Day Sunshine
397 Edgewood Ave.
New Haven, CT 065111

Beatnik Pop
9724 Washington Blvd., #200
Culver City, CA 90232
group

Beats International
1700 Broadway, 5th Fl.
New York, NY 10019
group

Beats, The
1304 Fletcher Rd.
Tifton, GA 31794
group

Beaumont, Jim & the Skyliners
141 Dunbar Ave.
Fords, NJ 08863
group

Beauties, The
9720 Wilshire Blvd., 4th Fl.
Beverly Hills, CA 90212
group

Beautiful South, The
322 King St.
Hammersmith, London W6 ORR U.K.
group

Beaver Records
P.O. Box 35044
Charlotte, NC 28235
Dave Fisher
independent record label

Beck Wood Records
9016 Wilshire Blvd., #427
Beverly Hills, CA 90211
Alan Beck
independent record label

Beck, Jeff
9830 Wilshire Blvd.
Beverly Hills, CA 90212
musician

Beck, Joe Trio
223 1/2 East 48th St.
New York, NY 10017
group

Becket
5125 Wisconsin Ave., #14
Washington, DC 20016
group

Becton, James
830 Glastonbury Rd., #614
Nashville, TN 37217
musician

Bedlam
P.O. Box 128037
Nashville, TN 37212
group

Bedlam Management
P.O. Box 1561
London W11 U.K.
artist management

Bedlam Rovers
P.O. Box 5187
Berkeley, CA 94705
group

Bee Gees (Maurice, Barry and Robin Gibb)
P.O. Box 8179
Miami, FL 33139
pop group

Beethoven Festival
Davies Symphony Hall
201 Van Ness Ave.
San Francisco, CA 94102

Beggars Banquet
274 Madison Ave., #804
New York, NY 10016
Peter Gordon
independent record label

Beghe, Francesca
114 Lexington Ave.
New York, NY 10016
singer

Bel-Vistas
1 Franklin Park North
Buffalo, NY 14202
group

Belafonte, Harry
c/o RCA
1133 Ave. of the Americas
New York, NY 10036
singer

Belew, Adrian
P.O. Box 8385, 2612 Eric Ave.
Cincinnati, OH 45208
musician

Believer
200 West 57th St., #910
New York, NY 10019
group

Belkin Personal Management
44 N. Main St.
Chagrin Falls, OH 44022
Mike Belkin, Chairman/CEO

Bell, Eddy & Valerie
142 8th Ave., N
Nashville, TN 37203
duo

Bell, Mark
500 S. Buena Vista St., Animation Bldg.
Burbank, CA 91505
singer

Bellamy Bros.
c/o MCA
70 Universal Plaza
Universal City, CA 91608
group

Bellamy Brothers Fan Club
c/o Lucy Musser
P.O. Box 801
San Antonio, FL 34266

Belle, Regina
51 W. 52nd St.
New York, NY 10019
singer

Bellson, Louie
223 1/2 East 48th St
New York, NY 10017
musician

Belltower
c/o Atlantic Records
75 Rockefeller Plaza
New York, NY 10019
group

Belmonts
141 Dunbar Ave.
Fords, NJ 08863
group

Beloved, The
c/o Atlantic Records
75 Rockefeller Plaza
New York, NY 10019
group

Belt Drive Records Ltd.
P.O. Box 101107
San Antonio, TX 78201
Fred Weiss, President
independent record label

Bemeg/Everett Management
P.O. Box 1327
Beverly Hills, CA 90211
Bill Everett
artist management

Bemshi
325-331 Lafayette St., 2nd Fl.
New York, NY 10012
group

Benatar, Pat (Andrejewski)
Gold Mountain Management
2575 Cahuengua Blvd., #470
Los Angeles, CA 90068
singer

Bendik
2100 Colorado Blvd.
Santa Monica, CA 90404
group

Bennett, Glenn
568 Broadway, #1104
New York, NY 10012
singer

Bennett, Tony
101 W. 55th St.
New York, NY 10019
singer

Bennett, William
San Francisco Symphony Orchestra
201 Van Ness Ave.
San Francisco, CA 94102
oboist

Bennu Productions Inc.
171 Madison Ave.
New York, NY 10016
Wayne J. Keeley, Producer/Director
video production

Benoit, David
9000 Sunset Blvd., #1200
Los Angeles, CA 90069
musician

Benson Music Group, The
365 Great Circle Rd.
Nashville, TN 37228
Jerry Park
independent record label

Benson, George
648 N. Robertson Blvd.
Los Angeles, CA 90069
musician

Bentely
315 Bainbridge St., #2
Brooklyn, NY 11233
group

Bentyne, Cheryl
51 W. 52nd St.
New York, NY 10019
singer

Beowulf
1616 Vista Del Mar
Hollywood, CA 90028
group

Berg, G.L. & Associates
110 S. 2nd St., #225
Waite Park, MN 56387
Gary Berg, Owner
artist management

Berganza, Teresa
APDO 137
SLD Escorial
E-28200 Madrid, Spain
mezzo-soprano

Bergman, Alan
c/o Lantz Office
888 7th Ave., #2501
New York, NY 10016
writer, lyricist

Bergman, Barry Management
2555 E. 12th St.
Brooklyn, NY 11235
artist management

Bergonzi, Carlo
A Ziliani ALCI
Via Paoloda Cannobio 2
120122 Milan, Italy
tenor

Berio, Luciano
Il Colombaio
Radicondoli, Siena, Italy
composer, conductor

Berkey, Jackson
9130 Mormon Bridge Rd.
Omaha, NE 68152
singer

Berlin Contemporary Jazz Orchestra
825 8th Ave., 26th Fl.
New York, NY 10019
group

Berlin, Steve
P.O. Box 128037
Nashville, TN 37212
musician

Berman, Laza
c/o Jacques Leiser
Dorchester Towers
155 W. 68th St.
New York, NY 10023
pianist

Bernard Hermann Society
c/o Kevin Fahey
5523 Denny Ave.
N. Hollwyood, CA 91601
society for late film composer

Bernard, Charles Julien
Calgary Philharmonic Society
205 8th Ave., SE
Calgary, Alberta, Canada T2G 0K9
cellist

Bernardi, Mario
Calgary Philharmonic Society
205 8th Ave. SE
Calgary, Alberta, Canada T2G
0K9
conductor

Bernhardt, Robert
Tucson Symphony Orchestra
443 S. Stone Ave.
Tucson, AZ 85701
music director, conductor

Bernheimer, Martin
Los Angeles Times
Times Mirror Square
Los Angeles, CA 90012
music critic

Bernstein Corporation
2170 S. Parker Rd.
Denver, CO 80231
R. Bernstein, President/CEO
artist management

Bernstein, Elmer
Screen Composers of America
2451 Nichols Canyon
Los Angeles, CA 90046
composer, conductor

Berry, Chuck (Charles Edward Anderson Berry)
Berry Park, 691 Buckner Road
Wentzville, MO 63385
singer, composer

Berry, Heidi
8533 Melrose Ave., #B
Los Angeles, CA 90069
singer

Berry, Walter
c/o Thea Dispeker Artists Representa-
tive
59 E. 54th St.
New York, NY 10022
baritone

**Bessie Bartlett Frankel Festival of
Chamber Music**
Scripps College
Claremont, CA 91711

Bessie Smith Society
c/o Professor Michael Roth
Franklin and Marshall College
Lancaster, PA 17604

Best Kissers in the World
89 5th Ave., 8th Fl.
New York, NY 10023
group

Bet-Car Management
307 Lake St.
San Frnacisco, CA 94118
Ora Harris
artist management

Bethlehem Bach Festival
423 Heckewelder Pl.
Bethlehem, PA 18018

Better Music
476 Broome St., #6A
New York, NY 10013
Michael Lang
artist management

**Betts, Dicky (Richard Forrest
Betts)**
40 W. 57th St.
New York, NY 10019
guitarist, songwriter, vocalist

Between the Ears Management
41 W. 72nd St., #3G
New York, NY 10023
Marc Nathan, President
artist management

Bevis Frond, The
1401 Haight St.
San Francisco, CA 94117
group

Bewitched
P.O. Box 25581
Chicago, IL 60625
group

Beyond Management
804 Spain St.
New Orleans, LA 70117
artist management

BFCS
1416 Second St.
Santa Monica, CA 90401
video production company

Bianco, Matt
75 Rockefeller Plaza
New York, NY 10019
musician

Bicycle Face
133 1/2 E. Franklin St.
Chapel Hill, NC 27514
group

Big Audio Dynamite
1775 Broadway, 7th Fl.
New York, NY 10019
group

Big Band Academy of America
c/o Milton Gerald Bernhart
Kelly Travel Service
6565 Sunset Blvd., #516
Los Angeles, CA 90028

Big Beat Bluesline
P.O. Box 1949
New Haven, CT 06510
magazine

Big Beat Productions Inc.
1515 University Dr., #108A
Coral Springs, FL 33071
Richard Lloyd, President
artist management

Big Beat Records
19 W. 21st St., #501
New York, NY 10010
Sean Pennington, Owner
independent record label

Big Blunder Management
641 S. Palm St., #D
La Habra, CA 90631
Jon St. James, CEO

Big Boy Records
P.O. Box 53297
Chicago, IL 60653
Bill Collins, President
independent record label

Big Brave Management
155 E. 55th, #6H
New York, NY 10022
Steve Shipp
artist management

Big Chief Records
611 Broadway, #907E
New York, NY 10012
independent record label

Big FD Entertainment
2001 Barrington Ave., #100
Los Angeles, CA 90025
Doug Goldstein
artist management

Big Life Records U.S.
73 Spring St., #601
New York, NY 10012
Jazz Summers, President
independent record label

Big Man's Fan Club
RR 8, Box 105
Benton, KY 42025
Clarence Clemons, sax player
E Street Band, fan club

Big Money Inc. Records
P.O. Box 2483 Loop Station
Minneapolis, MN 55402
Chris Johnson, President
independent record label

Big Talent
P.O. Box 8603
Portland, OR 97207
Mike King
artist management

Big Wedge Music
P.O. Box 29-0186
Nashville, TN 37229
Ralph Johnson, President
independent record label

Billboard
BPI Communications Publication
49 Music Square W.
Nashville, TN 37203
professional entertainment publication

**Billboard International Buyer's
Guide**
BPI Communications Publications
49 Music Square W
Nashville, TN 37203
directory

Billboard's Country Music Source Book-Directory
BPI Communications Publication
49 Music Square W
Nashville, TN 37203

Billboard's International Manufacturing & Packaging Directory
49 Music Square W
Nashville, TN 37203

Billingslea Sweeney & Associates
317 Rosecrans Ave., Second Fl.
Manhattan Beach, CA 90266
Tim Sweeney/Wes Billingslea
artist development

Billy "Crash" Craddock Fan Club
c/o Leola Butcher
P.O. Box 1585
Mt. Vernon, IL 62864

Billy Boy Productions
18653 Ventura Blvd., #745
Tarzana, CA 91356
Michael Faley, VP
artist management

Bing Crosby Historical Society
P.O. Box 216
Tacoma, WA 98401

Bing Records
947 Steiner St.
San Francisco, CA 94117
Kathy McBride
independent record label

Binkerd, Gordon Ware
Boosey & Hawkes Inc.
24 W. 57th St.
New York, NY 10019
composer

Biograph Records
16 River St.
Chatham, NY 12037
Arnold Caplin, President
independent record label

Bird Seed Productions
1946 N. Hudson Ave.
Chicago, IL 60614
Robin McBride
independent record label

Birmingham Festival of Arts
Commerce Center, #910
Birmingham, AL 35203
music festival

Bishop, Stephen
151 El Camino
Beverly Hills, CA 90212
singer, songwriter

Bismeaux Productions
P.O. Box 463
Austin, TX 78767
artist management

Bitter End, The
147 Bleecker St.
New York, NY 10012
club

Bix Beiderbecks Memorial Jazz Festival
The Bix Beiderbecks Memorial Society
2225 W. 17th St.
Davenport, IA 52804

Bizarre/Straight Records
740 N. LaBrea
Los Angeles, CA 90038
Bob Duffy
independent record label

Black & Blue Records
400D Putnam Pike, #152
Smithfield, RI 02917
Boris Ofterhaul, A&R
independent record label

Black & White Television
73 Spring St., #501
New York, NY 10012
Sherry Simpson, Administration
video production

Black Beat
Sterling's Magazines, Inc.
355 Lexington Ave., 13th Fl.
New York, NY 10017
black music magazine

Black Boot Records
5503 Roosevelt Way NE
Seattle, WA 98105
Brian Sykes, President
independent record label

Black Cat Entertainment
P.O. Box 10815
Oakland, CA 94610
Susie Donahue
artist management

Black Crowes, The
75 Rockefeller Plaza, 20th Fl.
New York, NY 10019
rock group

Black Dot Enterprises
1339 Vancouver Ave.
Ottawa, Quebec K1V 6T8 Canada
artist management

Black Dot Management
1019 S. Central
Glendale, CA 91204
Raymond A. Shields, Owner

Black Eagle Records
128 Front St.
Marblehead, MA 01945
Peter Bullis
independent record label

Black Label/Fallout Inc.
1506 E. Olive Way
Seattle, WA 98122
independent record label

Black Moon Music Productions
182 Bay Ave.
Highlands, NJ 07732
Jim Clark, President
independent record label

Black Park Management
400 W. Morgan St., #200
Raleigh, NC 27603
Ed Morgan, President

Black Rose Management
454 Main St., P.O. Box 216
Cold Spring Harbor, NY 11724
Tito Batista

Black Sacred Music
A Journal of Theomusicology
Duke University Press
P.O. Box 6697, College Station
Durham, NC 27708

Black Top Records
5340 Camp St.
New Orleans, LA 70115
Nauman S. Scott
independent record label

Black, Clint
30 Music Square W
Nashville, TN 37203
singer, musician

Blackheart Records Group
155 E. 55th St., #6H
New York, NY 10022
Kenny Laguna
independent record label

Blackout Records
P.O. Box 544
Yonkers, NY 10710
Bill Wilson, GM/President
independent record label

Blades, Ruben
c/o David Maldonado
1674 Broadway, #703
New York, NY 10019
singer, songwriter, composer

Blair, Lou Management
407-68 Water St.
Vancouver, BC V6B 1A4 Canada
artist management

Blak & Bloo
7574 Sunset Blvd.
Hollywood, CA 90028
gothic rock club

Blake & Bradford
901 Third St., #407
Santa Monica, CA 90403
Chris Blake
artist management

Blake Mevis Music
811 18th Ave. S.
Nashville, TN 37203
Blake Mevis, Owner
artist management

Blake, Ran
New England Conservancy
290 Huntington Ave.
Boston, MA 02115
jazz pianist, composer

Blanton/Harrell Inc.
2910 Poston Ave.
Nashville, TN 37203
E. Michael Blanton, President
artist management

Blast First!
262 Mott St., #324
New York, NY 10012
independent record label

Bley, Carla Borg
c/o Ted Kurland Associates
173 Brighton Ave.
Allston, MA 02134
jazz composer

Blind Pig Records
P.O. Box 2344
San Francisco, CA 94126
Jerry DelGiudice
independent record label

Blind Pig Records
Chicago
3022 N. Allen St.
Chicago, IL 60618

Bliss
P.O. Box 35709
Houston, TX 77235
artist management

Blockbuster Entertainment Corp.
901 E. Olas Blvd.
Ft. Lauderdale, FL 33301
H. Wayne Huizenga, Chairman and
CEO
U.S. leader in video rentals

Blomstedt, Herbert Thorson
San Francisco Symphony
Davies Symphony Hall
San Francisco, CA 94102
symphony director, conductor

Blood Sweat & Tears
9200 Sunset Blvd., #822
Los Angeles, CA 90069
group

Blossom Music Center
P.O. Box 1000
Cuyahoga Falls, OH 11000

Blue City Records
P.O. Box 1060
Massapequa, NY 11758
Cindy Keyser
independent record label

Blue Desert Pictures
5900 E. Thomas, #H-130
Scottsdale, AZ 85251
video production

Blue Fish Artist Management
782 Toliver St.
Marietta, GA 30060
Susan Zegers, Managing Director

Blue Island Records
1878 S. Santa Cruz St.
Anaheim, CA 92805
David Hulsey
independent record label

Blue Light Management Ltd.
875 Boulevard East
Weehawken, NJ 07087
Richard Lynn
artist management

Blue Muse Inc.
1683 Novato Blvd., #207
Novato, CA 94947
Gaynell Rogers, President
artist management

Blue Plate Music
4121 Wilshire Blvd., #204
Los Angeles, CA 90010
Dan Einstein, VP
independent record label

Blue Wave Records
3221 Perryville Rd.
Baldwinsville, NY 13027
Greg Spencer, Producer
independent record label

Blueberry Hill Records
6504 Delmar
University City, MO 63130
Joe Edwards
independent record label

Blues Factory Records and Artist Management
2911 Elmhurst Blvd.
Royal Oak, MI 48073
Mark Foreman

Blues Foundation, The
174 Beale St.
Memphis, TN 38103
Jay Sheffield, Executive Director

Blues Heaven Foundation
c/o the Cameron Organization, Inc.
P.O. Box 6926
Burbank, CA 91506
Willie Dixon, President and Founder

BMG Music/RCA
1133 Avenue of the Americas
New York, NY 10036
Michael Dornemann, Chairman/CEO
record company

BMG Music/RCA
Los Angeles
6363 Sunset Blvd.
Hollywood, CA 90028

BMG Music/RCA
Nashville
1 Music Square W
Nashville, TN 37203

BNA Entertainment
1 Music Circle N, #350
Nashville, TN 37203
Ric Pepin, VP/GM
independent record label

BNB & Associates
804 N. Crescent Dr.
Beverly Hills, CA 90210
Sherwin Bash
artist management

Bobby Blue Fan Club
P.O. Box 46666
Los Angeles, CA 90046

Bobby Vinton International Fan Club
153 Washington St.
Mt. Vernon, NY 10550

Bogard, James Associates
7608 Teel Way
Indianapolis, IN 46256
artist management

Boggiano, Anthony
23 New Mount St.
Manchester, M4 4DE U.K.
artist management

Bohdi Entertainment
18016 Western Ave., #228
Gardena, CA 90248
Tory Gullett
artist management

Bohemia Ragtime Society
5095 Picket Dr.
Colorado Springs, CO 80918
Nick Taylor, President

Bolcom, William Elden
University of Michigan School of Music
1339 Moore Hall
Ann Arbor, MI 48109
musician, composer, musician educator

Bolton, Michael
8980 Wilshire Blvd.
Beverly Hills, CA 90212
singer, songwriter

Bomp
(Who Put the Bomp)
P.O. Box 7112
Burbank, CA 91510
magazine

Bomp/Voxx Records
P.O. Box 7112
Burbank, CA 91510
Greg Shaw
independent record label

Bon Jovi
c/o Fan Club
P.O. Box 4843
San Francisco, California 94101
group

Bon Jovi, Jon
McGhee Entertainment
9145 Sunset Blvd., #100
West Hollywood, CA 90069
rock singer, composer

Bon Ton West
P.O. Box 8406
Santa Cruz, CA 95061
Marty Kirkman
artist management

Bonazzi, Elaine Claire
Trawick Artists
129 W. 72nd St.
New York, NY 10023
mezzo-soprano

Bond, Victoria Ellen
Roanoke Symphony Orchestra
P.O. Box 2433
Roanoke, VA 24010
conductor, composer

Boner Records
P.O. Box 2081
Berkeley, CA 94702
Tom Flynn
independent record label

Bono, Sonny Salvatore
P.O. Box 1786
32 E. Tahgutz-McCullum Way
Palm Springs, CA 92262
singer, composer

Bonsall, Joseph Sloan Jr.
c/o J. Halsey Co. Inc.
3225 S. Norwood Ave.
Tulsa, OK 74135
singer (Oak Ridge Boys)

Bonynge, Richard
Colbert Artists Mgmt.
111 W. 57th St.
New York, NY 10019
opera conductor

Boogie
221 Venetian Ave.
Gulfport, MI 39507
magazine

Bookhouse Promotions
3845 Harrison St., #114
Oakland, CA 94611
independent record label

Boomtown Music
P.O. Box 265 Station C
Toronto, Ontario M6J 3P4 Canada
artist management

Boone, Pat (Charles Eugene)
9200 Sunset Blvd., #1007
Los Angeles, CA 90069
singer

Boozer, Brenda Lynn
Columbia Artists Mgmt.
165 W. 57th St.
New York, NY 10019
mezzo-soprano

BOP
c/o Relativity
P.O. Box 10770
Oakland, CA 94610
group

Borge, Victor
c/o Gutman & Murtha Associates
162 W. 56th St.
New York, NY 10019
pianist, comedian

Borman Entertainment
9220 Sunset Blvd., #320
Los Angeles, CA 90069
Gary Borman
artist management

Bornand, Ruth Chaloux
Bornand Music
139 4th Ave.
Pelham, NY 10803
antique music box specialist

Bortini Management Associates
24449 Cedar Rd.
Beachwood, OH 44122
Frank Daniels, A&R

Boss, Adrian
19 All Saints Rd.
London W11 7HE U.K.
artist management

Boston Globe Jazz Festival
c/o Boston Globe
Boston, MA 02107

Bottom Line, The
15 W. 4th St.
New York, NY 10012
club

Boulder Bach Festival
P.O. Box 1896
Boulder, CO 80306

BouTime Entertainment Group
3325 Wilshire Blvd., #700
Los Angeles, CA 90010
Lopez Holmes Hill
independent record label

Bowdoin Summer Music Festival
Bowdoin College
Gibson Hall
Brunswick, ME 04011

Bowen, Andy
21 Upper Dean St.
Digbeth B5 45G U.K.
artist management

Bowie, David
Duncan Heath Associates
162 Wardour St.
London W1 U.K.
singer

Bowles, Eamon
426 2nd St., #1
Brooklyn, NY 11215
artist management

BOX
c/o Wild West
7201 Melrose Ave., #D
Los Angeles, CA 90046
group

Boyington Film Productions
5875 Blackwelder
Culver City, CA 90232
video production

Boylan, John Patrick
Great Ear Music Co.
5750 Wilshire Blvd., #590
Los Angeles, CA 90036
record producer, songwriter

Boyz II Men
729 7th Ave., 12th Fl.
New York, NY 10019
singing group

Bradshaw, Murray Charles
UCLA Department of Musicology
405 Hilgard Ave.
Los Angeles, CA 90024
musicologist

Brainard, Paul Henry
Yale Institute of Sacred Music
409 Prospect St.
New Haven, CT 06511
musicologist, music educator

Branca, John
Ziffren, Brittenham & Branca
2121 Ave. of the Stars, 32nd Fl.
Los Angeles, CA 90067
music attorney

Brass Management
10900 Wilshire Blvd., #1230
Los Angeles, CA 90024
Tony Ferguson
artist management

Bravo! Colorado at Vail/Beaver Creek
P.O. Box 1288
Vail, CO 81658
music festival

Bravura
P.O. Box 67461
Rochester, NY 14617
Scott Van Dusen, CEO/President
video production

Braw Music Management
16 Mentone Terrace
Edinburgh, EH9 2DF U.K.
Kenneth MacDonald
artist management

Breakthrough Entertainment Ltd.
60 E. 42nd St., #1350
New York, NY 10165
Michael Solomon
artist management

Bream, Julian
c/o Harold Holt, Ltd.
31 Sinclair Rd.
London W14 ONS U.K.
classical guitarist, lutist

Brenda Lee Fan Club
c/o John W. Smith, III
2038 Robert St.
Wilmington, IL 60481

Brendel, Alfred
Ingpen & Williams
14 Kensington Court
London, W8 U.K.
concert pianist

Brevard Music Center
P.O. Box 592
Brevard, NC 28712

Bridge Across the Pond
c/o Nancy Rosas
707 Flintlock Dr.
Bel Air, MD 21014
Tom Jones fan club

Bridge Records
P.O. Box 1864
New York, NY 10116
Michael Calvert, A&R
independent record label

Bright Ideas Productions
30879 Thousand Oaks Blvd., #161
Westlake Village, CA 91362
Marci Jaegle, Marketing Director
independent record label

Brightman, Sarah
9830 Wilshire Blvd.
Beverly Hills, CA 90212
singer

Brinkerhoff, Martin
17767 Mitchell
Irvine, CA 92714
video producer

Broadcast Music, Inc. (BMI)
320 W. 57th St.
New York, NY 10019
Frances W. Preston, CEO and President

Brock & Associates
7106 Moores Lane, #200
Brentwood, TN 37027
Darlene and Dan Brock
artist management

Brokaw, Michael Management
2934 Beverly Glen Circle, #383
Bel Air, CA 90077
artist management

Broken Records International
305 S. Westmore Ave.
Lombard, IL 60148
Roy Bocchiert, President
independent record label

Broken Rekids
P.O. Box 460402
San Francisco, CA 94110
Mike Millett
independent record label

Broken Spoke Records
3201 S. Lamar Blvd.
Austin, TX 78704
James White, Owner
independent record label

Brooks & Ciampi P.C.
1501 Broadway, #501
New York, NY 10036
Anthony Ciampi, Attorney
artist management

Brooks, Garth
1109 17th Ave. S
Nashville, TN 37212
singer

Brothers Management Associates
141 Dunbar Ave.
Fords, NJ 08863
Allen A. Faucera, President

Brown Cat Inc.
2351 College Station Rd., #504
Athens, GA 30605
Sam Lanier
artist management

Brown, Beatrice
Ridgefield Symphony Orchestra
P.O. Box 613
Ridgefield, CT 06877
symphony conductor

Brown, Bob Management
P.O. Box 779
Mill Valley, CA 94942
manager for Huey Lewis and the News

Brown, Iona
Los Angeles Chamber Orchestra
315 W. 9th St., Bldg. 801
Los Angeles, CA 90015
violinist, orchestra director

Brown, James
Brothers Management Associates
141 Dunbar Ave.
Fords, NJ 08863
singer, broadcasting executive

Brown, Downtown Julie
William Morris
1350 Avenue of the Americas
New York, NY 10019
Downtown Veejay

Brown, Patrick Management
4405 Martin Luther King Jr.
Blvd.
Los Angeles, CA 90008

Browne, Jackson
RR 1, Box 648
Del Valle, TX 78617
singer, songwriter

Browning, John
165 W. 57th St.
New York, NY 10019
pianist

BRT Video
505 W. 65 Court, #200
Ft. Lauderdale, FL 33309-6130
music video production

Bruckheimer, Bonnie
500 S. Buena Vista
Burbank, CA 91521
artist management

Bruckner Society of America
2150 Dubuque Rd.
Iowa City, IA 52240
Charles L. Eble, President
Gustav Mahler and Anton Bruckner
society

Bryan World Productions
125 S. Wilton Place
Los Angeles, CA 90004
Bob Bryan, Director
video production

Bryant, Felice
House of Bryant
P.O. Box 570
Gatlinburg, TN 37738
songwriter, vocalist

BS Productions
3010 West End Ave., #7C
Nashville, TN 37203
video production company

BSA Presentations
Div. of BSA Inc.
P.O. Box 1516
Champaign, IL 61824
Bill Stein, President
artist management

BSW Records
P.O. Box 2297
Universal City, TX 78148
Frank Willson, President
independent record label

Buckholtz Productions, Inc.
737 Eleonore St.
New Orleans, LA 70115
video production

Buckskin Company, The
7 Music Circle N
Nashville, TN 37203
David Skepner, President
artist management

Buddy Holly Memorial Society
3806 55th St.
Lubbock, TX 79413

Buddy Lee Attractions, Inc.
38 Music Square E, #300
Nashville, TN 37203
Tony Conway, President
artist management

Buffett, Jimmy
c/o Frontline Management
80 Universal City Plaza, 4th Fl.
Universal City, CA 91608
singer, songwriter

Bullet
The Charthouse 57 Ramsay Rd.
London, W3 8AZ U.K.
artist management

Bullethead Management
P.O. Box 637
New York, NY 10276
Scott Ambrose Reilly

Bullwinkle Entertainment Inc.
P.O. Box 1242
Voorhees, NJ 08043
Michael Minnick, President
artist management

Bumbry, Grace
165 W. 5th St.
New York, NY 10019
soprano

Bumstead Productions
1616 W. 3rd Ave.
Vancouver, BC V6J 1K2 Canada
Larry Wanagas
artist management

Bunetta, Al Management Inc.
4121 Wilshire Blvd., #204
Los Angeles, CA 90010
artist management

Burke, T.J. & Associates
P.O. Box 2512
Toluca Lake, CA 91610
Tim Burke
artist management

Burns Entertainment Inc.
2145 Avenue Rd.
Toronto, Ontario M5M 4B2 Canada
Jeff Burns, President
independent record label

Burton Management Inc.
250 W. 57th St., #1502
New York, NY 10107
Pamela Burton, President
artist management

Bust It Productions
80 Swan Way, #130
Oakland, CA 94612
Louis Burrell
independent record label

Music is harmony, harmony is perfection,
perfection is our dream, and our dream is heaven.
—AMIEL

C & M Productions
5114 Albert Dr.
Brentwood, TN 37027
Joy Cotton, President
artist management

C M Management
7957 Nita Ave.
Canoga Park, Ca 91304
Craig Miller, President

C'est la Mort Records
P.O. Box 91
Baker, LA 70714
Woodrow Dumas
independent record label

C-Hundred Filmcorp.
P.O. Box 423
Athens, GA 30603
video production

C-Level Recordings
11288 Ventura Blvd., #205
Studio City, CA 91604
Ian Rich
independent record label

C.M.O. Management
Unit 32 Ransomes Dock: 35-37 Park-
gate Rd.
London, SW11 4NP U.K.

C/Z Records
1407 E. Madison, #41
Seattle, WA 98122
Daniel House
independent record label

Cabaret Metro
3730 N. Clark
Chicago, IL 60613
Joe Shanahan
independent record label

Cabrillo Music Festival
6500 Soquel Dr.
Aptos, CA 95003

Cadence Jazz Records
Cadence Bldg.
Redwood, NY 13679
David Bernstein, Promotion
independent record label

Cadence
The Review of Jazz & Blues
Cadence Bldg.
Redwood, NY 13679
magazine

Cage, John
101 W. 18th St.
New York, NY 10011
composer

Cahn, Sammy
c/o Daniel Howard
8600 Melrose Ave.
Los Angeles, CA 90069
lyric songwriter

Cahn-Man Management
5332 College Ave., #202
Oakland, CA 94618
Ellot Cahn

**Cal Arts Contemporary
Music/World Music Festivals**
California Institute of the Arts
24700 McBean Parkway
Valencia, CA 91355

Caldwell, Sarah
Opera Company of Boston, Inc.
P.O. Box 50
Newton, MA 02258
opera producer, conductor, stage
director

Caledonia Foundation
Scottish Heritage Center
P.O. Box 564
Laurinburg, NC 28352
Miss Duncan McDonald, Secretary
society to further Scottish Opera

Caliber Records
12754 Ventura Blvd.
Studio City, CA 91604
Stephen Brown, President

Calico Ltd.
8843 Shirley Ave.
Northridge, CA 91324
Tom Burton, President
video production

Caligula Records
1151 Post St., #12
San Francisco, CA 94109
independent record label

Callaghan Group Ltd.
219 E. 31st
New York, NY 10016
Edward Callaghan, President
artist management

Calvary Music Group, The
Calvary Records
142 8th Ave. N
Nashville, TN 37203
Nelson Parkerson, President
independent record label

Calzatti/Clark Productions
4133 Mentone Ave.
Culver City, CA 90232
Jeff Clark, Executive Producer

Camaraderie Music
P.O. Box 15403, Kenmore Station
Boston, MA 02215
Curt Naihersey
independent record label

Camel Management
120 N. Victory Blvd., #206
Burbank, CA 91502
Bruce Bird

Camel Records
120 N. Victory Blvd., #206
Burbank, CA 91502
Bruce Bird, President
independent record label

Cameron Organization Inc.
2001 W. Magnolia Blvd.
Burbank, CA 91506
Scott A. Cameron President
artist management

Campagna, Mary Anne
1623 Crescent Place
Venice, CA 90291
artist management

Campbell, Glen
151 El Camino
Beverly Hills, CA 90212
singer, songwriter

Campbell, Ian David
San Diego Opera
P.O. Box 988
San Diego, CA 92112
opera company director

Canadian Friends of Mine
c/o Kevin C. Beyer
6620 Vintage Dr.
Hudsonville, MI 49426
Bachman Turner Overdrive, Guess
Who fan club

Canon, Robert Morris
Boston Opera Theater
300 Massachusetts Ave.
Boston, MA 02115
opera producer

**Cape and Islands Chamber Music
Festival**
P.O. Box 72
Yarmouth Port, MA 02675

Capitol Records
1750 N. Vine St.
Hollywood, CA 90028
Hale Milgram, President/Capitol
Joe Smith, President/CEO Capitol-
EMI Music
record label

Capitol Records
New York
810 7th Ave., 4th Fl.
New York, NY 10019

Capobianco, Tito
Pittsburgh Opera Inc.
711 Penn Ave., 8th Fl.
Pittsburgh, PA 15222
opera director

Capri Records Ltd.
19423 N. Turkey Creek Rd.
Morrison, CO 80465
Tom Burns, President
independent record label

**Caprice International Records &
Discs**
14 Rasberry Ln., P.O. Box 808
Lititz, PA 17543
Joey Welz, President
independent record label

Capricorn Records
120 30th Ave. N
Nashville, TN 37203
Phil Walden, President
independent record label

Caramoor Music Festival
P.O. Box R
Katonah, NY 10536

Cardenas/Fernandez
1254 N. Wells
Chicago, Il 60610
Henry Cardenas
artist managment

Cardenes, Andres Jorge
c/o American International Artists
515 E. 89th St., #6B
New York, NY 10028
violinist

Cardiac Records
1790 Broadway, 6th Fl.
New York, NY 10019
Cathy Jacobson, President
independent record label

Carey, Mariah
51 West 52nd St.
New York, NY 10019
singer

Carlyle Records Inc.
1217 16th Ave. S
Nashville, TN 37212
Laura Fraser, President
independent record label

Carman Productions
15456 Cabrito Rd.
Van Nuys, CA 91406
Tom Skeeter
artist management

Carmel Artist Management
P.O. Box 50353
Palo Alto, CA 94303
Jeanette Avenida, Promotion and
Marketing

Carmel Bach Festival
P.O. Box 575
Carmel, CA 93921

Carmel Records
P.O. Box 50353
Palo Alto, CA 94303
Jeanette Avenida, Promotion
independent record label

Caro Records
4901 Morena Blvd., #906
San Diego, CA 92117
independent record label

**Carol Lawrence Memorial
Fan Club**
3886 Shattuck Ave.
Columbus, OH 43220

Caroline Records
114 W. 26th St., 11th Fl.
New York, NY 10001
Keith Wood, President
independent record label

Carpenter, Richard
P.O. Box 1084
Downey, CA 90240
composer, arranger

**Carr, Vikki (Florencia Bisenta De
Casillas Martinez Cardona)**
P.O. Box 5126
Beverly Hills, CA 90209
singer

Carr/Sharpe Entertainment
9320 Wilshire Blvd., #200
Beverly Hills, CA 90212
Budd Carr/Wil Sharpe
artist management

Carreras, Jose
Opera Caballe
Via Augusta 59
Barcelona, Spain
tenor

Carroll, Diahann
9200 Sunset Blvd., #710
Los Angeles, CA 90069
singer

**Carson, Phil & Associates Unlim-
ited**
8455 Beverly Blvd., 6th Fl.
Los Angeles, CA 90048
Phil Carson
artist management

Carter Family Fan Club
P.O. Box 1371
Hendersonville, TN 37077

Carter, Benny (Lester Bennett)
P.O. Box 870
Hollywood, CA 90028
musician, composer, conductor.

Carter, Betty (Lillie Mae Jones)
Bet-Car Productions
117 St. Felix St.
Brooklyn, NY 11217
jazz singer, songwriter

Carter, Nell
151 El Camino
Beverly Hills, CA 90212
singer

Carter, Russell
Artist Management
755 First National Bank Bldg.
Decatur, GA 30030
artist management

Carter, William N.
Career Management
1114 17th Ave. S, Suite 204
Nashville, TN 37212
artist management

Case, Keith & Associates
59 Music Square W
Nashville, TN 37203
artist management

Casci, Nedda
American Guild of Musical Artists
1727 Broadway
New York, NY 10019
mezzo-soprano

Cash, Johnny
House of Cash, Inc.
P.O. Box 508
Hendersonville, TN 37077
singer

Cash, June Carter
House of Cash, Inc.
P.O. Box 508
Hendersonville, TN 37077
singer

Cashbox
6464 Sunset Blvd., #605
Hollywood, CA 90028
George Albert, Publisher
magazine

Casino Records
411 Powells Lane
New York, NY 11590
Phil Vance
independent record label

Cassidy Class
667 Center Ave.
Martinez, CA 94553
David, Shaun and Shirley Jones fan club

Cassilly, Richard
Boston University
855 Commonwealth Ave.
Boston, MA 02215
tenor

Castle Communications
28 Cross St.
Brookvale NSW 2100 Australia
John Evans, Managing Director
independent record label

Castle Hill Festival
P.O. Box 283
Ipswich, MA 01938
music festival

Catgut Acoustical Society
c/o Carleen Maley Hutchins
112 Essex Ave.
Montclair, NJ 07042
studies violin acoustics

Catwalk Management
P.O. Box 4666
Wilmington, DE 19807
Sallie S. Harris
artist management

Caustic Fish Co., The
P.O. Box 597
Denver, CO 80201
Kirk Drabing, President
independent record label

CBG Records
225 Parkhurst St.
Newark, NJ 07114
Ken Southworth, President
independent record label

CBS Records Inc.
51 West 52nd Street
New York, NY 10019
Walter Yetnikoff, President & CEO
record company

CD Presents Ltd.
1317 Grant Ave., #531
San Francisco, CA 94133
David Ferguson, President

CD Review Digest
Classical
The Peri Press
Hemlock Ridge, P.O. Box 348
Voorheesville, NY 12186

CD Review Digest
Jazz, Popular, etc.
Peri Press
Hemlock Ridge, P.O. Box 348
Voorheesville, NY 12186

CD Review Yearbook
WGE Publishing
Forest Rd., Box 278
Hancock, NH 03449

Celebresearch Inc.
7119 E. Shea Blvd., # 106-436
Scottsdale, AZ 85354
Joyce McRae
artist management

Celestine-Cloutier
8278 Sunset Blvd.
Los Angeles, CA 90048
hairstylist/makeup rep

Centaur Records Inc.
8867 Highland Rd., #206
Baton Rouge, LA 70808
Victor Sachse, President
independent record label

Center for Contemporary Opera
P.O. Box 10350, Gracie Station
New York, NY 10028
Richard Marshall, Director

Century II Promotions Inc.
523 Heather Place
Nashville, TN 37220
Sonny Simmons, President
artist management

Century Media Records
P.O. Box 2218
Van Nuys, CA 91404
Ivette Ruiz, Publicity
independent record label

Cexton Records
2740 s. Harbor Blvd., #K
Santa Ana, CA 92704
John Anello Jr., President
independent record label

CFY Records
P.O. Box 6271
Stanford, CA 94309
Eugene Robinson
independent record label

Cha Cha Records
902 N. Webster
Port Washington, WI 53074
Jospeh DeLucia, President
independent record producer

Challedon Records
Pembroke One Bldg., 5th Fl.
Virginia Beach, VA 23462
Rick Shapiro
independent record label

Chamber Music America
545 8th Ave.
New York, NY 10018
Dean K. Stein, Executive
Director

Chamber Music America Membership Directory
Chamber Music America
545 8th Ave., 9th Fl.
New York, NY 10018

Chamber Music Northwest
520 S.W. 6th Ave., #1112
Portland, OR 97204

Chambers, Victor
51 Lady Musgrave Rd.
Kingston, 10 Jamaica
artist management

Chameleon Music Group
6255 Sunset Blvd., #917
Hollywood, CA 90028
independent record label

Chameleon Music Group
New York
1740 Broadway, 23rd Fl.
New York, NY 10019

Champagne Pictures
437 Sherbourne St.
Toronto, ONT M4X 1K5
Canada
Andy Crosbie
video production

Chaos Recordings
51 W. 52nd St.
New York, NY 10019
Michael Bleeker
independent record label

Chapel Lane Productions
1916 28th Ave. S.
Birmingham, AL 35209
Michael Panepento, Director
video production

Chapman, Tracy
9229 W. Sunset Blvd., #718
West Hollywood, CA 90069
singer, songwriter

Chapter 22 Management
Unit 17, Newhall Place, 17 Newhall
Hill
Birmingham, B1 3JH U.K.
Craig Jennings

Char-Mel Management
61-29 Madison St., #2-L
Ridgewood, NY 11385
Serafin Rivera

Charismatic Productions
2604 Mozart Place NW
Washington, DC 20009
Charles Fishman
artist management

Charles Ives Center For the Arts
P.O. Box 2957
Danbury, CT 06813

Charles Ives Society
c/o Institute of Studies in American
Music
Conservatory of Music
CUNY Brooklyn College
Brooklyn, NY 11210
H. Wiley Hitchcock, President

Charles, Ray (Ray Charles Robinson)
2107 W. Washington Blvd., #200
Los Angeles, CA 90018
musician, singer, composer

Charley Pride Fan Club
P.O. Box 670507
Dallas, TX 75367

Charlie Daniels Band
Rte. 6, Box 156A
Lebanon, TN 37087
country band

Charo
P.O. Box 1007
Hanalei, Kauai, HI 96714
singer

Chase Group
34 King James Lane
Atlantic Highlands, NJ 07716
Chase Jackson
artist management

Chase Music Group
P.O. Box 11178
Glendale, CA 91226
William G. Stilfield, President
independent record label

Cheap Trick
315 W. Gorham St.
Madison, WI 53703
musicians

Cheap Trick International
P.O. Box 4321
Madison, WI 53711
fan club

Cheetah Records
605 E. Robinson St., #610
Orlando, FL 32801
Tom Reich, President
independent record label

Chen, Zuo Huan
Central Philharmonic Orchestra
China
He Pen Li
Beijing China
conductor

Cher
c/o Bill Sammeth Organization
9200 Sunset Blvd.
Los Angeles, CA 90069
singer

Cher'd Interest
c/o Linda Huston
5807 Hornet Dr.
Orlando, FL 32808
Cher Fan Club

Cherrie Records
56 Teresa St.
Daly City, CA 94014
Cleve White, President
indenpendent record label

Cherry Bear Organization
139 Mortimer Rd.
London NW10 U.K.
artist management

Cherry Street Records
P.O. Box 52681
Tulsa, OK 74152
Rodney Young, President
independent record label

Chesky Records
311 W. 43rd St., #202
New York, NY 10036
Norman Chesky
independent record label

Chestnut Hill Concerts
P.O. Box 183
Guildord, CT 06437

**Chet Atkins Appreciation
Society**
29 Ferris St.
South River, NJ 08882

Chi-Town Records Inc.
838 W. Grand Ave.
Chicago, IL 60622
Lewis A. Pitzele, Chairman
independent record label

Chiaroscuro Records
830 Broadway
New York, NY 10003
Jon Bates
independent record label

Chicago
80 Universal City Plaza, #400
Universal City, CA 91608
group

Chicago Concert Artists
431 S. Dearborn St., #906
Chicago, IL 60605
Jean Seidl, Managing Director
opera artist management

Chicago Fan Club
c/o Warner Bros.
75 Rockefeller Plaza
New York, NY 10019

Children's Group
561 Bloor St. W., #300
Toronto, Ontario M5S 1Y6 Canada
Ed Glinert
independent record label

China Club, The
2130 Broadway
New York, NY 10023
club

**Chinese Music Society of North
America**
1 Heritage Plaza
P.O. Box 5275
Woodridge, IL 60517
Sin-Yan Shen, President

Chisum PL Recordings
2300 5th Ave., 16th Fl.
New York, NY 10037
Andre Robbins
independent record label

Chorus America
2111 Sansom St.
Philadelphia, PA 19103
Kenneth Garner, Executive Director

Chou, Wen-Chung
Columbia University Center for US-
China Arts Exchange
423 W. 118th St., #1E
New York, NY 10027
composer

CHR Management
350 Fifth Ave., #501
New York, NY 10118
Chip Rachlin

Chriss, Joel and Co.
300 Mercer St., #3J
New York, NY 10003
artist management

Chrysalis Records, Inc.
9255 Sunset Blvd., #319
Los Angeles, CA 90069
John Sykes, President
recording company

Cielo Films
503 S. Catalina St.
Los Angeles, CA 90020
Joanna Bongiovanni
video productions

Cimirron/Rainbird Inc.
607 Piney Point Rd.
Yorktown, VA 23692
Lana Puckett, President
independent record label

Cincinnati Summer Opera Festival
Cincinnati Opera Association
Cincinnati Music Hall
1241 Elm St.
Cincinnati, OH 45210

Cine International Assoc.
222 E. 44th St.
New York, NY 10017
video production

Cinema Records
812 W. Darby Rd.
Havertown, PA 19083
Denny Somach, President
independent record label

Cinemagic Productions
537 Jones St., #898
San Francisco, CA 94102
video Production

Cinepop Management
20-A Victoria Rd.
Brighton Sussex BN1 3FS U.K.
Simon Watson

Circus
P.O. Box 265
Mt. Morris, IL 61054
hard rock magazine

Citrus Group
802 N. Citrus Ave.
Los Angeles, CA 90038
hairstylist/makeup rep

City Block Records
2015 Mass. Ave. NW
Washington, DC 20036
Charles X. Block, Chairman
independent record label

City Lights Management
P.O. Box 1309
Studio City, CA 91614
Roger Perry

City Spark Records
921 W. 44th St.
Kansas City, MO 64111
Tom Mardikes
independent record label

Cityzins for On-Linear Futures
P.O. Box 2026 Madison Square Station
New York, NY 10159
Sue Ann Harkey
independent record label

Clapton, Eric
9830 Wilshire Blvd.
Beverly Hills, CA 90212
guitarist, film score composer

Clarion Music Society
P.O. Box 1196
New York, NY 10276
Nancy Stout, Executive Director
performs rare classical operatic,
choral and orchestral music

Clarity Recordings
P.O. Box 411407
San Francisco, CA 94141
Ed Woods, Owner
independent record label

Clark, Dick
3003 West Olive Ave.
Burbank, CA 01505
producer

Clark, Douglas Associates Inc.
18 West Ct.
Sausalito, CA 94965
video production

Clark, Malcolm Inc.
1101 Western Ave., #520
Seattle, WA 98104
video production

Clark, Roy
c/o J. Halsey
3225 S. Norwood Ave.
Tulsa, OK 74135
singer, musician

Clark, Terry
Pablo Records
451 N. Canon Dr.
Beverly Hills, CA 90210
jazz musician

Class Act Productions
1514 Ed Bluestein Blvd., #107
Austin, TX 78721
Jeff Van Ryswyk, Owner
artist management

Classic Concepts
444 W. 35th St., #1-D
New York, NY 10001
Lionel C. Martin
video production

Classical Music Lover's Exchange
P.O. Box 31
Pelham, NY 10803
Tamara Monique Conroy, Founder
and President

Cleary, Dan
Management Associates
1801 Ave. of the Stars, #1105
Los Angeles, CA 90007
artist management

Clement, Michele
879 Florida St.
San Francisco, CA 94110
video producer

Cleve, George
San Jose Symphony Orchestra
99 Alamaden Blvd., #400
San Jose, CA 95113
conductor

**Cliburn, Van (Harvey Lavan
Cliburn, Jr.)**
2525 Ridgmar Blvd., #307
Fort Worth, TX 76116
concert pianist

**Cliff Richard Fan Club of
America**
8916 Skokie Blvd., #3
Skokie, IL 60077

Cliff, Jimmy
c/o Victor Chambers
51 Lady Musgrave Road
Kington, Jamaica
reggae singer

Cline, Patsy
Fan Club
P.O. Box 244
Dorchester, MA 02125

Close Encounter Productions
503 Crown Point
Buffalo Grove, IL 60089
video production

Cloutier
7201 Melrose Ave.
Los Angeles, CA 90046
hairstylist/makeup rep

Club Lingerie
6507 Sunset Blvd.
Hollywood, CA 90028
club

CMC International Inc.
106 W. Horton St.
Zebulon, NC 27597
Bill Cain
artist management

CMS Management
625 Main St.
Simpson, PA 18407
Carl Canedy

Coalition Entertainment
155 Toryork Dr., #15
Weston, Ontario M9L JX9
Canada
Robert Lanni, President
artist management

Coalition Entertainment
155 Toryork Dr., #15
Weston, Ontario M9L JX9
Canada
Robert Lanni, President
independent record label

Coasters, The
141 Dunbar Ave.
Fords, NJ 08863
group

Coats Music
315 Church St.
Sandpoint, ID 83864
Dennis Coats, Owner
artist management

Cocker, Joe
c/o A&M
1416 N. LaBrea Ave.
Hollywood, CA 90028
singer

Code of the West
P.O. Box 1013
Putnam, TX 76469
Gary Beckworth, President
artist management

Coffer, Raymond Management
Angley House, 5 The Lake
Bushey Herts WD1 1HS U.K.

Cohen, Marc
c/o Atlantic
75 Rockefeller Plaza
New York, NY 10019
singer

Cohen, Ted Management
1232 S. Genesee Ave.
Los Angeles, CA 90019

Cohn, Bruce Management
P.O. Box 878
Sonoma, CA 95476

Colbert Artists Management
111 West 57th St.
New York, NY 91505
Agnes Eisenberger, President

Cold Chillin'
1995 Broadway, #1800
New York, NY 10023
Dee Joseph Garner
independent record label

Cole Classic Management
4150 Riverside Dr., #207
Burbank, CA 91505
Earl Cole, Manager

Cole, Natalie
151 El Camino
Beverly Hills, CA 90212
singer

Coleman, Cy
161 W. 54th St.
New York, NY 10019
pianist, composer, producer

Coleman, Ornette
P.O. Box 12 Canal Street Station
New York, NY 10012
composer, instrumentalist

Collin, Barbara Artists
P.O. Box 10782
Beverly Hills, CA 90213
artist management

Collins Management Inc.
5 Bigelow St.
Cambridge, MA 02139
Tim Collins, President

Collins, Art Management
201 W. 85th St., #5B
New York, NY 10029
artist management

Collins, Phil
Hit and Run Music Ltd.
25 Ives St.
London SW3 2ND U.K.
singer, songwriter, drummer

Collision Records
P.O. Box 3556
San Rafael, CA 94912
independent record label

Color Me Badd
c/o Reprise Records
3300 Warner Blvd.
Burbank, CA 91505
group

Colorado Mahlerfest
1281 Linden Dr.
Boulder, CO 80304

Colorado Music Festival
1035 Pearl St., #302
Boulder, CO 80302

Colorado Springs Fine Arts Center
30 W. Dale St.
Colorado Springs, CO 80903
David S. Wagner, CEO and Executive
Director

Colossal Pictures
2800 Third St.
San Francisco, CA 94107
Drew Takahashi
video production

Columbia Records—Sony Music Entertainment
51 West 52nd Street
New York, NY 10019
Don Ienner, President
record company

Columbia Records—Sony Music Entertainment
Santa Monica
2100 Colorado Blvd.
Santa Monica, CA 90404

Comet, Catherine
Grand Rapids Symphony Orchestra
220 Lyon St., NW #415
Grand Rapids, MI 49503
conductor

Commissiona, Sergiu
Helsinki Philharmonic Orchestra
Karamzininkatu 4
SF-00100 Helsinki, Finland
conductor

Commodores, The
3151 Cahuenga Blvd., W, #235
Los Angeles, CA 90068
group

Communications Corporation of America
2501 N. Sheffield
Chicago, IL 60614
artist management

Community 3
438 Bedford Ave.
Brooklyn, NY 11211
Albert Garzon, Director
independent record label

Community 3/Germany
Andernacher Str. 23, D-8500
Nurnburg 10 Germany
Thomas Hartmann, Label Manager
independent record label

Como, Perry
c/o RCA
1133 Avenue of the Americas
New York, NY 10036
singer

Company Called W, A
P.O. Box 618, Church Street Station
New York, NY 10008
Walt Goodridge, President
independent record label

Company of Fifers and Drummers
P.O. Box 525
620 N. Main St.
Ivoryton, CT 06442
Ed Olsen, Curator

Composers Theatre
66 W. 12th St.
New York, NY 10011
Laura Foreman, President
society of professional composers and musicians

Computer Music Journal
MIT Press
55 Hayward St.
Cambridge, MA 02142
magazine

Conant, Robert Scott
Foundation for Baroque Music, Inc.
165 Wilton Rd.
Greenfield Center, NY 12833
harpsichordist

Concerted Efforts Inc.
P.O. Box 99
Newtonville, MA 02160
Paul Kahn, Director
artist management

Concerts America
1510 Forest Lane
McLean, VA 22101
Mike Schreibman, President
artist management

Concord Jazz
P.O. Box 845
Concord, CA 94522
Carl E. Jefferson, President
independent record label

Concord Jazz Festival
P.O. Box 6166
Concord, CA 93921

Concrete Management Inc.
301 West 53rd St., #11D
New York, NY 10019
Walter O'Brien, President

Concrete Productions
2811 McKinney Ave., #204
Dallas, TX 75204
Tina Sherriel, General Manager
make-up/hair for music videos

Confidential Records
1013 Evelyn Ave.
Albany, CA 94706
Joel Brandwein, President
independent record label

Conlee, John Enterprises
38 Music Square E
Nashville, TN 37203
Dave Roberts
artist management

Conlin, Thomas Byrd
Charleston Symphony Orchestra
P.O. Box 2292
1210 Virginia St. E
Charleston, WV 25328
conductor

Conlon, James Joseph
Columbia Artist Management
165 W. 5th St.
New York, NY 10019
conductor

Connecticut Early Music Festival
P.O. Box 329
New London, CT 06320

Connick, Harry Jr.
P.O. Box 4450
New York, NY 10101
jazz musician

Connie Francis International Fan Club
61 Westwood Dr.
Rochester, NY 14616

Conniff, Ray
P.O. Box 46395
West Hollywood, CA 90046
conductor, composer, arranger

Conscience Music
P.O. Box 740
Oak Park, IL 60303
Karen M. Schwartz, Personal Manager

Consensus Management
3479 NW Yeon St.
Portland, OR 97210
Morris McClellan

Constant Communications
1137 2nd St., #212
Santa Monica, CA 90403
Connie Hillman, President
artist management

Contemporary Artists
P.O. Box 48106
Los Angeles, CA 90048
artist management

Contemporary Christian Music
CCM Pubs. Inc.
1913 21st Ave. S
Nashville, TN 37212
magazine

Contemporary Entertainment Corporation
1401 S. Brentwood
St. Louis, MO 63144
Terry Williams
artist management

Conti, Bill
c/o Screen Composers Guild
2451 Nichols Canyon
Los Angeles, CA 90046
composer

Convenience
P.O. Box 66461
AMF O'Hare, IL 60666
John Maz, Director
independent record label

Cooder, Ry
c/o Warner Bros.
3300 West Warner Blvd.
Burbank, CA 91505
recording artist, guitarist

Cool-Moon Productions
43 Wolfe St.
Glen Cove, NY 11542
Ronald Royster, President
artist management

Coolidge, Rita
c/o Jason McCloskey
426 S. Fairview St.
Burbank, CA 91505
singer

Cooper, Alice
4135 E. Keim Dr.
Paradise Valley, AZ 85235
singer

Cooper, Jay Leslie
P.O. Box 5524
Beverly Hills, CA 90209
music lawyer

Coppos Films
118 N. Larchmont Blvd.
Los Angeles, CA 90004
video production

Core Entertainment
8101 Orion Ave., #18
Van Nuys, CA 91406
Keith Dressel, President
independent record label

Core Entertainment Group
7240 NE Drive, #104
Austin, TX 78723
Jim Ericson, A&R
independent record label

Corea, Chick (Armando)
2635 Griffith Park Blvd.
Los Angeles, CA 90039
pianist, composer

Corigliano, John Paul
c/o Michael Mace
315 W. 57th St.
New York, NY 10019
composer of NET Great Performances theme

Cornelius, Don
9255 Sunset Blvd., #420
Los Angeles, CA 90039
executive producer of "Soul Train"

Corner Stone Management
148 E. Lancaster Ave.
Wayne, PA 19087
Steve Mountain

Corvalan/Condliffe Management
1010 4th St., #5
Santa Monica, CA 90403
Maria Corvalan/Brian Condliffe

Cosh Management
P.O. Box 102
London E15 2HH U.K.
artist management

Cosmotone Records
P.O. Box 71988
Los Angeles, CA 90071
Rafael Brom, President
independent record label

Costello, Elvis (Declan Patrick McManus)
c/o Warner Bros.
3300 Warner Blvd.
Burbank, CA 91510
musician, singer

Country Breeze Music
1715 Marty
Kansas City, KS 66103
Ed Morgan, President
independent record label

Country Music Association
1 Music Circle S.
Nashville, TN 37203
Edwin Benson, Executive Director

Country Music Foundation
4 Music Sq. E.
Nashville, TN 37203
William Ivey, Director
educational foundation

Country Music Foundation Records
4 Music Sq. E
Nashville, TN 37203
Kyle Young, Deputy Dir.
independent record label

Country Music Showcase International
P.O. Box 368
Carlisle, IA 50047
Harold L. Luick, President
society for professional and amateur performers

Country Music Television
2806 Opryland Dr.
Nashville, TN 37214
country music video programming

Courage Management
2899 Agoura Road, #562
Westlake, CA 91361
John Courage
artist management

Courtright Management Inc.
201 E. 87th St., P.O. Box 248
New York, NY 10128
Hernando Courtright
manages producers/engineers/artists/ songwriters

Covert Communications
36 Wright Ave.
Toronto, Ontario M6R 1K8 Canada
artist management

Cowabunga Music
P.O. Box 630755
Miami, FL 33163
Jack Gale, President
independent record label

Cowperthwaite, Janet
320 Judah
San Francisco, CA 94122
artist management

Cowsills Fan Club
P.O. Box 83
Lexington, MS 39095

Cracks 90 Ltd.
P.O. Box 1115
London N8 7DX U.K.
Andy Ferguson
artist management

Crash Management
150 W. 56th St., # 2812
New York, NY 10019
Jon Goldwater
artist management

Cray, Robert
Hightone Records
220 Fourth St., #101
Oakland, CA 94607
guitarist, singer, songwriter

Crazed Management
210 Bridge Plaza Dr.
Manalapan, NJ 07726
Jon Zazula
artist management

Creative Image
6363 Wilshire Blvd., #500
Los Angeles, CA 90048
Tanya Du'Shay, Executive Director
casting/makeup/hair/for music videos

Creative Music Foundation
P.O. Box 671
Woodstock, NY 12498
Karl H. Berger, Co-Director
concentrates on technical skill

Creative Musical Alternatives
1800 Dwight Way
Berkeley, CA 94703
Marcy Straw, Director
artist management

CREEM
John T. Edwards Publishing Ltd.
519 8th Ave., 15th Fl.
New York, NY 10018
Dan Halpern, Publisher
magazine

Crespin, Regine
c/o Breslin
119 W. 57th St.
New York, NY 10019
soprano

Crewcuts Fan Club
c/o Judith Gorecki
601 Irvington Ave.
Hillside, NJ 07205

Crisis Management
1763 E. Pender St., #209
Vancouver, BC V5L-1W5 Canada
Ken Lester

Criss Cross Jazz
P.O. Box 1214, 7500 BE
Enschede Netherlands
Gerry Teekens
independent record label

Critique Records
800 W. Cummings Park, #2500
Woburn, MA 0181
independent record label

Crockford, Paul Management
59 Islington Park
London N1 U.K.
artist management

Crooked Crooked Beat Management
3441 Cahuenga Blvd.
Hollywood, CA 90068
artist management

Crosby, John O'Hea
Santa Fe Opera
P.O. Box 2488
Santa Fe, NM 87504
conductor

Crosby, Stills & Nash
1588 Crossroads of the World
Los Angeles, CA 90028
musicians

Cross & Associates
22470 Foothill Blvd., #34
Hayward, CA 94541
Rebecca Cross
artist management

Cross, Christopher
P.O. Box 63
Marble Falls, TX 78654
singer, songwriter

Crosseyed Bear Productions
278 Haverstraw Rd.
Suffern, NY 10901
Phillip Bear
artist management

Crossfire Entertainment
P.O. Box 128037
Nashville, TN 37212
Will Botwin
artist management

Crossover Entertainment
200 E. 24th St., #1908
New York, NY 10010
Adrienne Lenhoff, President
artist management

Crossroads Management
P.O. Box 221, Parkville Station
Brooklyn, NY 11204
Valerie Sicignano
artist management

Crosstown Music
449 1/2 Moreland Ave. NE
Atlanta, GA 30307
Jim Barber
artist management

Crowley, Mike
Artist Management
122 Longwood Ave.
Austin, TX 78734

Cruz Records
P.O. Box 7756
Long Beach, CA 90807
Greg Ginn
independent record label

Crystal
4237 Los Nietos Dr.
Los Angeles, CA 90027
hairstylist's rep

Crystal Management
318 W. 20th St.
New York, NY 10011
Albert Mongillo
artist management

CSA Management
101 Chamberlin Rd.
London, NW 10 U.K.
Clive Stanhope
artist management

CSI Video Center
6225 Sunset Blvd., Suite 624
Los Angeles, CA 90028
video production

Cult of the Virgin
65 Hillside Ave., #B-A
New York, NY 10040
Black Virgin fan club

**Cultural Exchange Society of
America**
445 E. 68th Ave., #12L
New York, NY 10021
Helen Demitroff, Secretary/Treasurer
foreign exchange for musicians

Culture Club
34 Green Lane
Northwood, Middlesex, U.K.
defunct pop group

Cummings, Bob Productions, Inc.
1204 Elmwood Ave.
Nashville, TN 37212
video production

Curb Records
3907 Alameda Ave., 2nd Fl.
Burbank, CA 91505
Mike Curb, Chairman/President
record company

Current Events Management
P.O. Box 20839
New York, NY 10009
Scott Ambrose Reilly

Curry, Adam
c/o MTV
1515 Broadway, 23rd Fl.
New York, NY 10036
MTV video countdown veejay

Curtis Management
207 1/2 First Ave. S, #300
Seattle, WA 98104
Kelly Curtis
artist management

Curtis Wood/Eagle International Records
4416 Eaton Creek
Nashville, TN 37218
independent record label

Cutting Records Inc.
104 Vermilyea Ave., #B2
New York, NY 10034
Amado Marin, President
independent record label

CWP Inc.
210 2nd St. N., #007
Minneapolis, MN 55401
Christopher Nason, President/CEO
video production

Cybervoc Records
73 N. Palm St.
Ventura, CA 93001
independent record label

Cycle of Fifths Management Inc.
331-H Dante Court
Holbrook, NY 11741
John Reilly
artist management

Cyclone Pictures
314 W. 56th St., #LD
New York, NY 10019
Jefferson Spady
video production

Cyntone Records
14875 NE 20th Ave.
Miami, FL 33181
James Hazley
independent record label

Cyrus, Billy Ray
c/o Mercury
825 8th Ave.
New York, NY 10019
singer

*Composers should write tunes that chauffeurs
and errand boys can whistle.*
—THOMAS BEECHAM

D Management
P.O. Box 121682
Nashville, TN 37212
Doug Casmus
artist management

D.A.S. Communications Ltd.
83 Riverside Dr.
New York, NY 10024
David Sonenberg, President
artist management

D.I.S. Company
250 W. 57th, #2428
New York, NY 10107
David Salidor, Owner
artist management

D.J. Jazzy Jeff (Jeff Townes)
1133 Ave. of the Americas
New York, NY 10036
singer

Dagene Records
P.O. Box 410851
San Francisco, CA 94141
David Alston, President
independent record label

Daily Variety
5700 Wilshire Blvd., #120
Los Angeles, CA 90036
Michael Silverman, Publisher
entertainment trade paper

Dallaire, Gary Management
498 W. End Ave., #1A
New York, NY 10024
artist management

Dallas Music Videos
6932 Greenville Ave., P.O. Box 135
Dallas, TX 75231
Kathy Blaylock
video production

Dalton, Lacy J.
c/o Capitol
1750 Vine St.
Hollywood, CA 90028
singer

Daltrey, Roger
Left Services
157 W. 57th St.
New York, NY 10019
musician

Damage Management Ltd.
16 Lambton Place
London, W11 2SU U.K.
Ed Bicknell
artist management

Damone, Vic
P.O. Box 2999
Beverly Hills, CA 90013
singer

Dancing Buffalo
1301 Ocean Ave.
Santa Monica, CA 90401
video production

Daniels, Charlie
17060 Central Pike
Lebanon, TN 37087
musician, songwriter

Dare Management
227 Waverly Pl., #6C
New York, NY 10014
Jim Fouratt
artist management

Dark Light Music Ltd.
686 Richmond St. W
Toronto, Ontario M6J 1C3 Canada
Serge Sloimovits, President
independent record label

Darkhorse Entertainment
3903 SW Kelly
Portland, OR 97201
Michael Mavrolas, President
artist management

Darknite Management
3260 Netherland Ave.
Riverdale, NY 10463
Cindy Feldman

Darren, James
P.O. Box 1088
Beverly Hills, CA 90213
singer

Darvarova, Elmira
Metropolitan Opera Orchestra
Lincoln Center
New York, NY 10023
violinist, 1st woman concertmaster of
Met Opera

Davies, Dennis Russell
Brooklyn Philharmonic
30 Lafayette Ave.
Brooklyn, NY 11217
conductor

Davies, Raymond Douglas
MCA Records
70 Universal City Plaza
Universal City, CA 91608
musician, songwriter, "The Kinks"

Davies, Roger Management
3575 Cahuenga West, #580
Los Angeles, CA 90068
artist management

Davimos Advisors
6380 Wilshire Blvd.
Los Angeles, CA 90048
John Davimos
artist management

Davis, Chip
American Gramaphone Records
9130 Mormon Bridge Rd.
Omaha, NE 68152
record producer, arranger

Davis, Clive Jay
Arista Records, Inc.
6 W. 57th St.
New York, NY 10019
record company executive

Davis, Leonard
New York Philharmonic
132 W. 65th St.
New York, NY 10023
violist

Davis, Mac
9100 Wilshire Blvd., 1000W
Beverly Hills, CA 90212
singer

DAW
40 Main St., #1B
Westport, Ontario K0G 1X0 Canada
David Daw, President
independent record label

DB Records
432 Moreland Ave. NE
Atlanta, GA 30307
Randy Crittenton
independent record label

DBM Management
172 Arlington Rd.
London NW1 7HL U.K.
Dave Balfe
artist management

DCC Compact Classics
8300 Tampa Ave., #G
Northridge, CA 91324
Marshall Blonstein, President
independent record label

De Paola Productions
1560 Benedict Canyon
Beverly Hills, CA 90210
video production

DE-EL Entertainment Inc.
456 West 57th St., #1A
New York, NY 10019
Diane Gowman, President
artist management

Dea, Joe
8254 Fountain Ave., #D
Los Angeles, CA 90046
video producer

Dead Dead Good Records Ltd
2 Witton Walk
Northwich, Cheshire CW9 5AT London
Steve Harrison
independent record label

Dealmeida, Cynthia Koledo
Pittsburgh Symphony Society
Heinz Hall
600 Penn Ave.
Pittsburgh, PA 15222
oboist

DeBarge, El
6255 Sunset Blvd., #624
Los Angeles, CA 90028
singer

Debbie Harry Collector's Society
124 S. Locust Point Rd.
Mechanicsburg, PA 17055

Debby Boone Fan Club
c/o Ms. Chris Bujnovsky
526 Boeing Ave.
Reading, PA 19601

Decent Management
7932 Hillside Ave.
Los Angeles, CA 90046
Martin Schwartz
artist management

Dederich-Pejovich, Susan Russell
Dallas Symphony Orchestra
2301 Flora St., #300
Dallas, TX 75201
harpist

Dedicated Records
37 Uxbridge St.
London W87 TQ U.K.
independent record label

Dee-Mura Enterprises, Inc.
269 West Shore Dr.
Massapequa, NY 11758
Doreen Nakamura
artist management

Deep Purple
P.O. Box 254
Sheffield, S6 1DF, U.K.
group

Dees, Rick
KIIS FM
6255 Sunset Blvd.
Los Angeles, CA 90069
radio personality

Def American
3500 W. Olive Ave., #1550
Burbank, CA 91505
Rick Rubin, President
independent record label

Def Jam
652 Broadway
New York, NY 10012
independent record label

Def Leppard
P.O. Box 670 Old Chelsea Station
New York, NY 10113
group

Deff House Records
1 Paloma Ave., #2
Pacifica, CA 94044
Bob Keane, President
independent record label

Del Reeves Fan Club
c/o Patricia Williams
Rt. 2, 12615 U.S. 30, W
Upper Sandusky, OH 43351

Del Shannon Appreciation Society
6777 Hollywood Blvd., 9th Fl.
Hollywood, CA 90028

Del-Fi Records Inc.
P.O. Box 69188
Los Angeles, CA 90069
Bob Keane, President
independent record label

DeLarrocha, Alicia
c/o Columbia Artists Mgmt.
165 W. 57th St.
New York, NY 10019
concert pianist

DeLauro Management
1756 Broadway, #22-J
New York, NY 10019
Tony DeLauro
artist management

Delicious Vinyl
6607 Sunset Blvd.
Los Angeles, CA 90028
Rick Ross, GM
independent record label

Delmark/Pearl Records
4121 N. Rockwell Ave.
Chicago, IL 60618
Bob Koester, Owner
independent record label

Delos International Inc.
1645 N. Vine St., #340
Hollywood, CA 90028
Amelia Haygood, President
independent record label

Delta Music Inc.
2275 S. Carmelina Ave.
Los Angeles, CA 90064
Bob Koester
independent record label

Demann Entertainment
8000 Beverly Blvd.
Los Angeles, CA 90048
Freddy DeMann
artist management

Demonstration Records
P.O. Box 2930 Loop Station
Minneapolis, MN 55402
demo co

**Denver, John (Henry John
Deutschendorf, Jr.)**
8942 Wilshire Blvd.
Beverly Hills, CA 90211
singer, songwriter

Dep International
92 Fazly St.
Birmingham B5 5RD U.K.
video production

DePasse, Suzanne
5750 Wilshire Blvd., #610
Los Angeles, CA 90036
record company executive

Depot Recordings
P.O. Box 11
Kaneville, IL 60144
Joann Murdock
independent record label

DePreist, James Anderson
Oregon Symphony
711 SW Alder St., #200
Portland, OR 97205
conductor

Depth of Field Management
1501 Broadway, #1506
New York, NY 10036
Darryl Pitt, President
artist management

Derek Savage Management
12 Putney Bridge St.
Wadsworth, London SW18 1HU
U.K.
Stephen Taylor
artist management

Dern, Bill Management
8455 Fountain Ave., #550
Los Angeles, CA 90069
artist management

**Des Moines Metro Summer
Festival of Opera**
Des Moines Metro Opera
106 W. Boston
Indianola, IA 50125

DesBarres, Michael
P.O. Box 4160
Hollywood, CA 90078
singer

Desert Artist Management
6080 N. Oracle Rd., Suite G
Tucson, AZ
Jimmy Greenspoon

Desert Sky
28205 Agoura Rd., #A
Agoura Hills, CA 91301
video production

Design & Direction Inc.
437 San Vicente Blvd., #C
Santa Monica, CA 90402
video production

DeStefano, Debbie
Personal Management
P.O. Box 88225
Los Angeles, CA 90009
artist management

Detko, Bill Management
127 Shamrock Dr.
Ventura, CA 93003
artist management

Detroit Waldhorn Society
1014 Marshfield
Ferndale, MI 48220
Lowell Greer, Founder
valveless horn enthusiasts

DeWaart, Edo
RFO NOB-Muziekcentrumvan
de Omroep Postbus 10
1200 JB Hilversum, The Netherlands
conductor

Dhanus Ltd.
P.O. Box 2147
Sioux City, IA 51104
Morrie Miller
artist management

Diamante Negro Records
P.O. Box 641312
San Jose, CA 95164
Rafael Ibarra
independent record label

Diamond, Neil Leslie
8730 Sunset Blvd., PH-W
Los Angeles, CA 90069
singer, songwriter

Diddley, Bo
P.O. Box 474
Archer, FL 32618
musician

DiFranco, Loretta Elizabeth
Metropolitan Opera Association
Lincoln Center
New York, NY 10023
lyric coloratura soprano

Digital Music Products
P.O. Box 15835 Park Square Station
Stamford, CT 06901
Paul Jung
independent record label

Dileo, Frank Management Ltd.
152 W. 57th St.
New York, NY 10019
artist management

Dinah Shore Fan Club
c/o Kay Daly
3552 Federal Ave.
Los Angeles, CA 90066

Dionysus Records
P.O. Box 1975
Burbank, CA 91507
Lee Joseph, Head Cheese
independent record label

Dire Straits
10 Southwick Mews
London W2 U.K.
group

Direct Images
P.O. Box 29392
Oakland, CA 94604
Bill Knowland, Producer/Director
video production

Direct Management
P.O. Box 121759
Arlington, TX 76012
Danny Wilkerson, Owner
artist management

Direct Management Group
947 N. La Cienega Blvd., #G
Los Angeles, CA 90069
Martin Kirkup
artist management

Directory of Record & CD Retailers
Power Communications
P.O. Box 786
Wharton, NJ 07885

Dirt Band, The
P.O. Box 1915
Aspen, CO 81611
group

Dirty Linen Ltd.
P.O. Box 66600
Baltimore, MD 21239
Paul Hartman
independent record label

Dischord Records
3819 Beecher St. NW
Washington, DC 20007
Ian MacKaye
independent record label

Discovery International
6546 Hollywood Blvd., #210
Hollywood, CA 90028
Al Franklin
artist management

Discovery Records
2052 Broadway
Santa Monica, CA 90404
independent record label

Ditoro Films
8721 Sunset Blvd., #212
Los Angeles, CA 90069
video production

Diva Entertainment World
8491 Sunset Blvd., #252
W. Hollywood, CA 90069
Marc Joseph Krasnow, Managing
Director
artist management

Diva Entertainment World
8491 Sunset Blvd., #252
W. Hollywood, CA 90069
Marc Joseph Krasnow, Managing
Director
independent record label

Dixieland Jazz International
P.O. Box 11652
Houston, TX 77293
magazine

DJ International
727 W. Randolph St.
Chicago, IL 60661
Rocky Jones
independent record label

DJ Times
Testa Communications, Inc.
25 Willowdale Ave.
Pt. Washington, NY 11050
magazine for mobile and club DJs

Django Reinhardt Society
10 W. Jackson Ave.
Middletown, NY 10940
Mike Peters, President
gypsy jazz guitarist society

DMA Entertainment
2020 Century Park East, #600
Los Angeles, CA 90067
artist management

DMF Entertainment
135 W. 96th St., #14-A
New York, NY 10025
Diana Finley
artist management

DNA Records
725 Pomona Ave.
Albany, CA 94706
Danny Carnahan
independent record label

Doctor Dream Records
841 W. Collins Ave.
Orange, CA 92667
David Hayes, President
independent record label

Dog, Tim
c/o Sony Music
51 W. 52nd St.
New York, NY 10019
musician

Dollywood Ambassadors and Dollywood Foundation
1020 Dollywood Lane
Pigeon Forge, TN 37863
fan club for Dolly Parton and Dollywood

Domingo, Placido
c/o Stafford
26 Mayfield Rd.
Weybridge Surrey KT13 8XB U.K.
tenor

Domino Records
547 W. 27th St., 6th Fl.
New York, NY 10001
Arnie Goodman, General Manager
independent record label

Domino, Fats (Antoine)
9229 Sunset Blvd., 4th Fl.
Los Angeles, CA 90069
pianist, singer, songwriter

Don't Records
P.O. Box 11513
Milwaukee, WI 53211
Brian Wooldridge
independent record label

Donny Osmond International Network
P.O. Box 1448
Provo, UT 84603
fan club

Donovan
P.O. Box 472
London SW7 2QB U.K.
singer

Doobie Brothers
15140 Sonoma Highway
Glen Ellen, CA 95442
group

Doom Inc.
814 1/2 Highland Ave.
Los Angeles, CA 90038
Thomas Mignone, President
music commercial production

Down Beat
Maher Pubs.
180 W. Park Ave.
Elmhurst, IL 60126
magazine

Doyle/Lewis Management
1109 17th Ave. S
Nashville, TN 37212
Pam Lewis
artist management

Dragon Street Records
P.O. Box 670714
Dallas, TX 75367
David Dennard, President
independent record label

Dread Zeppelin Fan Club
c/o Birdcage Records
Sierra Madre, CA 91024
fan club for Reggae band that does
cover versions of Led Zeppelin

Dressel, Jon and Associates
6473 Brackett Rd.
Eden Prairie, MN 55346
artist management

Driehuys, Leonardus Batiaan
Charlotte Symphony Orchestra
1415 S. Church St., #S
Charlotte, NC 28203
conductor

Drifters, The
10 Chelsea Court
Neptune, NJ 07753
group

Drinker Library of Choral Music
Free Library of Philadelphia, Music
Department
Logan Square
Philadelphia, PA 19103
Mary Elizabeth VendernBerge,
Director of Music Department

Driven Rain Management
330 Washington Blvd., #607
Marina del Rey, CA 90292
Gail A. Gellman, Manager
artist management

Drum Corps International
P.O. Box 548
Lombard, IL 60148
Don Pesceone, Executive Director

Drumtape Ltd.
15/17 Old Compton St.
London, W1V 6JR U.K.
Joe D'Morrais
artist management

Dryer, Richard & Associates
4885 Hamberg
St. Louis, MO 63123
artist management

Dual Quad Entertainment
P.O. Box 692028
Los Angeles, CA 90069
Vinny Kostiw
artist management

Duerksen, George Louis
University of Kansas Department of
Music Education and Music Therapy
311 Bailey Hall
Lawrence, KS 66045
music educator, music therapist

Duke Ellington Society, The
P.O. Box 31, Church Street Station
New York, NY 10008
Marris Hodara, President

Dunlop Mfg. Inc.
P.O. Box 846
Benicia, CA 94510
custom logo guitar picks

Dunn, Susan
c/o Breslin
119 W. 57th St.
New York, NY 10019
singer

Duran Duran
P.O. Box 600
London NW18 1EN U.K.
group

Dylan, Bob
P.O. Box 870
New York, NY 10276
singer, composer

Dynamic Tom Jones Fan Club
c/o Martha Pess
55 Trapper Lane
Levittown, NY 11756

Dynasty Management Group
P.O. Box 11879
Chicago, IL 60611
Cookie Abrahamson
artist management

Dynasty Records
5397 Eglinton Ave. W, #106
Toronto, Ontario M9C 5K6 Canada
Neill Dixon, President
independent record label

The heart of the melody can never be put down on paper.

—PABLO CASALS

E G Management
9157 Sunset Blvd.
Los Angeles, CA 90069
artist management

E L Management
10100 Santa Monica Blvd., #2340
Los Angeles, CA 90067
Edward Leffler, President
artist management

E! Entertainment Television, Inc.
5670 Wilshire Blvd., 2nd Fl.
Los Angeles, CA 90036
Lee Masters, President/CEO
cable network

E, Sheila
9830 Wilshire Blvd.
Beverly Hills, CA 90212
musician

Eardrum Records
327 6th Ave. SE, #108
Minneapolis, MN 55414
independent record label

Early Morning Productions, Inc.
207-1365 Yonge Street
Toronto, Ontario M4T 2P7 Canada
Barry Harvey
artist management

Earth Tracks Artists
4712 Avenue N, #286
Brooklyn, NY 11234
David Krinsky, A & R Director
artist management

Earthbeat! Records
P.O. Box 1460
Redway, CA 95560
Leib Ostrow, President
independent record label

Earwig Music
1818 West Pratt Blvd.
Chicago, IL 60626
Michael Frank, President
artist management

Earwig Music Company
1818 W. Pratt Blvd.
Chicago, IL 60626
Michael Frank, President
independent record label

East Coast Rocker
P.O. Box 137
7 Oak Place
Montclair, NJ 07042
James Rensenbrink, Editor and Publisher
magazine

East End Lights
The Quarterly Magazine for Elton
John Fans
Voice Communications Corp.
P.O. Box 760
31950 23 Mile Road
New Baltimore, MI 48047
Tom Stanton, Editor

East End Management
8209 Melrose Ave., 2nd Fl.
Los Angeles, CA 90046
Tony Dimitriades
artist management

East Media Group
5831 Sunset Blvd.
Hollywood, CA 90028
artist management

Eastern Front Records
253 Central St.
Holliston, MA 01746
Jerry Potts
independent record label

Eastern Music Festival
Eastern Philharmonic Orchestra
P.O. Box 22026
Greensboro, NC 27420

Eastern Way Records
5831 Sunset Blvd.
Hollywood, CA 90028
independent record label

Eastlawn Compact Discs and Cassettes
P.O. Box 36487
Grosse Pointe Farms, MI 48236
Richard Spangler
independent record label

Easton, Sheena
151 El Camino
Beverly Hills, CA 90212
singer

Ebb Productions
9102 17th Ave. NE
Seattle, WA 98115
Andrew Ratshin, President
artist management

Ebb, Fred
c/o Dramatists Guild
234 W. 44th St.
New York, NY 10036
lyricist

Eberley, Helen-Kay
EB-SKO Productions
1726 Sherman Ave.
Evanston, IL 60201
opera singer, classical record company
executive

Echo Records Inc./Dancefloor Distribution
111 Cedar Lane
Englewood, NJ 07631
Jeffrey Collins, President
independent record label

Eckstine, Billy (William Clarence Eckstine)
c/o Polygram Records
810 7th Ave.
New York, NY 10019
singer

Eclipse Management
8439 Sunset Blvd., #406
Los Angeles, CA 90069
Anita Camarata
artist management

ECM Records
825 8th Ave., 26th Fl.
New York, NY 10019
independent record label

Ectasy Records
444 N. 3rd St.
Philadelphia, PA 19123
John Hodian
independent record label

Eddie Rabbitt Fan Club
P.O. Box 125
Lewistown, OH 43333

Edge Productions
109 Jackstaff
Hendersonville, TN 37075
video production

Edge Records
6464 Sunset Blvd., #850
Hollywood, CA 90028
Rick Frio, President
independent record label

Edge, The
260 California Ave.
Palo Alto, CA 94306
club

Edible Records
621 E. Green
Champaign, IL 61820
independent record label

Egg Cream Films
70-A Greenwich Ave., #203
New York, NY 10011
video production

Ego Management
6464 Sunset Blvd., #850
Hollywood, CA 90028
Rick Frio, President
artist management

Eichner Entertainment Company, The
810 7th Ave., 36th Fl.
New York, NY 10019
artist management

Elastic
P.O. Box 17598
Anaheim, CA 92817
Amin Gashgai
independent record label

Elder, Mark Philip
Rochester Philharmonic Orchestra Inc.
108 East Ave.
Rochester, NY 14604
conductor

Electric Records
33-45 Murray Ln.
Flushing, NY 11354
Tina K. Pryor, A&R
independent record label

Electro Motive Records
P.O. Box 14461
Berkeley, CA 94701
P. Conheim
independent record label

Electro-voice
600 Cecil St.
Buchanan, MI 49107
microphone specialists

Elektra Records (also Asylum, Nonesuch)
75 Rockefeller Plaza
New York, NY 10019
Bob Krasnow, Chairman
record label

Elektra Records (also Asylum, Nonesuch)
Beverly Hills
345 Maple Dr., #123
Beverly Hills, CA 90210
record label

Elfman, Danny
c/o Kraft
6525 Sunset Boulevard, #402
Los Angeles, CA 90028
composer, singer

Elias, Rosalind
c/o R. Lombardo
61 W. 62nd St., #65
New York, NY 10023
mezzo-soprano

Elkhorn Music Festival, Inc.
P.O. Box 1914
Sun Valley, ID 83353

Ellington, Mercer Kennedy
c/o Niwes
360 Central Park West, #166
New York, NY 10025
trumpeter, conductor, composer

Elliot, Willard Somers
Chicago Symphony Orchestra
220 S. Michigan Ave.
Chicago, IL 60604
musician, composer

Ellipse Production Company
P.O. Box 665
Manhattan Beach, CA 90266
L.S. Elsman
artist management

Ellisclan Ltd.
17 Hereford Mansions, Hereford Road
London W2 5BA U.K.
Ernest Chapman
artist management

Elmer Bird International Fan Club
Rte. 2, Box 130
Hurricane, WV 25526
fan club for clawhammer, frailing banjo performer

Elvis Forever TCB Fan Club
P.O. Box 1066
Pinellas Park, FL 34665

Elygra Music
Group International
913 20th Ave., S, #23
Nashville, TN 37212
Argyle Bell, President
video production

Elysian Fields Management
250 West 57th St., #2428
New York, NY 10107
David Salidor
artist management

EMA-Telstar
Carl Milles VAg 7 Box 1018
Lidingo, S-18121 Sweden
Thomas Johansson
artist management

Emarco Management & Publishing
23241 Ventura Blvd.
Woodland Hills, CA 91365
Mark Robert, President
artist management and publishing

Emerald City Creative Services
12251 Des Moines Memorial Dr.
Seattle, WA 08168
Melkor M. Odom, President
artist management

Emerald Records
830 Glastonbury Rd., #614
Nashville, TN 38217
Cliff Ayers, President
artist management

Emerald Records
830 Glastonbury, Rd., #614
Nashville, TN 37217
Cliff Ayers, President
independent record label

Emergo Records
225 Lafayette St., #407
New York, NY 10012
Doug Keogh, Label Manager
independent record label

EMF (Mark Decloedt, James Atkin, Zac Foley, Ian Dench, Derry)
Brownson
810 Seventh Ave.
New York, NY 10022
group

EMI Records Group (also SBK, Chrysalis)
810 7th Ave., 8th Fl.
New York, NY 10019
Charles Koppelman, Chariman/CEO
record label

EMI Records Group (also SBK, Chrysalis)
Los Angeles
8730 Sunset Blvd., 5th Fl.
Los Angeles, CA 90069

Emigre
4475 D. St.
Sacramento, CA 95819
Tim Starback
independent record label

Emka
43 Portland Rd.
London, W11 4LJ U.K.
Steve O'Rourke
artist management

Emotion Pictures
935 N. Leavitt, #2S
Chicago, Il 60622
Bill Ward
video production

Empire Artist
154 Stanton St.
New York, NY 10002
Neil Esterby
artist management

Empire Entertainment
P.O. Box 1756
Sebastopol, CA 95473
Oliver Laudahn
independent record label

En Pointe Compact Discs
182 S. Raymond Ave.
Pasadena, CA 91105
Gene Shiveley, VP
independent record label

En Vogue
75 Rockefeller Plaza, 4th Fl.
New York, NY 10019
group

Encounter Audiophile Recordings Inc.
P.O. Box 8132
Philadelphia, PA 19101
Jim Miller, President
independent record label

End, The
1030 N. Cole
Hollywood, CA 90038
video production

Endangered Species
P.O. Box 20469 Columbus Circle Station
New York, NY 10023
Fred Porter, President
artist management

Enemy/Brake Out Records
11-36 31st Ave., #4R
Long Island City, NY 11106
Michael Knuth, President
independent record label

Energy Productions
12700 Ventura Blvd., 4th Fl.
Studio City, CA 91604
video production

Energy Records
260 Beverly, #200
Beverly Hills, CA 90212
Robert Joyce
independent record label

Engelbert's "Goils"
10880 Kader Dr.
Cleveland, OH 44130
Engelbert Humperdinck fan club

English Management Ltd.
915 Calle Amanecer
San Clemente, CA 92673
Tony English
artist management

Enhancement Entertainment Group
P.O. Box 7581
Torrance, CA 90504
Rockin Rod Long, President/CEO
artist management

Enigma Records
136 West 18th St., 2nd Fl.
New York, NY 10011
William Hein, President
record label

Eno, Brian (Brian Peter George St. John DeLaSalle Eno)
Opal Ltd.
6834 Camrose Dr.
Los Angeles, CA 90068
composer, musician, producer

Ensey, Leta Productions
International Inc.
P.O. Box 530685
Grand Prairie, TX 75053
artist management

Ensey, Leta Productions International Inc.
P.O. Box 530685
Grand Prairie, TX 75053
Leta Ensey, President
independent record label

Entertainment Management
P.O. Box 716
Ojai, CA 93023
Howard Silverman
artist management

Entertainment Services Unlimited
Main St. Plaza 1000, #303
Voorhees, NJ 08043
Larry Mazer
artist management

Entner, Warren Management
5550 Wilshire Blvd., #302
Los Angeles, CA 90036
artist management

Entourage Entertainment
5325 Newcastle Ave., Box D
Encino, CA 91316
Stu Sobol
artist management

Entremont, Philippe
Amaro-Chantaco
64500 Saint-Jean-de-Lux
France
conductor, pianist

Epic Records
Sony Music Entertainment
P.O. Box 4450
New York, NY 10101
Dave Glew, President
record label

Epic Records (also WTG)
Sony Music Entertainment
2100 Colorado Blvd.
Santa Monica, CA 90404

Epicenter Communications
3 West 102 St., #1A
New York, NY 10025
Timothy Barry
video production

Epicenter Communications
3 West 102 St., #1A
New York, NY 10025
Timothy Barry
artist management

Epitaph
6201 Sunset Blvd., #111
Hollywood, CA 90028
Brett Gurewitz
independent record label

Epithet Productions
P.O. Box 6367
Stanford, CA 94309
Becket S. Dillard
artist management

Epithet Productions
P.O. Box 6367
Stanford, CA 94309
Becket S. Dillard
independent record label

Epoch Films
11731 Crescenda St.
Los Angeles, CA 90049
video production

Epstein, David Mayer
MIT Music Department
Cambridge, MA 02139
composer, conductor

EQ
P.O. Box 0532
Baldwin, NY 11510
recording studio technical magazine

Equator Music
17 Hereford Mansions, Hereford
Road
London W2 5BA U.K.
Ernest Chapman
artist management

Erector Set Studios
1150 S. La Brea Ave.
Los Angeles, CA 90019
Richard Rosenthal, President/General
Manager
video production

ERI Management, Inc.
180 W. Broadway
New York, NY 10013
Kurt Von Schlossberg
artist management

Ernest Bloch Society
34844 Old Stage Rd.
Gualala, CA 95445
Lucienne Bloch Dimitroff, Secretary/Treasurer
studies legendary pianist

Ertegun, Ahmet Munir
Atlantic Records
75 Rockefeller Plaza
New York, NY 10019
record company executive

Escape Entertainment
1019 N. Cole Ave., #4
Hollywood, CA 90038
video production

ESG Recordings
2905 Yorktown
Mesquite, TX 75149
Tony Johnson
independent record label

Eskimo Records
924 5th St., #9
Santa Monica, CA 90403
independent record label

ESP Management
1790 Broadway, Penthouse Suite
New York, NY 10019
Bud Prager
artist management

Esperian, Kallen Rose
c/o Breslin
119 W. 57th St.
New York, NY 10019
soprano

ESS.A.Y. Recordings
145 Pausade St.
Dobbs Ferry, NY 10522
Richard Kapp, President
independent record label

Estefan, Gloria Maria
6205 Bird Rd.
Miami, FL 33155
singer, songwriter

Estonian Music Center
243 E. 34th St.
New York, NY 10016
Mrs. Juta Kurman, President

Eternal Talent
1598 E. Shore Dr.
St. Paul, MN 55106
Bob Yezek
artist management

Etheridge, Melissa
c/o Island Records
14 E. 4th St.
New York, NY 10012
singer, songwriter

Etiquette Records
2442 NW Market St., #273
Seattle, WA 98107
Buck Ormsby, Owner
independent record label

Eureka Records
1 Franklin Park N
Buffalo, NY 14202
Rich Wall, Director
independent record label

EuroExport Entertainment
P.O. Box 4735
Austin, TX 78765
L.A. Evans, President/CEO
artist management

European Jazz Directory
P.O. Box 777 Times Square Station
New York, NY 10108

Eurythmics (Annie Lennox/Dave Stewart)
P.O. Box 245
London N8 90G U.K.
group

Eurythmics Fan Club
6363 Sunset Blvd., #437
Hollywood, CA 90028

Evans, Jeff
2457 Yalle Ave.
Memphis, TN 39112
artist manager

Ever Rap/Ever Rat/Ever Dread
P.O. Box 99284
Scattle, WA 98199
David Portnow, Publisher
independent record label

Everyone Everywhere
97 Bellevue St.
Cammeray NSW 2062 Australia
artist management

Ewing, Maria Louise
c/o Harold Holt
31 Sinclair Rd.
London W14 0NS U.K.
soprano

Excell Productions
1900 S. Sepulveda Blvd., Third Fl.
Los Angeles, CA 90025
Kevin Gorman
artist development

Eye On Production
Hemisphere Center Route 1
Newark, NJ 07114
video production

F-Stop Productions
6311 Romaine St.
Hollywood, CA 90038
Ken Dupuis
video production

F.W.A. Productions
444 W. 35th St., #1D
New York, NY 10001
video production

Fabulous Thunderbirds Fan Club
P.O. Box 17006
Austin, TX 78760

Face the Music
RD 3, Woods Ridge Rd.
Lake Katonah, NY 10536
Joanna Fitzpatrick
artist management

Facteau, Andre
P.O. Box 170117
San Francisco, CA 94117
artist manager

Factory Communications Ltd.
1 Charles St.
Manchester M17 EB U.K.
video production

Fair's Fair
3 Hamilton Dr. S
North Caldwell, NJ 07006
Gigi Freddy
artist management

Fairbanks Summer Arts Festival
P.O. Box 80845
Fairbanks, AK 99708
music festival

Falcon Management International
P.O. Box 710
East Northport, NY 11731
Michael Bosnic
artist management

Falcon Productions
133 Aragon Ave.
Coral Gables, FL 33134
video production

Falsified Records
P.O. Box 1010
Birmingham, MI 48012
Bill Boyer
independent record label

Fan Club Directory
2730 Baltimore Ave.
Pueblo, CO 81003

Fantasma Productions Inc.
2000 S. Dixie Hwy.
West Palm Beach, FL 33401
Jon Stoll, President
artist management

Fantasy Inc.
2600 10th St.
Berkeley, CA 94710
Ralph Kaffel, President
independent record label

Fargnoli, Steve
35 Harwood Rd.
London SW6 4QP U.K.
artist manager

Fassbaender, Brigitte
c/o Jennifer Selby
Ittisstrasse 57
8000 Munich 82, Germany
opera singer

Fat Boys, The
250 West 57th St., #1723
New York, NY 10107
rap group

Fat City Artists
1226 17th Ave. S, #2
Nashville, TN 37212
Rusty Michael
artist management

Fat Daddy Records Inc.
7701 Greenbelt Rd., #200
Greenbelt, MD 20770
Clayton J. Powell, Jr.
independent record label

Fat Eye Music
4140 W. 63rd St.
Los Angeles, CA 90043
Ronnie Richardson
independent record label

Fat Productions
42-15 Crescent, #503
Long Island City, NY 11101
video production

Faulkner, Julia Ellen
Vienna State Opera
1010 Vienna, Austria
opera singer

Favorite Country Stars
Media Holdings, Inc.
545 Mainstream Dr., #101
Nashville, TN 37228
magazine

Favors, Malachi
Art Ensemble of Chicago
818 E. 48th St.
Chicago, IL 60615
jazz musician, bassist

Feather Records
P.O. Box 132
Boston, MA 02123
Lauren Passarelli, Owner
independent record label

Federal Music Society
132 E. 71st St.
New York, NY 10021
Frederick R. Selch, President
Society for Music of the American
Federal Period, 1789-1840

Feinstein, Michael
8942 Wilshire Blvd.
Beverly Hills, CA 90211
entertainer, musicologist

Feliciano, Jose
c/o Thomas Cassidy
417 Marawood Dr.
Woodstock, IL 60098
singer

Fender, Freddy (Baldemar Huerta)
3225 S. Norwood Ave.
Tulsa, OK 74135
singer

Ferguson, Gene
Route 1, Box 113
Louisburg, TN 37091
Artist manager

Ferguson, Maynard
P.O. Box 716
Ojai, CA 93023
trumpeter

Ferrante & Teicher
P.O. Box 12403, NS Station
Atlanta, GA 30355
musicians

Ferris State University Festival of the Arts
Ferris State University
Big Rapids, MI 49307
music festival

Ferry, Bryan
JEM Records Group
3619 Kennedy Rd. South
Plainfield, NJ 07080
singer, songwriter

Festival Music Society of Indiana, Inc.
6471 Central Ave.
Indianapolis, IN 46220

Festival at Sandpoint, The
P.O. Box 695
Sandpoint, ID 83864

Festival Casals
P.O. Box 41227, Minillas Station
Santurce, PR 00940

Festival of Arts
Arts Council of Great Grand Rapids
205 B Waters Bldg.
Grand Rapids, MI 49503
music festival

Festival of Contemporary Music
University of Nevada—Las Vegas
Department of Music
4505 Maryland Pkwy.
Las Vegas, NV 89154

Festival of New American Music
6000 Jay St.
Sacramento, CA 95819

Festival of the Arts
Northern Illinois University
School of Music
De Kalb, IL 60115
music festival

Festival of the Arts
c/o Lake Oswego Chamber of Commerce
P.O. Box 368
Lake Oswego, OR 97034
music festival

Festival of the Sun
Office of Cultural Affairs
University of Arizona
800 E. University Blvd., #110
Tucson, AZ 85719
music festival

Festival Records
3271 Main St.
Vancouver, BC V5V 3M6 Canada
independent record label

Fiction O.D.
4933 Cartwright Ave.
N. Hollywood, CA 91601
Mo Green
independent record label

Fiesta Sound/Fiesta Records
1655 S. Compton Blvd.
Los Angeles, CA 90021
R.G. Robeson
independent record label

Fifth Column Records
915 F. St. NW
Washington, DC 20004
Craig Albertson, GM
independent record label

**50,000,000,000,000,000,000,000
Watts**
5721 SE Laguna Ave.
Stuart, FL 34997
M.C. Kostek
independent record label

Film Impressions North
126 Lakeview Dr.
McMurray, PA 15317
video production

Filmspace Inc.
615 Clay Lane
State College, PA 16801
video production

Filmworks Corp.
265 Aragon Ave.
Miami, Fl 33134
video production

Fine Young Cannibals
1680 N. Vine St., #1101
Hollywood, CA 90028
group

Finer Arts Records Co.
2170 S. Parker Rd., #115
Denver, CO 80231
Richard Bernstein, President
independent record label

Fingerprint Records
P.O. Box 197
Merrimac, MA 01860
Dan Russell, President
independent record label

Finkelstein Management Company
151 John St., #301
Toronto, Ontario, Canada
Bernie Finkelstein, President

Finn, Robert
1801 Superior Ave. E
Cleveland, OH 44114
music critic

**Firefly Festival for the Performing
Arts at St. Patrick's County Park**
202 S. Michigan St., lower level
South Bend, IN 46601

First Chair America
c/o Mary Martin
P.O. Box 474
Greenwood, MS 38930
recognition for 1st chair in orchestras
and bands

First Class Productions
111 Westland Place
West Monroe, LA 71291
John K. Wilson, President
artist management

First Global Management
1370 Avenue of the Americas, 15th Fl.
New York, NY 10019
Jonathan First, President
artist management

First Strike Management
625 Main St., #844
New York, NY 10044
Johnny Jones, President
artist management

First Video Productions Inc.
4235 Centergate
San Antonio, TX 78217
video production

First Warning
594 Broadway, #1104
New York, NY 10012
Michael Lembo, President
independent record label

Firth, Everett Joseph
323 Whiting Ave.
Dedham, MA 02026
timpanist

Fishof Productions
61 W. 62nd St., #18-L
New York, NY 10023
David Fishof
artist management

Fitzgerald, Ella
c/o Granz
451 N. Canon Dr.
Beverly Hills, CA 90210
singer

Fitzpatrick, Robert Organization
P.O. Box 667
Sunset Beach, CA 90742
artist management

Five Roses Music Company
P.O. Box 417, Studio R
White Sulpher Springs, NY 12787
Sammie Lee Marler, President
independent record label

Flack, Roberta
c/o Atlantic Records
75 Rockefeller Plaza
New York, NY 10019
singer

Flag Management
132 Liverpool Rd.
London N1 1LA U.K.
Mike Collins
artist management

Flagstaff Festival of the Arts
P.O. Box 1607
Flagstaff, AZ 86002
music festival

Flash Multimedia Productions
460 St. Johns St.
Central Islip, NY 11722
Gabe Gabrielsen, Owner
video production

Flashframe Films
841 Broadway, #504
New York, NY 10003
Len Epand
video production

Flat Town Music Company
P.O. Drawer 10
Ville Platte, LA 70586
Jin Soileau
independent record label

Fleetwood Mac
29169 W. Heathercliff, #574
Malibu, CA 90265
on again, off again group

Fleetwood, Mick
c/o Warner Brothers
3300 W. Warner Blvd.
Burbank, CA 91505
musician

Fleischmann, Ernest Martin
Los Angeles Philharmonic Orchestra
135 N. Grand Ave.
Los Angeles, CA 90012
music administrator

Fleming Tamulevich & Assoc.
733-735 North Main
Ann Arbor, MI 48104
Jim Fleming/David Tamulevich
artist management

Fletch Woodward
Motion Pictures
3125 Piedmont Road
Atlanta, GA 30305
Michael Woodward
video production

Flip Side Sound and Film
3616B Falls Rd.
Baltimore, MD 21211
video production

Flipside
P.O. Box 363
Whittier, CA 90608
independent record label

Florence Ballard Fan Club
P.O. Box 36A02
Los Angeles, CA 90036

Flower Films
10341 San Pablo Ave.
El Cerrito, CA 94530
Les Blank
video production

Flying Fish Records
1304 W. Shubert Ave.
Chicago, IL 60614
Bruce Kaplan, President
independent record label

Flying Heart Records
4026 NE 12th Ave.
Portland, OR 87212
Jan Celt
independent record label

FM Productions
160 25th St. NW
Naples, FL 33964
Mark R. Nowack, President
artist management

Fogelberg, Daniel Grayling
c/o Epic Records
1801 Century Park West
Los Angeles, CA 90067
composer, recording artist

Folklore Productions
1671 Appian Way
Santa Monica, CA 90401
Mitch Greenhill
artist management

Folsom Management
P.O. Box 23710
New Orleans, LA 70130
Edward Feldsott, President
artist management

Force of Habit Productions
521 Waller St.
San Francisco, CA 94117
video production

Forced Exposure
P.O. Box 9102
Waltham, MA 02254
Roger Miller
independent record label

Forceful Enterprises
P.O. Box 284
Brooklyn, NY 11203
Jeffrey Aber
artist management

Ford, Jim Management
P.O. Box 158
Arvonia, VA 23004
artist management

Forefront Records
222 Monroe St., #2FN
P.O. Box 1964
Hoboken, NJ 07030
Michael Young
independent record label

Foreigner
1790 Broadway, PH
New York, NY 10019
group

Forrester, Roger
Management Ltd.
77 Harley Hse, Marylebone Rd.,
Regents Pk.
London NW1 5HF U.K.
artist management

Forsythe Management
3141 76th St.
Jackson Heights, NY 11370
Allyson Forsythe
artist management

Forte Records & Productions Ltd.
320 Spadina Rd.
Toronto, Ontario M5R 2V6 Canada
Dawna Zeeman
independent label and producer

Forti/Layne Entertainment
7355 NW 41st St.
Miami, FL 33166
video production

40 Acres & a Mule
8 St. Felix St., 1st Fl.
Brooklyn, NY 11217
independent record label

Forward Productions/Artist Alliance
P.O. Box 145
Angeles Camp, CA 95222
Mark Dyken
independent record label

Fountain, Pete (Peter Dewey Fountain, Jr.)
2 Poydras St.
New Orlean, LA 70140
clarinettist

4 AD Inc.
8533 Melrose Ave., #B
Los Angeles, CA 90069
Robin Hurley, U.S. Director
independent record label

Four Buddies/Billdia Music
1180 E. Philadelphia St., #3
Pomona, CA 91766
W. Campbell, President
independent record label

Four Dots Records
P.O. Box 233
Denton, TX 76202
Carl Finch
independent record label

Four Freshman
P.O. Box 70404
Las Vegas, NV 89160
nostalgia harmony group

415 Records
888 7th Ave., 37th Fl.
New York, NY 10106
independent record label

415 Records/Popular Metaphysics
150 Bellham Blvd., #255
San Rafael, CA 94901
Sean Pergerson, A&R
independent record label

Four Seasons
P.O. Box 262
Carteret, NJ 07008
group

Fox Management
1375 Forty Foot Road
Kulpsville, PA 19443
David Cooper
artist management

Fox, Mitchell Management
66 Music Square W
Nashville, TN 37203
artist management

Foxworthy Management
4002 Liggett Dr.
San Diego, CA 92106
Douglas Foxworthy, President
artist management

Fragile Films
653 N. Fairfax Ave.
Los Angeles, CA 90036
Rhea Rupert
video production

Frampton, Peter
c/o Atlantic Records
75 Rockefeller Plaza
New York, NY 10019
singer, musician

Franco Artist Management
163 Morningside Dr.
Anselmo, CA 94960
Rob Franco, President
artist management

Frankie Laine Society
P.O. Box 145
Lindenhurst, NY 11757
fan club

Franklin, Aretha
8450 Linwood St.
Detroit, MI 48206
singer

Franklin, David & Associates
999 Peachtree St., #2680
Atlanta, GA 30309
artist management

Freckle Records
P.O. Box 4005
Seattle, WA 98104
Jack Burg
independent record label

Free Hand Management
14639 Ventura Blvd.
Sherman Oaks, CA 91403
Dale Jaffe, President
artist management

Free to Run
24415 Vanowen St., #45
West Hills, CA 91307
Jon Sutherland
artist management

Freedman, Peter Entertainment
1775 Broadway, 7th Fl.
New York, NY 10019
artist management

Freedomain Music
890 Rd. 102
Carbondale, CO 81623
R. Earthsong
independent record label

Freefall Talent Group
18 Grandview St.
Huntington, NY 11743
Mark Puma
artist management

Freestyle Media Group
1526 W. 259th St. , #6
Harbor City, CA 90710
video production

Fresh Prince (Will Smith)
1133 Ave. of the Americas
New York, NY 10036
rapper

Fresh Sounds Inc.
P.O. Box 36
Lawrence, KS 66044
Bill Rich
independent record label

Fresh!
Ashley Communications, Inc.
19431 Business Ctr. Dr., #27
Northridge, CA 91324
magazine for black teenagers trying to
break into entertainment

Fresher Management
81 Harley House, Marylebone Rd.
London NW1 5HT U.K.
artist management

Freshwater Records
P.O. Box 27713
Los Angeles, CA 90027
independent record label

Fretted Instrument Guild of America
c/o Ann Pertoney
2344 S. Oakley Ave.
Chicago, IL 60608
banjo, mandolin, guitar guild

Frey, Glenn
151 El Camino
Beverly Hills, CA 90212
songwriter, vocalist, guitarist

Fricke, Janie
P.O. Box 680785
San Antonio, TX 78268
singer

Friends of Bobby Vee
P.O. Box 443
Girard, OH 44420
fan club

Friends of Dennis Wilson
1381 Maria Way
San Jose, CA 95117
fan club

Friends of Jackie Wilson
P.O. Box 262
Carteret, NJ 07008
fan club

Friends of Julio International
c/o Isabel Butterfield
28 Farmington Ave.
Longmeadow, MA 01106
Julio Iglesias fan club

Fringe Project
P.O. Box 670, Station A
Toronto, Ontario M5W 1G2 Canada
Ben Hoffman, President
independent record label

Fritz, Ken Management
648 N. Robertson Blvd.
Los Angeles, CA 90069
artist management

From the Hood Filmworks
1658 E. Washington Ln.
Philadelphia, PA 19138
Ronald White
video production

Front Line Assembly
1659 N. Damon Ave.
Chicago, IL 60647
artist management

Frontier Records
P.O. Box 22
Sun Valley, CA 91353
Lisa Fancher, President
independent record label

Frontline Records
4041 MacArthur Blvd., #300
Newport Beach, CA 92660
Brian Tong, President
independent record label

Fun House America Inc.
599 Broadway, 5th Fl.
New York, NY 10012
Mike Yoshida
independent record label

Future Star Entertainment
333 S. Beverly Dr., #110
Beverly Hills, CA 90212
Paul S. Shenker, President
artist management

If music be the food of love, play on.
—SHAKESPEARE

G Fine
P.O. Box 180, Cooper Station
New York, NY 10276
P. Fine, President
independent record label

G.E.M. Entertainment Management
14431 Ventura Blvd., #195
Sherman Oaks, CA 91423
Beth A. Miller
artist management

G.G. Greg Artist Management
1288 E. 168th St.
Cleveland, OH 44110
artist management

G.H.B. Jazz Foundation
1206 Decatur St.
New Orleans, LA 70116
Ernie Bivens, President
independent record label

G.M.I.
144 S. Beverly Dr., #503
Beverly Hills, CA 90212
artist management

G.T.A. Inc.
3128 Cavendish Dr.
Los Angeles, CA 90064
Jim Golden, President
artist management

Gabour, Jim Moving Pictures
2401 Rue Chartres
New Orleans, LA 70117
video production

Gabriel, Peter
Probono
132 Liverpool Rd.
London N1 1LA U.K.
vocalist, composer.

Gallagher/Thompson
662 N. Baness Ave., #201
Los Angeles, CA 90004
Tess Thompson, Producer
video production

Gallin/Morey Associates
8730 Sunset Blvd., PH-W
Los Angeles, CA 90069
Sandy Gallin/Jim Morey
artist management

Galway, James
P.O. Box 1077
Bucks, SL2 4DB U.K.
flutist

Gangland Artists
707-710 W. Broadway
Vancouver, BC V5Z 1J8 Canada
Allen Moy
artist management

Garcia, Jerry
P.O. Box 12979
San Rafael, CA 94913
musician

Gardner Howard Entertainment
9255 Sunset Blvd., #308
Los Angeles, CA 90069
Andi Howard/Mike Gardner
artist management

Gardner/Borress
401 2nd Ave., #12-G
New York, NY 10010
Hirsh Gardner/Gary Borress
artist management

Garfield Group, The
325-331 Lafayette St., 2nd Fl.
New York, NY 10012
Bruce Garfield, President
artist management

Garfunkel, Art
c/o Columbia
51 W. 52nd St.
New York, NY 10019
singer

Garneau Video Productions
2330 Pacific Coast Highway
Lomita, CA 90717
video production

Garrett, Leif
9000 Sunset Blvd., #515
Los Angeles, CA 90069
former teen idol

**Garth Newel Chamber Music
Series**
P.O. Box 427
Hot Springs, VA 24445

Gary, John
Grenier and Moore Productions,
Inc.
32500 Concord Dr.
Madison Heights, MI 48071
singer

Gates Music Inc.
1850 Winton Road S.
Rochester, NY 14618
Joe DiMaria, Manager
artist management

Gatlin Enterprises Inc.
7003 Chadwick Dr., #360
Brentwood, TN 37027
Steve Gatlin
artist management

Gattie, Erma Charlotte
Tornay Mgmt. Inc.
127 W. 72nd St.
New York, NY 10023
singer

Gavin Kern & Associates
7080 Hollywood Blvd., #1009
Hollywood, CA 90028
Michael Houbrick, Agent
artist management

**Gay and Lesbian Association of
Choruses**
1617 E. 22nd Ave.
Denver, CO 80205
Helen Speegle, President

Gayle Enterprises Inc.
51 Music Square E
Nashville, TN 37203
Bill Gatzimos, President
artist management

Gayle, Crystal
57 Music Sq. E.
Nashville, TN 37203
singer

**Gazell/Storyville/Silkheart
Records**
P.O. Box 527
Mansfield Center, CT 06250
Sam Charters
independent record label

GBS Records
38 Music Square E., #216
Nashville, TN 37201
Ernie Bivens
independent record label

Geffen/DGC Records
9130 Sunset Blvd.
Los Angeles, CA 90069
David Geffen, Chairman
record label

Geffen/DGC Records
New York
1755 Broadway, 6th Fl.
New York, NY 10019

Geldof, Sir Bob
Davington Priory
Faversham, Kent U.K.
singer

**Gene Pitney International Fan
Club**
c/o David P. McGrath
8901 6 Mile Rd.
Caledonia, WI 53108

**Gene Summers International Fan
Club**
P.O. Box 475184
Garland, TX 75047

Generic Records Inc.
433 Limestone Rd.
Ridgefield, CT 06877
Gary Lefkowith
independent record label

GENES Compact Disc Co.
P.O. Box 7778
Silver Spring, MD 20907
Jon Curlin, VP
independent record label

Genesis
81-83 Walton St.
London SW3 U.K.
group

Genesis Entertainment
6201 Sunset Blvd., #176
Los Angeles, CA 90028
Humphrey Riley
artist management

Genesis Information
c/o Brad Lentz
P.O. Box 12250
Overland Park, KS 66212
fan club

Genius Records
P.O. Box 481052
Los Angeles, CA 90048
Marcy Blaustein
independent record label

Gentry, Teddy
c/o Morris and Assoc.
818 19th Ave. S.
Nashville, TN 37203
country musician

**George Michael International Fan
Club**
P.O. Box 882884
San Francisco, CA 94188

George Strait Fan Club
P.O. Box 2119
Hendersonville, TN 37077

George, Garry
Management
9107 Wilshire Blvd., #475
Beverly Hills, CA 90210
artist management

Gerber & Associates
5260 Southridge Ave.
Los Angeles, CA 90043
David Gerber
artist management

Gerrard Associates Inc.
2911 W. Olive Ave.
Burbank, CA 91505
Louis Gerrard
video production

Gerry & The Pacemakers
28A Manor Row
Brodford, BDL 4QU U.K.
one of original British invasion
groups

Get Hip Recordings Inc.
P.O. Box 666
Canonsburg, PA 15317
Gregg Kostelich, President
independent record label

Geto Boys
c/o Priority
P.O. Box 2186
Hollywood, CA 90078
rappers

Ghiglia, Oscar Alberto
197 Quaker Lane S.
Hartford, CT 06119
classical guitarist

ghs Strings
2813 Wilber Ave.
Battle Creek, MI 49015
guitar string specialists

Giant Records
8900 Wilshire Blvd., #200
Beverly Hills, CA 90211
Irving Azoff, Owner
record label

Giant Records
New York
75 Rockefeller Plaza, 21st Fl.
New York, NY 10019

Giant Records
Nashville
45 Music Square W
Nashville, TN 37203

Gibb Family Friendship
Club
c/o Brenda Cornwell
301 Mackic Lane
Louisville, KY 40214
Bee Gees fan club

Gibb, Barry
P.O. Box 8179
Miami, FL 33139
vocalist, songwriter

Gibb, Maurice
P.O. Box 8179
Miami, FL 33139
vocalist, songwriter

Gibb, Robin
Borman Sternberg Enterprises
9220 Sunset Blvd., #320
Los Angeles, CA 90069
vocalist, songwriter

Gibson Productions
375 N. Broadway, #201
Hericho, NY 11753
Diane Gibson
artist management

Gibson, Debbie
P.O. Box 489
Merrick, NY 11566
singer, songwriter

Giddins, Gary Mitchell
Village Voice
36 Cooper Sq.
New York, NY 10003
music critic

Gifford, Virginia Snograss
Library of Congress
Music Section—SMCD
Madison Bldg., Rm. 547
Washington, DC 20540
music cataloger and bibliographer

Gigantic
618 S. Broadway, #A
Redondo Beach, CA 90277
Larry Bayless
artist management

Gigantic
618 S. Broadway, #A
Redondo Beach, CA 90277
Larry Bayless
independent record label

Gilbert, Pia S.
Juilliard School of Music
60 Lincoln Center Plaza
New York, NY 10023
Schoenberg award winning composer

Giles, Anne Diener
Los Angeles Philharmonic
135 N. Grand Ave.
Los Angeles, CA 90012
flutist

Gilley, Mickey
Interests, Inc.
P.O. Box 23162
Nashville, TN 37202
singer

Gimbel, Norman
P.O. Box 50013
Montecito, CA 93150
lyricist

Giordano, John Read
Ft. Worth Symphony Orchestra
4401 Trail Lake Dr.
Fort Worth, TX 76109
conductor

Giraldi Suarez Productions
Los Angeles Office
329 N. Wetherly Drive
Beverly Hills, CA 90211
Will Lafayette
video production

Giraldi Suarez Productions
581 6th Ave.
New York, NY 10011
Bob Giraldi
video production

Girl Groups Fan Club
P.O. Box 69A04
West Hollywood, CA 90069
Honeycone, Orlons, Dee Dee Shapr,
Martha and the Vandellas, Ronnettes,
Marvelettes, etc.

Gladrock Artists
1222 16th Avenue South, #21
Nashville, TN 37212
Johnson Bell, Personal Manager
artist management

Glass, Philip
International Production Associates
853 Broadway, #2120
New York, NY 10003
composer, musician

Glazunov Society
17320 Park Ave.
Sonoma, CA 95476
Donald J. Venturini, President
society studies Russian composer
Alexander Glazunov

Glen Campbell Fan Club
10351 Santa Monica Blvd., #300
Los Angeles, CA 90025

Glenn Miller Birthplace Society
P.O. Box 61
Clarinda, IA 51632

Glenn Miller Society
18 Crendon St.
High Wycombe, Bucks, U.K.

Glitch Records
P.O. Box 4429
Austin, TX 78765
Keith Ayres, President
independent record label

Global Pacific Records
270 Perkins St.
Sonoma, CA 95476
Howard Sapper, President
independent record label

Globe Records
P.O. Box 5523
Mill Valley, CA 94942
Tim Eschliman, President
independent record label

Gloria Estefan and the Miami Sound Machine
8390 S.W. 4th St.
Miami, FL 33144
group

GM Recordings Inc.
167 Dudley Rd.
Newton Centre, MA 02159
Bruce Millard
independent record label

Gniewek, Raymond
Metropolitan Opera
Lincoln Center
New York, NY 10023
violinist

GNP/Crescendo Record Co. Inc.
8400 Sunset Blvd., #4A
Los Angeles, CA 90069
Gene Norman
independent record label

Go Discs Ltd.
322 King St., Hammersmith
London W6 ORR U.K.
Andy Macdonald
artist management

Go Go's
345 N. Maple Dr., #325
Beverly Hills, CA 90210
group

Godin, Michael
Management Inc.
418-810 W. Broadway
Vancouver, BC V5Z 4C9 Canada
artist management

Godsdog Records
520 Washington Blvd.
Marina del Rey, CA 90292
Nik Venet
independent record label

Goetz, Lindy
Management
11116 Aqua Vista, #39
Studio City, CA 91602
artist management

Gold Mountain Entertainment
3575 Cahuenga West, #450
Los Angeles, CA 90068
Ron Stone
artist management

Goldsmith, Jerry
Savitsky, Stain and Geibelson
2049 Century Park E, #3700
Los Angeles, CA 90067
composer

Gong Sounds Inc.
3000 Biscayne Blvd., #400
Miami, FL 33137
Gladstone Gilbert, President
independent record label

Goodman, Marv
Creative Bloc Music Ltd.
2170 Broadway, #2292
New York, NY 10024
music publisher

Gordon, Edward
Ravinia Festival Association
1575 Oakwood Ave.
Highland Park, IL 60035
music association executive

Gospel Music Association
P.O. Box 23201
Nashville, TN 37202
Bruce Koblish, Executive Director

Gospel Music Workshop of America
3908 W. Warren St.
Detroit, MI 48208
Edward M. Smith, Exec. Secty.

Gospelrama Gospel Expo
P.O. Box 1342
Washington, DC 20013
Dr. Henry A. Thomas, Founder and
Chairman

GP Productions
362 3rd Ave., Suite 1B
New York, NY 10016
Gill R. Pessoa, President
artist management

GP Productions
362 3rd Ave., #1B
New York, NY 10016
Gill R. Pessoa, President
independent record label

**GPA Films (Grodin Production
Associates)**
137 E. 25th St., 7th Fl.
New York, NY 10010
Lenny Grodin, President
video production

Gramavision Records
33 Katonah Ave.
Katonah, NY 10536
independent record label

**Grand Canyon Chamber Music
Festival**
P.O. Box 1332
Grand Canyon, AZ 86023

Grand Ole Opry
2804 Opryland Dr.
Nashville, TN 37214

Grand Ole Opry Fan Club
2804 Opryland Dr.
Nashville, TN 37214

Grand Prairie Festival of the Arts
Grand Prairie Arts Council, Inc.
P.O. Box 65
Stuttgart, AR 72160
music festival

Grand Teton Music Festival
P.O. Box 490
Teton Village, WY 83025

Granite Studio
326 1/2 La Cienega
Los Angeles, CA 90048
Jim Bailey, Brian Carney—Owners
recording studio

Grant Park Concerts
Grant Park Symphony Orchestra
425 E. McFetridge Dr.
Chicago, IL 60605

Grant, Amy
P.O. Box 50701
Nashville, TN 37205
singer

Grass Recording and Sound
800 Arbor Place
Del Rey Oaks, CA 93940
Michael Grass, Owner
independent record label

Grateful Dead, The
P.O. Box 1566, Main Office Street
Montclair, New Jersey 07043
group

Graves, Denyce Antoinette
Tramick Artists
129 W. 72nd St.
New York, NY 10023
mezzo-soprano

Great Gulfcoast Arts Festival
Pensacola Arts Council
P.O. Box 731
Pensacola, FL 32594
music festival

Great Jones (a subsidiary of Island Records)
14 East Fourth St.
New York, NY 10012
Mike Bone, President
record label

Great Northwest Music Co., The
P.O. Box 4740
Seattle, WA 98104
Jerry Dennon, President
independent record label

Great Southern Record Co.
P.O. Box 13977
New Orleans, LA 70185
John Berthelot
independent record label

Great White
P.O. Box 67487
Los Angeles, CA 90067
band

Great Woods Center for the Performing Arts
P.O. Box 810
Mansfield, MA 02048
music festival

Green Linnet
70 Turner Hill Rd.
New Canaan, CT 06840
Wendy Newton
independent record label

Green Monkey
P.O. Box 31983
Seattle, WA 98103
Tom Dyer
independent record label

Green, Adolph
211 Central Park W
New York, NY 10024
lyricist

Green, Al
151 El Camino
Beverly Hills, CA 90212
gospel singer

Greengrass Enterprises Inc.
16 E. 48th St.
New York, NY 10017
Ken Greengrass, President
artist management

Greenspan Management
7224 Hillside Ave., #6
West Hollywood, CA 90046
Nance Greenspan
artist management

Greenville Arts Festival
c/o Mrs. Harold C. Clark Jr.
109 Byrd Blvd.
Greenville, SC 29605
music festival

Greenwood Productions
1 W. Foster St.
Melrose, MA 02176
video Production

Griffin, Merv
9860 Wilshire Blvd.
Beverly Hills, CA 90210
singer

Grillo, Joann Danielle
Ambassadors of Opera
240 Central Park S., #16M
New York, NY 10019
mezzo-soprano

Groov Marketing & Consulting
6253 Hollywood Blvd., #917
Hollywood, CA 90028
Neil E. Gorov, President
artist management

Groove Tip Recordings Ltd.
P.O. Box 13361
Arlington, VA 22219
James A. Lumpkin III
independent record label

Gross Management Organization
930 3rd St., #102
Santa Monica, CA 90403
Barry Gross, President
artist management

Gross, David Management
P.O. Box 40124
San Francisco, CA 94140
artist management

Ground Zero
9265 Old Eighth Rd.
Cleveland, OH 44067
Mark Litten
artist management

GRP Records
555 W. 57th St.
New York, NY 10019
Larry Rosen, President
independent record label

Grusin, Dave
c/o Warner Brothers
400 Warner Blvd.
Burbank, CA 91522
film composer, record producer

Guild of Carillonneurs in North America
c/o Richard D. Gegner
3718 Settle Rd.
Cincinnati, OH 452227
players of carillons and chimes

Guinn, John Rockne
Detroit Free Press Inc.
321 W. Lafayette Blvd.
Detroit, MI 48226
music critic

Guitar Foundation of America
c/o Gunnar Eisel
P.O. Box 878
Claremont, CA 91711

Guitar Recordings
10 Midland Ave.
Port Chester, NY 10573
Peter Primont
independent record label

Guns N' Roses
9130 Sunset Blvd.
Los Angeles, CA 90069
group

Gunzenhauser, Stephen Charles
Delaware Symphony Orchestra
P.O. Box 1870
Wilmington, DE 19899
conductor

Guthrie, Arlo
The Farm
Washington, MA 01223
singer, songwriter

Gutter, Robert Harold
Philharmonic of Greensboro
200 N. Davie St.
Greensboro, NC 27401
conductor

Guy, Buddy
Legends
754 S. Wabash Ave.
Chicago, IL 60605
blues guitarist

Guy, Jasmine
14755 Ventura Blvd., #1-710
Sherman Oaks, CA 91403
singer

Gwynn, Cat
907 N. Matlman Ave.
Los Angeles, CA 90026
video production

I am never merry when I hear sweet music.
—SHAKESPEARE

H-Gun
2024 S. Wabash, 7th Fl.
Chicago, IL 60616
video production

Haden, Charles
Blue Note Records
1750 Vine St.
Los Angeles, CA 90028
jazz bassist, composer

Hadley, Jerry
c/o Lyric Arts Group
204 W. 10th St.
New York, NY 10014
opera singer

Haffkine, Ron Enterprises Inc.
P.O. Box 121017
Nashville, TN 37212
country artist management

Hafitz, Michael Esq.
107 Appleton St.
Boston, MA 02116
music attorney

Hag Inc.
P.O. Box 536
Palo Cedro, CA 96073
artist management

Haggard, Merle
P.O. Box 536
Palo Cedro, CA 96073
singer

Halem, Chaim
2219 1/2 Artesia Blvd.
Redondo Beach, CA 90278
hairstylist

Hall & Oates
130 W. 57th #2A
New York, NY 10019
duo

Hall, Daryl
Champion Entertainment
130 W. 57th St., #12B
New York, NY 10019
musician

Hall, David
P.O. Box 257
Castine, ME 04421
sound archivist

Hall, Tom T.
P.O. Box 1246
Franklin, TN 37065
songwriter, performer

Halmark Direction Co.
1819 Broadway
Nashville, TN 37203
John Dorris
artist management

Halsey, Jim Co.
P.O. Box 40703
Nashville, TN 37203
artist management

Hamilton, Chico (Forestorn Hamilton)
321 E. 45th St., PH A
New York, NY 10017
drummer

Hamlisch, Marvin
c/o Guttman & Pam
8500 Wilshire Blvd., #801
Beverly Hills, CA 00211
composer, musician

Hammer (formerly M.C.)(Stanley Kirk Burrell)
1750 N. Vine St.
Hollywood, CA 90028
rapper

Hancock, Herbie
9830 Wilshire Blvd.
Beverly HIlls, CA 90212
composer, pianist

Handler, Beryl
179 Aguetong Rd.
New Hope, PA 18038
jazz artist management

Hangen, Bruce Boyer
Omaha Symphony Orchestra
310 Aguila Ct. Bldg.
1615 Howard St.
Omaha, NE 68102
conductor

Hank Williams Jr. Fan Club
P.O. Box 1350
Paris, TN 38242

Happy Dog Management
11684 Ventura Blvd., #200
Studio City, CA 91604
Joel Gilbert
artist management

Happy Feet Productions
425 N. Oakhurst Dr., #207
Beverly Hills, CA 90210
video production

Happy Hour Music
5206 Benito St.
Montclair, CA 91761
Judith Wahnon
independent record label

Happy Squid Records
P.O. Box 94565
Pasadena, CA 91109
John Talley-Jones
independent record label

Hard Attack Management
5214 Western Blvd., 1st Fl.
Raleigh, NC 27606
Belva Parker
artist management

Hard Hat Records
519 N. Halifax Ave.
Daytona Beach, FL 32118
Bobby Lee Cude
independent record label

Hard to Handle Management
64 Lee Road, #106
Wayne, PA 19087
Steven Barnett
artist management

Hardanger Fiddle Association of America
325 Howtz St.
Duluth, MN 55811
Thorwald Quale, Director

Hardly Records
5120 Walnut St.
Philadelphia, PA 19139
Scott Herzog, President
independent record label

Harman, J.A. Management Group
7216 34th Ave.
Kenosha, WI 53142
artist management

Harmonic Hall
2639 S. King St.
Honolulu, HI 96826
Thomas Pereira
independent record label

Harmony
P.O. Box 400
Stittsville, Ontario K2S 1A5 Canada
Joanne Samler, Executive Secretary
barbershop quartet club

Harmony Artist Inc.
8833 Sunset Blvd., PH-W
Los Angeles, CA 90069
Mike Dixon, President
artist management

Harnick, Sheldon Mayer
Kraft, Haiken and Bell
551 Fifth Ave., 9th Fl.
New York, NY 10176
lyricist

Harper, David Management
137 Talgaith Rd.
London, W14 9DA U.K.
artist management

Harper, Heather Mary
20 Milverton Rd.
London NW6 7AS U.K.
soprano

Harrell, Lynn Morrie
c/o IMG
22 E. 71st St.
New York, NY 10021
cellist

Harris, Emmylou
c/o Monty Hitchcock
P.O. Box 159007
Nashville, TN 37215
singer

Harrison, George
Handmade Films Ltd.
26 Cadogan Sq.
London SW1 U.K.
singer

Harrison, Steve Management Inc.
70 Witton St.
Northwich Cheshire CW9 5A3 U.K.
artist management

Harry Connick, Jr. Fan Club
260 Brookline St., #200
Cambridge, MA 02139

Harry, Debbie (Deborah Ann Harry)
c/o Overland
1775 Broadway
New York, NY 10019
singer

Hartford, John Cowan
c/o The Case Co.
1016 16th Ave. S
Nashville, TN 37212
composer, singer

Harth, Robert James
Music Associates of Aspen
P.O. Box AA
Aspen, CO 81612
music festival executive

Harth, Sidney
c/o Sheldon Souffer Mgmt.
130 W. 56th St.
New York, NY 10019
musician, educator

Hawkins, Sophie B.
51 W. 52nd St.
New York, NY 10019
singer

Hayes, Isaac
c/o Columbia Records
51 W. 52nd St.
New York, NY 10019
composer, singer

Heart Beat Records
1 Camp St.
Cambridge, MA 02140
Duncan Brown, President
independent record label

Heart Fan Club
219 1st Ave., #333
Seattle, WA 98109

Heart Music Inc.
P.O. Box 160326
Austin, TX 78716
Tab Bartling, Owner
independent record label

Hearts of Space
1324 Noriega St.
San Francisco, CA 94122
Leyla R. Hill, GM
independent record label

Helen Forrest Fan Club
1040 De Haro St.
San Francisco, CA 94107

Helion Records
8306 Wilshire Blvd., #216
Beverly Hills, CA 90211
Greg Knowles, Producer
independent record label

Hell Fire Management
P.O. Box 75995
Oklahoma City, OH 73147
Scott Booker
artist management

Hellerman, Fred
250 W. 57th St.
New York, NY 10102
folksinger, composer

HellYeah
P.O. Box 1975
Burbank, CA 91507
Lee Joseph
independent record label

Helvering Agency, The
P.O. Box 2940
Anderson, IN 46018
John Helvering
artist management

Henderson Group Music
125 Powell Mill Rd., #D
Spartanburg, SC 29301
Dr. Barry Henderson, President
artist management

Henderson, Florence
9000 Sunset Blvd., #1200
Los Angeles, CA 90069
singer

Henderson, Skitch (Lyle Russel Cedric)
New York Pops
Carnegie Hall
881 17th Ave., #903
New York, NY 10019
pianist, conductor

Hendricks, Barbara
c/o Harrison/Parrot Ltd.
12 Penzance Place
London W11 4PA U.K.
opera singer, recitalist

Henley, Don
9130 Sunset Blvd.
Los Angeles, CA 90069
singer, songwriter

Hensler, Guenter Manfred
BMG Classics
1133 Ave. of the Americas
New York, NY 10036
record company executive

Herbert, Herbie Management
2051 Third St.
San Francisco, CA 94107
artist management

Herman, Jerry
c/o ASCAP
1 Lincoln Plaza
New York, NY 10023
composer, lyricist

Herndon, Mark
Morris and Assoc.
818 19th Ave., S
Nashville, TN 37203
drummer

Herschel Freeman Agency
1404 Vickers Ave.
Durham, NC 27707
artist management

Hervey & Company
9034 Sunset Blvd., #107
Los Angeles, CA 90069
Ramon Hervey II
artist management

Hewitt, Love
c/o London & Lichtenberg
11601 Wilshire Blvd., #400
Los Angeles, CA 90025
singer

Heyday Records
2325 3rd St., #339
San Francisco, CA 94107
Ron Gompertz, President
independent record label

Hickey, David Agency
P.O. Box 330160
Ft. Worth, TX 76163
rhythm & blues artist management

Hideoki Productions Ltd.
236 W. 26th St.
New York, NY 10001
video production

High Five Productions
3255 Cahuenga Blvd. W., #102
Los Angeles, CA 90068
Bud Schaetzle, Producer/Director
video production

High Noon Entertainment
89 5th Ave., 8th Fl.
New York, NY 10023
Russell Rieger
artist management

Higher Octave Music
8033 Sunset Blvd., #41
Los Angeles, CA 90046
Scott Bergstein, Senior VP
independent record label

Higher We Fly John Denver
Appreciation Society, The
5026 39th Ave.
Kenosha, WI 53144
fan club

Hightone Records
220 4th St., #101
Oakland, CA 94607
Darrell Anderson
independent record label

Hill, Andrew William
JAZZFUND
606 NW Front Ave.
Portland, OR 97209
jazz musician, composer

Hines, Gregory
9830 Wilshire Blvd.
Beverly Hills, CA 90212
singer

Hinton, Bruce C.
MCA Records
1514 South St.
Nashville, TN 37212
record company executive

Hip Magazine
Square Foot Publications
P.O. Box 1212
Orange, CT 06477
magazine

Hit & Run Music Ltd.
25 Ives St.
London SW3 2ND U.K.
Tony Smith
artist management

Hit City
707 E. 54th St.
Indianapolis, IN 46220
Scott Sanders
independent record label

Hit List Records
548 W. 28th St., 6th Fl.
New York, NY 10001
Arnie Goodman
independent record label

Hit Parader
Hit Parade Publ. Inc.
40 Violet Ave.
Poughkeepsie, NY 12601
heavy metal magazine

**Hit Video Country/Pollaro
Media Productions**
400 W. Main St.
Denison, TX 75020
Stephanie Clift, Producer
video production

Hitman of Design
8306 Wilshire Blvd., #2550
Beverly Hills, CA 90211
Robert E. Fusfield
video production

HLA
75 Kenton Street
London WC1 U.K.
Adam Johnson
video production

HMS Bookings
8620 West 3rd St.
Los Angeles, CA 90048
hairstylist/makeup artist rep

Ho, Don (Donald Tai Loy)
Hula Hut
286 Beach Walk
Honolulu, HI 96815
singer

Hoffman Bros. Management
1050 Bethlehem Pike
P.O. Box 249
Montgomeryville, PA 18936
Marc Hoffman
artist management

Holliday, Jennifer Yvette
c/o Mike Keller
1133 Broadway, #911
New York, NY 10010
singer

Hollywood Bowl Summer Festival
135 N. Grand Ave.
Los Angeles, CA 90012
music festival

Hollywood Records
500 S. Buena Vista St., Animation
Bldg.
Burbank, CA 91505
Peter Paterno, President
record label

Hollywood Reporter, The
6715 Sunset Blvd., #612
Hollywood, CA 90028
Tichi Wilkerson Kassel, Publisher
daily "trade" publication

Holtz, Glenn Edward
Geminhardt
P.O. Box 788
Elkhart, IN 46515
band instrument manufacturing executive

Holzman, D. Keith
First Media Music, Discovery
Records
2052 Broadway
Santa Monica, CA 90404
record company executive

Home Cooking Records
P.O. Box 980454
Houston, TX 77098
Roy C. Ames, Owner
independent record label

Homeland Recording and Publishing, Inc.
1011 16th Ave. S
Nashville, TN 37212
Beth Hemphill
independent record label

Homestead Records
P.O. Bopx 800
Rockville Center, NY 11571
Ken Katkin
independent record label

Hood, Sherri
21-29 35th St.
Astoria, NY 11105
artist management

Hooker Enterprises International
8285 Sunset Blvd., #10
Los Angeles, CA 90046
Jake Hooker, President
artist management

Hooker Enterprises International
8285 Sunset Blvd., #10
Los Angeles, CA 90046
Jake Hooker, President
independent record label

Hooker, John Lee
P.O. Box 210103
San Francisco, CA 94121
singer, guitarist

Hopkins Center
Dartmouth College
HB 6041
Hanover, NH 03445
music festival

Horizon Entertainment Management
130 W. 57th St., #12B
New York, NY 10019
Brian Doyle
artist management

Horizon Studio
1317 S. 295th Place
Federal Way, WA 00000
Roger Wood, Owner
video production

Horn, Paul Joseph
P.O. Box 6193, Station C
Victoria, British Columbia V8P 5L5
Canada
musician

Horn, Shirley
Verve Records/Worldwide Plaza
825 8th Ave.
New York, NY 10019
vocalist, pianist

Hornblow Group, The
24 Hudson Ave.
Edgewater, NJ 07020
Jamie Kitman
artist management

Horne, Lena
c/o White
5950 Canoga Ave.
Woodland Hills, CA 91367
singer

Horne, Marilyn
Metropolitan Opera Association
147 W. 39th St.
New York, NY 10019
mezzo-soprano

Hornsby, Bruce
c/o BMG
6363 Sunset Blvd.
Hollywood, CA 90028
musician

Hot Shot Productions
P.O. Box 1297
Kapa's Kanai, HI
video production

Hottrax Records
1957 Kilburn Dr.
Atlanta, GA 30324
Al Janoulis, President
independent record label

Houston International Festival, The
2 Houston Center
909 Fannin, #P330
Houston, TX 77010
music festival

Houston, Whitney
Solters, Roskind, Friedman, Inc.
45 W. 34th St.
New York, NY 10001
singer

Howard, Glenn Audio
5909 Ranchito Ave.
Van Nuys, CA 91404
independent record label

Howling Wind
Strangelove Press
6202 N. 16th St.
Phoenix, AZ 85016
magazine

HSI Productions
1611 Electric Ave.
Venice, CA 90291
video production

Hudson, William L.
Fairfax Symphony Orchestra
P.O. Box 1300
Annandale, VA 22003
conductor

Humble Adobe Productions
7000 Santa Monica Blvd.
Hollywood, CA 90038
Paul Schwartz, CEO
independent record label

Humboldt Records
P.O. Box 713
Trinidad, CA 95570
Robby Jarvis
independent record label

Hummingbird Productions
McClurg Ct. Center
333 E. Ontario
Chicago, IL 60611
video production

Hurricane Management
132 Surrey Ct.
Ramsey, NJ 07446
Scott K. Perkins
artist management

Husa, Karel Jaroslav
Cornell University Department of
Music
Ithaca, NY 14853
composer, conductor, educator

Huskinson Productions Inc.
904 Tower Bldg., 7th and Olive Way
Seattle, WA 98101
video production

Hutcherson, Bobby
The Berkeley Agency
2490 Channing Way, #418
Berkeley, CA 94704
jazz vibraphonist

Hyper Kinetics
53 Park Rd.
London N8 8SY U.K.
Kenny Smith
artist management

Hypnotic Management
96 Spadina Ave., 9th Fl.
Toronto, Ontario M5V 2J6 Canada
Tom Treumuth
artist management

I

Only sick music makes money today.
—Nietzsche

I-Beam, The
1748 Haight St.
San Francisco, CA 94117
club

I.R.S. Records
3939 Lankershim Blvd.
Universal City, CA 91604
Miles Copeland, President
record label

I.R.S. Records
New York
594 Broadway, #901
New York, NY 10012

I.S.I.S. Promotions and Management
545 8th Ave., #401-141
New York, NY 10018
Nefritari, President
artist management

ICC Fine Arts Festival
Illinois Central College
East Peoria, IL 61635
music festival

Ice Cube
c/o Priority
P.O. Box 2186
Hollywood, CA 90078
rapper

Ice-T
c/o Sire Records
75 Rockefeller Plaza
New York, NY 10019
rapper

Ichiban Records Inc.
P.O. Box 724677
Atlanta, GA 30339
John Abbey, President
independent record label

Idol, Billy
c/o EMI/Chrysalis
810 7th Ave., 8th Fl.
New York, NY 10019
singer

Idolmakers Management
42-15 Crescent St., #503
Long Island City, NY 11101
Herby Azor
artist management

Idyllwild Music Festival
Idyllwild School of Music and the Arts
P.O. Box 38
Idyllwild, CA 92349

Iglesias, Julio (Julio Jose Iglesias DeLaCueva)
c/o Columbia
P.O. Box 4450
New York, NY 10109
singer

IKA Media
30 W. 61st St.
New York, NY 10023
video production

Illinois Entertainer
Bam Network
2200 E. Devon, #192
Des Plaines, IL 60018
magazine

Illustrative Auteur Media
P.O. Box 2430
Santa Clara, CA 95055
Eric Predoehl, Producer/Director
video production

Image G Corporation
945 N. Highland Ave.
Hollywood, CA 90038
video production

Image Marketing
7958 Beverly Blvd.
Los Angeles, CA 90048
Lee Ann Myers
marketing consultants

Image Recording Co.
152 W. 5th St., 44th Fl.
New York, NY 10019
Kate Hyman
independent record label

Imagemaker Productions
220 Great Circle Rd., #118
Nashville, TN 37228
video production

Imaginary Entertainment
923 Westmount Dr.
West Hollywood, CA 90069
Jay Levey
artist management

**Imaginary Entertainment/Mood
Swing Production**
332 N. Dean Rd.
Auburn, AL 36830
Lloyd E. Townsend, Jr.
independent record label

Imagine! Records
4432 Telegraph Ave., #83
Oakland, CA 94602
Russ Ketter
independent record label

Imani Entertainment Inc.
P.O. Box 139
Brooklyn, NY 11215
Alfred Johnston, Director
independent record label

Immaculate Mary Fan Club
645 Titus Ave.
Rochester, NY 14617

Impact Recording
P.O. Box 146
Alexandria, IN 46001
Bill Traylor, GM
independent record label

Impact Records
6255 Sunset Blvd., #2100
Hollywood, CA 90028
Allen Kovac, CEO
independent record label

Imperial Records Inc.
P.O. Box 2642
Santa Maria, CA 93457
Joe Valenta, President
independent record label

IMPS Music
70 Route 202 N
Peterborough, NH 03458
independent music producers syndicate

In Appreciation of the Hollies
c/o Mark James Meli
14 Bucky Dr.
Rochester, NY 14624
fan club

In-a-Minute Records
1025 W. MacArthur Blvd.
Oakland, CA 90013
Jason Blaine
independent record label

Independent Productions
57 Middle St.
Gloucester, MA 01930
video production

Independent Project
544 Mateo St.
Los Angeles, CA 90013
Bruce Licher
independent record label

Independent Record Charts
43 Music Square E
Nashville, TN 37203
Wayne Hodge, President
independent country musicians

Industrial Management
3450 3rd St., #2A
San Francisco, CA 94124
Alfred Johnson
artist management

Ingram, James
c/o Warner Brothers Records
3300 Warner Blvd.
Burbank, CA 91505
rhythm and blues songwriter, performer

Ink Spots, The
1385 York Ave., #15H
New York, NY 10021
group

Insight Productions
1008 Sahara Way
Las Vegas, NV 89108
Rob Devlin, Owner
artist management

**Inspiration Point Fine Arts Colony
Opera Festival**
P.O. Box 127
Eureka Springs, AR 72632

Instant Veal Records
63 Carlton St.
Johnson City, NY 13790
Brian Dudla
independent record label

Instinct Entertainment
2700 Neilson Way, #1521
Santa Monica, CA 90405
Michael Rosen, President
artist management

Instinct Records
222 W. 14 St., #8B
New York, NY 10011
Jared Hoffman
independent record label

Institute of the American Musical
121 N. Detroit St.
Los Angeles, CA 90036
Miles Krueger, President and Curator
archives

Inter-American Music Council
c/o Prof. Efrain Paesky
1889 F St., NW, #230-C
Washington, DC 20006
music study and education

Interarts Hawaii
1221 Griffiths Street
Honolulu, HI 96826
music festival

Intercollegiate Men's Chorus
A National Association of Male Cho-
ruses
Kansas State University
McCain Auditorium
Manhattan, KS 66506
Gerald Polic, Exec. Officer

Interlochen Arts Festival
Interlochen Center for the Arts
P.O. Box 199
Interlochen, MI 49643
music festival

International Al Jolson Society
2981 Westmoor Dr.
Columbus, OH 43204

**International Alban Berg Soci-
ety**
c/o Prof. Barry Brook
33 W. 42nd St.
City University of New York
New York, NY 10036
studies and performs the works of the
Austrian composer

**International Bluegrass Music
Association**
326 St. Elizabeth St.
Owensboro, KY 42301
Dan Hayes, Executive Director

**International Buddy Rich Fan
Club**
P.O. Box 2014
Warminster, PA 18974

International Clarinet Society
Clarinetwork International
P.O. Box 7683
Shawnee Mission, KS 66207

**International Conference of Sym-
phony and Opera Musicians**
6607 Waterman
St. Louis, MO 63130
Brad Buckley, Chairman

**International Contemporary
Music Exchange**
500 E. 85th St., #14H
New York, NY 10028
Igor Buketoff, Director
studies contemporary classical music

**International Council for Tradi-
tional Music**
c/o Center for Ethnomusicology
Columbia University
New York, NY 10027
Dieter Christensen, Secretary General

International Double Reed Society
c/o Lowry Riggins
626 Lakeshore Dr.
Monroe, LA 71203

**International Fan Club Organiza-
tion**
P.O. Box 177
Wild Horse, CO 80862

**International Federation of Chil-
dren's Choirs**
120 S. 3rd St.
Shallway Bldg.
Connellsville, PA 15425
L. Fry, President

**International Federation of
Ragtime**
c/o Nick Taylor
5095 Picket Dr.
Colorado Springs, CO 80918

International Guild of Symphony, Opera and Ballet Musicians
c/o R.L. Baunton
5802 16th NE
Seattle, WA 98105

International Guitar Week
Lamont School of Music, University of Denver
Houston Fine Arts Center
7111 Montview Blvd.
Denver, CO 80220

International Horn Society
c/o Ellen Powley
2220 North 1400 East
Provo, UT 84604

International Klaus Tennstedt Society
504 NW 89th St.
Gainesville, FL 32607
David M. Grundy, Publisher
interpretation of German
conductor/composer

International Management Services
818 19th Ave. S
Nashville, TN 37203
artist management

International Marketing Group
1900 Elm Hill Pike
Nashville, TN 37210
Robert Jones
independent record label

International Polka Association
4145 S. Kedzie Ave.
Chicago, IL 60632
Fred Hudy, President

International Rhythm and Blues Association
P.O. Box 288571
Chicago, IL 60628
William C. Tyson, President

International Rock 'N' Roll Music Association
P.O. Box 158946
Nashville, TN 37215
Bernard G. Walters, President

International Sinatra Society
P.O. Box 5195
Anderson, SC 29623
fan club

International Society for Contemporary Music
c/o American Music Center
30 W. 26th St., #1001
New York, NY 10019
Robert Yekovich, President

International Society for Organ History and Preservation
P.O. Box 104
Harrisville, NH 03450
Alan M. Laufman, President

International Society of Bassists
4020 McEwen, #105
Dallas, TX 75244
John Clayton, President

International Society of Folk Harpers and Craftsmen
4718 Maychelle Dr.
Anaheim, CA 92807
Sylvia Fellows, Secretary

International Steel Guitar Convention
9535 Midland Blvd.
St. Louis, MO 63114
Dewith A. Scott, Sr., President

International Talent & Touring Directory
49 Music Square W.
Nashville, TN 37203
lists managers, talent, facilities, etc. for tours

International Trombone Association
c/o Vern Kagarice
North Texas State University
School of Music
Denton, TX 76203

International Trumpet Guild
Western Michigan University
School of Music
Kalamazoo, MI 49008
Dr. Stephen Jones, President

International Willie Nelson Fan Club
P.O. Box 7104
Lancaster, PA 17604

Interscope Records
10900 Wilshire Blvd., 12th Fl.
Los Angeles, CA 90024
Jimmy Iovine, Head of Label
record label

Intrepid Records
65 Jefferson Ave., #205
Totonto, Ontario M6K 1Y3 Canada
Stuart Raven-Hill, President
independent record label

Invasion Records
114 Lexington Ave., 2nd Fl.
New York, NY 10016
independent record label

Iron Butterfly Information Network
c/o Easy Action
P.O. Box 1658
Fontana, CA 92334
fan club

Iron John Management
360 N. Sycamore Ave., #5
Los Angeles, CA 90036
John Axelrod, President
artist management

Iron Maiden
P.O. Box 391
London, W4 1LZ U.K.
group

Ironwood Studios
601 NW 80th St.
Seattle, WA 98117
video production

Isaak, Chris
c/o Warner Bros./Reprise
3300 Warner Blvd.
Burbank, CA 91510
singer

Island Records
400 Lafayette St.
New York, NY 10003
Chris Blackwell, Chairman
record label

Island Records
Los Angeles
8920 Sunset Blvd., 2nd Fl.
Los Angeles, CA 90069

Israel & Bray
919 Third Ave., 6th Fl.
New York, NY 10022
music attorneys

It's a Gas
1172 Laurel Dr.
Toms River, NJ 08735
Vinny Rich
artist management

Ives, Burl (Icle Ivanhoe)
427 N. Canon Dr., #205
Beverly Hills, CA 90210
singer

J

Of all noises, I think music is the least disagreeable.
—SAMUEL JOHNSON

J Artist Management
P.O. Box 16681
Cleveland, OH 44116
John Malm
artist management

J. Cast Productions
330 Johnson St., Suite 3
Sausalito, CA 94965
John J. Castonia, President
artist management

J. Harman Publishing Co.
7216 34th Ave.
Kenosha, WI 53142
J. Harman, CEO
independent record label

Jack of all Trades Records
411 Venderbilt Ave., #6
Staten Island, NY 10304
Dexter Hazelton
artist management

Jack of All Trades Records
411 Vanderbilt Ave., #6
Staten Island, NY 10304
Dexter Hazelton, Partner
independent record label

Jackson, Bags (Milton)
Concord Records
P.O. Box 845
Concord, CA 94522
jazz musician

Jackson, David Management
2900 E. 26th St., #308
Sioux Falls, SD 97103
Bruce E. Colfin
artist management

Jackson, Isaiah
Dayton Philharmonic Orchestra
Montgomery County Memorial Hall
125 E. 1st St.
Dayton, OH 45422
conductor

Jackson, Janet (Damita)
338 N. Foothill Rd.
Beverly Hills, CA 90210
singer

Jackson, Joe
c/o Direct Mgmt. Group
947 N. La Cienega Blvd.
West Hollywood, CA 90069
musician, singer, songwriter

Jackson, Michael
c/o Gallin/Morey Assoc.
8730 Sunset Blvd., PH W
Los Angeles, CA 90069
singer

Jagger, Mick
c/o RZO
110 W. 57th St.
New York, NY 10019
rock performer

Jaguar Productions Inc.
235 E. 34th St.
New York, NY 10016
video production

Jake Barner Studios
120 S. Barner
Centralia, WA 98531
Allen Fadness
independent record label

Jam Presents
P.O. Box 6588
San Antonio, TX 78209
Joe Miller
artist management

James Turner Productions
1431 Duke St.
Alexandria, VA 22314
Chip Seligman
artist management

James, Carolyne (Clarity James)
Radford University Department of Music
Radford, VA 24142
mezzo-soprano

Janie's Friends
P.O. Box 680785
San Antonio, TX 78268
Janie Fricke fan club

Janis Ian Fan Club
P.O. Box 475
New York, NY 10023

Jarman, Joseph
P.O. Box 62
Brooklyn, NY 11205
jazz musician

Jarreau, Al
c/o Patrick Rains
9034 Sunset Blvd., #250
West Hollywood, CA 90069
musician

Jarrett, Keith
c/o GRP
555 W. 57th St.
New York, NY 10019
pianist, composer

Jarvi, Neeme
Detroit Symphony Orchestra
3711 Woodward Ave.
Detroit, MI 48201
conductor

Jaw Bone Music
5554 Radford Ave.
N. Hollywood, CA 91607
Michael Rourke, Producer
Christian-oriented video production

Jay Jay Records
35 NE 62nd St.
Miami, FL 33138
Walter Jagiello, President
independent record label

Jazi Jaz Entertainment
P.O. Box 326
New York, NY 10023
Juanita Gaskin
artist management

Jazz Composers Orchestra Association
598 Broadway, 7th Fl.
New York, NY 10012
Timothy Marquand, President

Jazz Interactions
P.O. Box 268
Glen Oaks, NY 11004
D. Payne, Co.-President
promotes appreciation and under-
standing of jazz

Jazz World Society
c/o Jan A. Byrczek
250 W. 57th St., #1212
New York, NY 10107
promotes jazz

Jazzbeat Productions
P.O. Box 153
Exeter, NH 03833
Dick Hollyday, President
artist management

Jazzmobile
154 W. 127th St.
New York, NY 10027
S. David Bailey, Exec. Director
brings jazz to neighborhoods in
mobile units

**JCI Records/Artful Balance
Records**
21550 Oxnard St., #920
Woodland Hills, CA 91367
independent record label

Jean, Kenneth
Florida Symphony Orchestra
1900 N. Mills Ave., #3
Orlando, FL 32803
conductor

Jerry Jeff Walker Fan Club
c/o Tried and True Music
P.O. Box 39
Austin, TX 78767

Jet Lag Inc.
155 E. 55th St., #6H
New York, NY 10022
Kenny Laguna
artist management

Jet Lag Magazine
8419 Hals Ferry
Mailman Bldg.
St. Louis, MO 63147
alternative music magazine

Jethro Tull
12 Stratford Place
London, W1N 9AF U.K.
group

Jewish Music Alliance
1133 Broadway, #1023
New York, NY 10010
J. Goldberg, Exec. Officer
19 local singing societies, preserving
Yiddish music

**Jewish Music Council of the Jew-
ish Community Center**
Association of North America
15 E. 26th St.
New York, NY 10010
Paula G. Gottlieb, Director

Jim Blashfield and Associates
1801 NW Upshur
Portland, OR 97209
video production

**Jimi Hendrix Information Man-
agement Institute**
P.O. Box 374
Des Plaines, IL 60016
fan club

Jimmy Page/Robert Plant
International Newsletter
1660 Broadmoor Dr. E
Seattle, WA 98112
Led Zeppelin fan club

Jive Records
Zomba Enterprises
137-139 W. 25th St., 8th Fl.
New York, NY 10001
Clive Calder, Chairman
record label

Jive Records
Zomba Enterprises—New York
6777 Hollywood Blvd., 6th Fl.
Hollywood, CA 90028

Jive Records
Zomba Enterprises—Chicago
323 E. 23rd St.
Chicago, IL 60616

JK JAM Music
6 Kingsly Ave.
Gansevoort, NY 12831
Jamie Keats, Owner
independent record label

Joe Public
51 W. 52nd St.
New York, NY 10019
group

Joel, Billy (William Martin)
Maritime Music Inc.
200 W. 57th St.
New York, NY 10019
singer, songwriter

Johanos, Donald
Honolulu Symphony Orchestra
1441 Kapiolani Blvd., #1515
Honolulu, HI 96814
conductor

John, Elton (Reginald Kenneth Dwight)
c/o John Reid
32 Galena Rd.
London W6 0LT U.K.
singer, songwriter

Johnny Cash and June Carter Cash International Fan Club
Rt. 12, Box 350
Winston-Salem, NC 27107

Johnson, Neville L. & Associates
11726 San Vicente Blvd., #418
Los Angeles, CA 90049
Neville L. Johnson, Esq.
attorney and manager

Johnson, Roland A.
Madison Symphony Orchestra
Oscar Mayer Theatre
211 N. Carroll St.
Madison, WI 53703
conductor, music director

JOKR Records
733 W. Naomi Ave., #1-154
Arcadia, CA 91007
John Piccari
independent record label

Jones, Etta
Houston Person
160 Goldsmith Ave.
Newark, NJ 07112
singer

Jones, George
c/o Buddy Lee Attractions
38 Music Alley
Nashville, TN 37212
country music singer, songwriter

Jones, Gwyneth
Box 556
CH-8037 Zurich Switzerland
soprano

Jones, Jack
8019 1/2 Melrose Ave., #3
Los Angeles, CA 90046
singer

Jones, Quincy
P.O. Box 48249
Los Angeles, CA 90048
composer, producer

Jones, Shirley
c/o Roy Gerber
500 Vernon Ave.
Venice, CA 90291
singer

Jones, Tom
10100 Santa Monica Blvd., #205
Los Angeles, CA 90067
singer

Jordan, Stanley
c/o Blue Note Records
1750 N. Vine St.
Hollywood, CA 90028
musician, developer of the two-
handed clapping guitar technique

Journey
P.O. Box 404
San Francisco, CA 94101
group

Joy Art Ltd.
540 N. Lakeshore Dr.
Chicago, Il 60611
Butch Stewart
video production

Joyce Linehan Mgmt.
P.O. Box 435 Kenmore Station
Boston, MA 02215
artist management

JP Ideas
1510 Calle Del Norte, #200
Laredo, TX 78041
Jorge Flores
"Tejano" artist management

JRS Records
7758 Sunset Blvd.
Los Angeles, CA 90046
independent record label

Juba Productions
3623 Canal St., 7th Fl.
New Orleans, LA 70119
Greer E. Goff
artist management

Jubilation—Paul Anka
Admiration Society
c/o Margaret Ann Aker
2136 Lincoln Ave., Apt. J
Alameda, CA 94501
fan club

Judd, Naomi
P.O. Box 17087
Nashville, TN 37217
singer

Judy Garland Memorial
Club
153 5th St.
Lock Haven, PA 17745

Juice Newton Fan Club
P.O. Box 293323
Lewisville, TX 75029

Juillet, Chantal
c/o Marie-Claude Beauchamp
2200 Place Rigaud/Chomedey,
Laral, PQ Canada H7S 1A4
violinist

Junior's Motel Entertainment
5435 Wyandotte
Kansas City, MO 64112
Mike Hollinger
artist management

JVC Jazz Festival New York
P.O. Box 1169 Ansonia Station
New York, NY 10023

K

Music has been called medicine, and some of it is hard to take.
—ANONYMOUS

Kactus
3473 Cahuenga Blvd. W
Los Angeles, CA 90068
video production

**Kalnia Honua Performing Arts
Center/Retreat**
P.O. Box 4500
Kalapana, HI 96778
music events and workshops

Kander, John Harold
c/o Dramatists Guild
234 W. 44th St.
New York, NY 10036
composer

Kantner, Paul
Little Dragon Publ.
3145 Geary Blvd., #416
San Francisco, CA 94118
musician "Jefferson Airplane"

Kaos, Inc.
9808 Wilshire Blvd., #304
Beverly Hills, CA 90212
Tom Mohler
artist management

Kapalua Music Festival
500 Office Rd.
Kapalua, Maui, HI 96761

Kaplan, Allan Enterprises
P.O. Box 9429
San Rafael, CA 94912
new age/jazz artist management

Kasem, Casey
c/o Stern
11755 Wilshire Blvd., #2320
Los Angeles, CA 90025
DJ

**Kate Smith—God Bless America
Foundation**
P.O. Box 3575
Cranston, RI 02910
fan club

Kaye, Tony Films Inc.
9155 Sunset Blvd., #7
W. Hollywood, CA 90069
Tony Kaye, Director
video production

Kazan, Lainie (Lainie Levine)
151 El Camino
Beverly Hills, Ca 90212
singer

Keating, Cornelius Francis
Columbia House Co.
51 W. 52nd St.
New York, NY 10019
chairman, record club company

Keene, Christopher
New York City Opera
20 Lincoln Center
New York, NY 10023
conductor, author, librettist, musician

Kenny G (Gorelick)
648 N. Robertson Blvd.
Los Angeles, CA 90048
saxophonist

Kensington Sound/Quantum Records
170A Baldwin St.
Toronto, ONT M5T 1L8 Canada
Mike Alyanak, President
video production

Kershaw, Stewart
Evansville Philharmonic Orchestra
Vanderburgh Auditorium
P.O. Box 84
Evansville, IN 47701
conductor

Keshaw
1718 N. First St., 3rd Fl.
Milwaukee, WI 53212
Mark McCran
artist management

Kewley, Fred Management
1711 18th Ave. S, #D3
Nashville, TN 37212
artist management

Khan, Chaka
c/o Geffen Records
9130 Sunset Blvd.
West Hollywood, CA 90069
singer

Khanzadian, Vahan
3604 Broadway, #2N
New York, NY 10031
tenor

Kimball, Robert Eric
180 W. 58th St.
New York, NY 10019
author, music historian

Kinetic Videos
23501 Park Sorrento, #103
Calabasas, CA 91302
Luke O'Reilly
video production

King King, The
91 8th Ave., #4
Brooklyn, NY 11215
Barry King
video production

King, B.B. (Riley B. King)
c/o Sidney A. Seidenberg
1414 Ave. of the Americas
New York, NY 10019
singer, guitarist

King, Carole
Free Flow Productions
1209 Baylor St.
Austin, TX 78703
composer, singer

King, Morgana
Associated Talent International
9744 Wilshire Blvd., #306
Beverly Hills, CA 90212
jazz vocalist

Kingbee Management
143 S. Cedros Ave., #V
Solana Beach, CA 92075
Kevin Morrow
artist management

Kingsnakes
205 Lake Blvd.
Sanford, FL 32773
Bob Greenlee
artist management

Kingston Korner
230 Cohasset Rd., #6S
Naperville, IL 60540
Kingston Trio fan club

Kingston Trio, The
107 Degas Road
Portola Valley, CA 94025
group

Kip Gynn Sound
15 Horizon Ave.
Venice, CA 90066
Cliff Gynn, Owner
video production

KISS
P.O. Box 840
Westbury, NY 11590
group

Kiss Konnection Fan Club
P.O. Box 5626
San Angelo, TX 76902

Kitt, Eartha Mae
General Artists Mgmt.
162 W. 56th St.
New York, NY 10019
singer

**Kneisel Hall Summer
Chamber Music School and Festival**
P.O. Box 648
Blue Hill, ME 04614

Kness, Richard Maynard
240 Central Park, #16M
New York, NY 10019
tenor

Knight, Gladys (Maria)
c/o Shakeji Inc.
1589 Golden Arrow Dr.
Las Vegas, NV 89109
singer

Kojian, Varujan Haig
Santa Barbara Symphony
214 E. Victoria St.
Santa Barbara, CA 93101
conductor

Kolarek, Frank Film and Video
286 Fifth Ave.
New York, NY 10001
video production

Koppelman, Charles
SBK Records
1290 Ave. of the Americas
New York, NY 10104
singer, turned record co. exec.

Kopple Artist Management
1040 W. Granville, #222
Chicago, IL 60660
artist management

Kragen & Company
1112 N. Sherbourne Dr.
Los Angeles, CA 90069
Ken Kragen
country artist management

Kramer, Jay
135 E. 55th St., 6th Fl.
New York, NY 10022
Jay Kramer
rap artist management

Kris Cross
51 W. 52nd St.
New York, NY 10019
group

Kris Kristofferson International Fan Club
313 Lakeshore Dr.
Marietta, GA 30067

Kristofferson, Kris
c/o CBS Special Records
51 W. 52nd St.
New York, NY 10019
composer, singer

Kriwanek & Associates
2600 Tenth St.
Berkeley, CA 94710
Partick Kriwanek
video production

Krosnick, Joel
Juilliard String Quartet
c/o Colbert Artists Mgmt.
111 W. 57th St.
New York, NY 10019
cellist

KRT Management
1776 Broadway, #1710
New York, NY 10019
video production

Kuchara Group, The
624 N. Fifth St.
Phoenix, AZ 85004
video production

Kurland, Ted Associates
173 Brighton Ave.
Allston, MA 02134
artist management

Kurt Weill Foundation for Music
7 E. 20th St.
New York, NY 10003
David Farneth, Director

Kushnick/Passick Management
1556 Third Ave., #301
New York, NY 10128
artist management

Kushnick/Passick Management
Los Angeles
914 S. Robertson Blvd.
Los Angeles, CA 90035

Popular music just has to come from the brain of the composer.
Nothing else has stuff like that in it.

—ANONYMOUS

L Stop/Highlife Group
6108 S. Kimbark
Chicago, IL 60637
Ralph Johnson, President
video production

L'Ensemble Chamber Music Center
Content Farm Road
Cambridge, NY 12816

LA Reps
8149 Kirkwood Dr.
Los Angeles, CA 90046
hairstylist/makeup rep

La's (Lee Mavers, Neil Mavers, Cammy Power, John Power)
825 Eighth Avenue
New York, New York 10022
group

Labate Management
926 Belvidere Ave.
Plainfield, NJ 07060
Donna A. Labate
metal artist management

LaBelle, Patti
c/o MCA Records
100 Universal City Plaza
Universal City, CA 91608
singer

Lacy J. Dalton Fan Club
P.O. Box 1109
Mount Juliet, TN 37122

Lacy, Steve
c/o BMG
1133 Ave. of the Americas
New York, NY 10036
jazz musician

Lacy/Los Angeles
8446 Melrose Place
Los Angeles, CA 90069
Peter Vieira
video production

Laine, Cleo (Clementina Dinah Dankworth)
c/o Sonoma-Hope Inc.
P.O. Box 282
Hope, NJ 07844
singer

Lake George Opera Festival
P.O. Box 2172
Glens Falls, NY 12801

Lang, K.D.
c/o Sire Records
75 Rockefeller Plaza
New York, NY 10019
country music singer, composer

Larger than Life
7201 Melrose Ave.
Los Angeles, CA 90046
video production

Larkin, Nelson Inc.
916 19th Ave. S
Nashville, TN 37212
country artist management

Larry Gatlin and Gatlin Brothers International Fan Club
P.O. Box 153452
Irving, TX 75015

Last Laugh Production Co. Ltd., The
19 Meard St.
London W1 U.K.
Chris Cook
artist management

Latvian Choir Association of the U.S.
7886 Anita Dr.
Philadelphia, PA 19111
Arija Sulcs, Vice-President

Lauper, Cyndi
c/o Dave Wolff
853 7th Ave.
New York, N.Y. 10019
singer

Laura Branigan Fan Club
P.O. Box 615
Springfield, OR 97477

Laurents, Arthur
P.O. Box 582
Quoque, NY 11959
lyricist

Lauritz Melchior Heldentenor Foundation
322 E. 55th St., #B
New York, NY 10022
discovers and provides grants to Wagnerian tenors

Lawrence, Steve
151 El Camino
Beverly Hills, CA 90212
singer

Lead Belly Society
P.O. Box 6679
Ithaca, NY 14851
Huddie Ledbetter fan club

Ledbetter & Co.
301 Cherry Blossom Lane
Gretna, LA 70054
Mary Ledbetter
artist management

Lee, Brenda (Brenda Mae Tapley)
P.O. Box 101188
Nashville, TN 37210
singer

Lefkowitz, David Management
3470 19th St.
San Francisco, CA 94110
alternative artist management

Leinsdorf, Erich
c/o Savino
P.O. Box 364
Malverne, NY 11565
orchestra conductor

Lembo Entertainment
25 Necco St.
Boston, MA 02210
Peter Lembo
artist management

Lennon Sisters Fan Club
P.O. Box E-1492
Binghamton, NY 13902

Lennon Sisters, The
944 Harding Ave.
Venice, CA 90291
singers

Lennox, Annie
Box 245
London N89 QG U.K.
singer

Leopold Stokowski Society of America
106 E. Curtis St.
Mount Vernon, OH 43050
Robert M. Stumpf, II, President

Leppard, Raymond John
Indianapolis Symphony Orchestra
45 Monument Circle
Indianapolis, IN 46204
conductor, harpsichordist

Lesbian and Gay Bands of America
P.O. Box 57099
Washington, DC 20037
John R. Macauley, President

Leschetizky Association
c/o Arminda Canteros
333 W. 86th St.
New York, NY 10024
pianists who studied under Theodor Leschetizky

Lesh, Philip Chapman
c/o Grateful Dead Productions
P.O. Box 1073
San Rafael, CA 94915
musician, composer

Lesley Gore Fan Club
c/o Jack Natoli
141 Vernon Ave.
Paterson, NJ 07503

Levalier, Dotian
National Symphony Orchestra
JFK Center Performing Arts
Washington, DC 20566
harpist

Leventhal, Harold Management
250 W. 57th St.
New York, NY 10107
folk artist management

Levi, Yoel
Atlanta Symphony Orchestra
1293 Peachtree St. NE, #300
Atlanta, GA 30309
orchestra conductor

Levine, James
Metropolitan Opera Association Inc.
Metropolitan Opera House, Lincoln Center
New York, NY 10023
conductor, pianist

Levine, Michael
8730 Sunset Boulevard, 6th Floor
Los Angeles, CA 90069
author, "The Music Address Book"

Levy, John Enterprises
5455 Wilshire Blvd., #2208
Los Angeles, CA 90036
blues/jazz artist management

Levy, Rick Management
Luxury Records
1602 Shenandoah Ct.
Allentown, PA 18104
artist management

Lewis, Huey
P.O. Box 819
Mill Valley, CA 94942
singer

Lewis, Jerry Lee
P.O. Box 3864
Memphis, TN 37173
country-rock singer, musician

Liberace Club of Las Vegas
c/o Pauline Lachance
5195 Caliente St., #71
Las Vegas, NV 89119

Liberace Museum
1775 E. Tropicana
Las Vegas, NV 89119
Joel Strote, President
pianos and candlelabra galore

Liberty Records
Capitol Records
3222 West End Ave.
Nashville, TN 37203
Jimmy Bowen, President
record label

Liederkranz Foundation
6 E. 87th St.
New York, NY 10028
Prof. John Balme, Vice-President
seeks to achieve high musical stan-
dards in the U.S.

Light, Christopher Upjohn
Old Kent Bank Bldg.
136 E. Michigan Ave.
Kalamazoo, MI 49007
computer musician

Lightfoot, Gordon (Meredith)
40 W. 57th St.
New York, NY 10019
singer, songwriter

Lightstone Productions Inc.
237 Lafayette St., #7-W
New York, NY 10012
Demian Lichtenstein,
President/CEO
video production

Limelight Film
6806 Lexington Ave.
Los Angeles, CA 90038
Steven Barron, Director
video production

Limelight Ltd.
3 Bromley Place
London W1P 5HB U.K.
Adam Whittaker
video production

**Lincoln Center Community Holi-
day Festival**
Lincoln Center for the Performing
Arts, Inc.
140 W. 65th St.
New York, NY 10023

Lincoln, Abbey (Aminata Moseka)
c/o Fantasy Records
2600 10th St.
Berkeley, CA 94710
jazz singer

Linstedt, Buono & Gordon
200 SW Market St., #1600
Portland, OR 97201
Bart Day
artist management

Lippman Entertainment
8900 Wilshire Blvd., #340
Beverly Hills, CA 90211
Jane Wallace
producers/mixers/engineers management

Little Orchestra Society
220 W. 52nd St., 18th Fl.
New York, NY 10036
John Kordel, Managing Director
sponsors Peabody award-winning
series of Happy Concerts for Young
People

**Little Richard (Richard Wayne
Penniman)**
c/o BMI
8730 Sunset Blvd., 3rd Fl.
Los Angeles, CA 90069
pianist, songwriter

Little River Band
87-91 Palmerstin Cres.
Albert Park
Melbourne Victoria 3206 Australia
group

Live Ways
234 E. 46th St.
New York, NY 10017
video production

Livengood, Victoria Ann
c/o Barrett Mgmt.
1776 Broadway, #1610
New York, NY 10019
opera singer

Livingston, Jay Harold
c/o ASCAP
1 Lincoln Plaza
New York, NY 10023
composer, lyricist

LKB Group, The
P.O. Box 8152
New York, NY 10116
T.A. Hubbard
video production

**LL Cool J (Ladies Love Cool
James)**
298 Elizabeth St.
New York, NY 10012
rapper

Lloyd Webber, Andrew
19/22 Tower St.
London WC2H 9NS U.K.
composer

**Loggins, Kenny (Kenneth Clarke
Loggins)**
151 El Camino
Beverly Hills, CA 90212
singer, songwriter

Lone Wolf Management Co.
P.O. Box 16390
Austin, TX 78716
Bill Ham
artist management

Long Term Management Inc.
11347 Park Central Place
Dallas, TX 75230
Bart Barton
artist management

Lopez-Cobos, Jesus
Cincinnati Symphony Orchestra
1241 Elm St.
Cincinnati, OH 45210
conductor

Loretta Lynn Fan Club
P.O. Box 177
Wild Horse, CO 80862

Los Angeles Festival
P.O. Box 5210
Los Angeles, CA 90055
music festival

Los Lobos
P.O. Box 1304
Burbank, CA 91507
group

Lost Arts Management
1077 Racine St.
Aurora, CO 80011
Tammy Olson
alternative/college oriented artist
management

Lost Planet
113 Spring St., 4th Fl.
New York, NY 10012
video production

**Lou Christie International Fan
Club**
c/o Harry Young
P.O. Box 748
Chicago, IL 60690

Loughnane, Lee David
c/o Howard Rose
2029 Century Park E., #450
Los Angeles, CA 90067
trumpeter "Chicago"

Louise Mandrell Fan Club
P.O. Box 718
Antioch, TN 37013

**Louisiana State University Festi-
val of Contemporary Music**
Louisiana State University
School of Music
Baton Rouge, LA 70803

Louma L.A.
8536 Venice Blvd.
Los Angeles, CA 90034
Andy Romanoff, President
video production equipment

Lowell, Howard
P.O. Box 445
N. Hollywood, CA 91603
jazz fusion artist management

**Lucasarts Commercial Produc-
tions**
1040 N. Las Palmas Blvd., Bldg. 13
Los Angeles, CA 90038
video production

Ludwig, Christa
Heidrum Artmuller
Goethgasse
1010 Vienna Austria
mezzo-soprano

Lupone, Patti
232 N. Canon Dr.
Beverly Hills, CA 90212
singer

Lute Society of America
P.O. Box 1328
Lexington, VA 24450
Beedle Hincly, Administrator

Luvers of David Jones United
2690 Associated Rd., #89
Fullerton, CA 92635
and Monkees

Lynne, Loretta
c/o MCA Records Inc.
70 Universal City Plaza
Universal City, CA 91608
singer

Music is an attempt to express emotions that are beyond reach.
—ANONYMOUS

M City Music & Art
225 W. Swift Ave.
Clovis, CA 93612
Roy Rendahl, Owner/Engineer
video graphics/recording

M-5 Management Inc.
23 4th St SE, #202
Minneapolis, MN 55414
Micah McFarlane
artist management

M-80 Management
5214 Western Blvd., #C
Raleigh, NC 27606
Dick Hodgin
artist management

Ma, Yo Yo
40 W. 57th St.
New York, NY 10019
cellist

Maag Productions, Inc.
126 N. Third St., #409
Minneapolis, MN 55401
video production

Mac Bennett Inc.
200 2nd Ave. South
Nashville, TN 37201
video production

Macal, Zdenek
Milwaukee Symphony Orchestra
330 E. Kilbourn, #900
Milwaukee, WI 53202
conductor

MacDonald, Ian Productions
Lantana Ctr., 3000 Olympic Blvd.
Santa Monica, CA 90404
video production

Macero, Ted
P.O. Box 932
Quogue, NY 11959
composer, conductor, producer

Macroscope Productions
18034 Ventura Blvd., #170
Encino, CA 91340
D. Knight, President
video production

Macurdy, John Edward
Metropolitan Opera
Lincoln Center
New York, NY 10023
basso

Madewood Arts Festival
420 Julia St.
New Orleans, LA 70130
music festival

Madhouse Management
P.O. Box 15108
Ann Arbor, MI 48106
Douglas Banker
artist management

Madonna (Madonna Louise Veronica Ciccone)
75 Rockefeller Plaza
New York, NY 10019
singer

Mahal, Taj (Henry St. Clair Fredericks)
Folklore Productions
1671 Appian Way
Santa Monica, CA 90401
composer, musician

Maine Festival, The
c/o Maine Arts Inc.
29 Forest Ave.
Portland, ME 04101
music festival

Major League Productions Inc.
111 E. Chestnut St., #42B
Chicago, IL 60611
video production

Major Production
288 E. Maple Rd., #331
Birmingham, MI 48009
Brian Sefansky, Executive Producer
video production

Makris, Andreas
National Symphony Orchestra
Kennedy Center
Washington, DC 20566
composer

Maltby, Richard Eldridge Jr.
c/o Flora Roberts
157 W. 57th St.
New York, NY 10019
lyricist

Maltese Productions
850 3rd Ave., 14th Fl.
New York, NY 10022
video production

Mamas and Papas Fan Club
P.O. Box 58
Annandale, MN 55302

Manchester Music Festival
P.O. Box 735
Manchester Village, VT 05254

Mancini, Henry
9200 Sunset Blvd., #823
Los Angeles, CA 90069
film music composer

Mandrell, Barbara Ann
World Class Talent
1522 Demonbreun St.
Nashville, TN 37203
singer

Mangione, Chuck (Charles Frank Mangione)
1850 Winton Road S.
Rochester, NY 14618
jazz musician, composer

Manhattan Film and Tape Works
907 Braodway
New York, NY 10010
video production

Manhattan Transfer, The
3575 Cahuengua Blvd., W., #450
Los Angeles, CA 90068
group

Manilow, Barry
Stiletto Ltd.
6640 Sunset Blvd., #110
Los Angeles, CA 90028
singer, songwriter, arranger

Mann, Herbie
c/o Chesky Records
P.O. Box 1268 Radio City Station
New York, NY 10101
flutist

Mannheim Steamroller
c/o American Gramaphone
9130 Mormon Bridge Rd.
Omaha, NE 68152
group

Maple Leaf Club
105 Ricky Court
Grass Valley, CA 95949
Dick Zimmerman, President
dedicated to the preservation of classic Ragtime

March, Ozan James
Pianists Foundation of America
P.O. Box 64115
Tucson, AZ 85281
concert pianist

Marcus, Greil Gerstley
San Francisco Focus
2601 Mariposa St.
San Francisco, CA 94110
music critic

Marie, Teena
c/o Sony Music
51 W. 52nd St.
New York, NY 10019
singer

Marks, Joe Film & Video
3728 SW 55th
Portland, OR 97221
video production

Marky Mark (Mark Wahlberg)
10900 Wilshire Blvd.
Los Angeles, CA 90024
rapper

Marlboro Music Festival
Marlboro, VT 05344

Marquis
203-R Harrison St. SE
Leesburg, VA 22075
Joe Ritenour
artist management

Marriner, Sir Neville
Academy of St. Martin in the Fields
109 Boundary Rd.
London NW8 ORG U.K.
conductor

Marsalis, Branford
c/o The Tonight Show
3000 W. Alameda
Burbank, CA 91523
musician

Marsalis, Wynton
9000 Sunset Blvd., #1200
Los Angeles, CA 90069
musician

Marsee, Susanne Irene
c/o Robert Lombardo
61 W. 62nd St., #6F
New York, NY 10023
lyric mezzo-soprano

Marsh, Ozan James
P.O. Box 64115
Tucson, AZ 85740
concert pianist

Marshall, Grant Company
P.O. Box 492
Hernando, MS 38632
country artist management

Martin, Dean (Dino Crocetti)
8942 Wilshire Blvd.
Beverly Hills, CA 90212
singer

Martinez, Susan & Co.
53 Melbourne Ave. SE
Minneapolis, MN 55143
public relations

Marton, Eva
Orgn. Int. Opera et Concert
19 Rue Vignon
F-75008 Paris France
singer

Marx, Richard
1750 N. Vine St.
Hollywood, CA 90028
singer

Mary Wilson Fan Club
P.O. Box 451
Lake Zurich, IL 60047

Massenet Society
9 Drury Lane
Ft. Lee, NJ 07024
Robert A. Frone, President
studies, performs the works of Jules
Massenet

**Masters Festival of Chamber
Music**
Hidden Valley Opera
P.O. Box 116
Carmel Valley, CA 93924

Masur, Kurt
New York Philharmonic
Avery Fisher Hall
132 W. 65th St.
New York, NY 10023
conductor

Mathis, Johnny
c/o Rojon Productions
3500 W. Olive Ave., #750
Burbank, CA 91505
singer

Matrix: Midland Festival
1801 W. St. Andrews Dr.
Midland, MI 48640
music festival

Mattea, Kathy
c/o Robert T. Titley
706 18th Ave. S
Nashville, TN 37212
vocalist, songwriter

Matz, Peter S.
Breaker Enterprises, Inc.
8170 Beverly Blvd.
W. Hollywood, CA 90048
composer, conductor, arranger

Mauceri, John Francis
c/o CAMI
165 W. 5th St.
New York, NY 10019
conductor

Maverick Sunday Concerts
P.O. Box 102
Woodstock, NY 12498

Max Steiner Memorial Society
P.O. Box 45713
Los Angeles, CA 90045
Albert K. Bender, Director and
Founder
preserves Academy Award winner
Steiner's film scores

Mayfield, Curtis
P.O. Box 724677
Atlanta, GA 30339
musician

MCA Records
70 Universal Plaza
Universal City, CA 91608
Al Teller, Chairman
record label

MCA Records
New York
1755 Broadway
New York, NY 10019

MCA Records
Nashville
1514 South St.
Nashville, TN 37212

McCartney, Paul
MPL Communications Ltd.
1 Soho Sq.
London W1V 6BQ U.K.
singer, composer

McCave International
25 W. 45th St., 10th Fl.
New York, NY 10036
video production

McClelland, Kirk Productions
831D Mecca Dr.
Sarasota, FL 34234
video production

McCraw/Creed Management
1718 N. First St., 3rd Fl.
Milwaukee, WI 53212
Mark McCraw
artist management

McCune Audio/Visual/Video
2200 Army St.
San Francisco, CA 94124
Jim Draper, Studio Manager

McEntire, Reba
1514 South Street
Nashville, TN 37212
singer

McFadden Artists Corp.
818 18th Ave. S
Nashville, TN 37203
Joe McFadden
country artist management

McFaul, Mary Booking & Management
P.O. Box 30081
Seattle, WA 98103
artist management

McFerrin, Bobby
ProbNoblem Music
Original Artists
128 W. 69th St.
New York, NY 10023
singer, musician

McGhee Entertainment
9145 Sunset Blvd., #100
Los Angeles, CA 90069
Doc McGhee
hard rock/metal artist management

McGhee Entertainment
New York
240 Central Park S, #2C
New York, NY 10019

McGlinn, John
c/o ICM
40 W. 57th St.
New York, NY 10019
conductor, music restorer

McGuire Sisters
100 Rancho Circle
Las Vegas, NV 89119
perennial singing group.

McKnight, Brian
c/o Mercury Records
825 8th Ave.
New York, NY 10019
singer

McKuen, Rod
P.O. Box 2783
Los Angeles, CA 90078
composer

McLean, Don
Benny Bird Co
Black Rock Turnpike
Fairfield, CT 06430
singer, instrumentalist, composer

McLean, Jackie
c/o Artists Collective, Inc.
35 Clark St.
Hartford, CT 06120
jazz saxophonist, educator, composer

McNair, Sylvia
c/o Colbert Artists Mgmt.
111 W. 57th St.
New York, NY 10019
classical vocalist

McRae, Carmen
c/o RCA Novus Records
1133 Ave. of the Americas
New York, NY 10036
singer

McVie, Christine Perfect
c/o Warner Bros. Records
3300 W. Warner Blvd.
Burbank, CA 91505
musician

Media Arts Center/Nickel Studios
753 Capitol Ave.
Hartford, CT 06106
Jack Stang
artist management

Media Five Entertainment
400 Northhampton St., #600
Easton, PA 18042
David Sestak
artist management

Medtner Society, United States of America
c/o Dimitry Feofanov
The Music Center of North Shore
300 Green Bay Rd.
Winnetka, IL 60093
studies, performs Nikolay Medtner,
Russian/German pianist

Meet the Composer
2112 Broadway, #505
New York, NY 10023
John Duffy, Director and President
promotes music of living American
composers

Meglosaurus Management
2016 Henley St.
Glenview, IL 60025
artist management

Mehta, Zubin
New York Philharmonic
Avery Fisher Hall
New York, NY 10023
conductor

Mel Tillis National Fan Club
48 Music Sq. E.
Nashville, TN 37203

Mellencamp, John Cougar
Champion Entertainment
130 W. 57th St., #12B
New York, NY 10019
singer, songwriter

Melodius Accord
801 W. End Ave., #9D
New York, NY 10025
Cynthia Shaw, Managing Director
involves people in the process of
music making

Men at Work
Box 289
Abbotsford, Victoria 3067 Australia
group

Menken, Alan
500 S. Buena Vista St.
Burbank, CA 91521
composer

Menotti, Gian Carlo
Spoleto Festival USA
P.O. Box 157
Charleston, SC 29402
composer

Menuhin, Yehudi
c/o H. Holt
122 Wigmore St.
London, W1 U.K.
violinist

Mercenary Films
211 E. 51st St., #8F
New York, NY 10022
video production

Mercury Records
PolyGram Label Group
Worldwide Plaza, 825 8th Ave.
New York, NY 10019
Ed Eckstine, President
record label

Mercury Records
PolyGram Label Group—Los Angeles
11150 Santa Monica Blvd., 10th Fl.
Los Angeles, CA 90025

Merrill, Robert
79 Oxford Rd.
New Rochelle, NY 10804
baritone

Messiah Festival of Music and Art
Bethany College
Department of Music
Lindsborg, KS 67456

Metal Muscle
Faces Magazine, Inc.
63 Grand Ave., #230
River Edge, NJ 07661
magazine

Metallica
75 Rockefeller Plaza
New York, NY 10019
group

Metheny, Patrick Bruce
c/o T. Kurland
173 Brighton Ave.
Boston, MA 02134
musician

Metropolitan Entertainment
7 N. Mountain Ave.
Montclair, NJ 07042
John Scher
artist management

Metropolitan Opera Association
Lincoln Center
New York, NY 10023
Joseph Volpe, General Director
sponsors school tours, keeps archives,
strives to make opera available to
everyone

Metropolitan Opera Guild
70 Lincoln Center Plaza, 6th Fl.
New York, NY 10023
G. Palmer LeRoy, Managing Director
supporters of the Met

Mettalix
Pilot Communications
25 W. 39th St.
New York, NY 10018
heavy metal magazine

Michael, George
Ixworth Place, 1st Fl.
London, SW1, U.K.
singer

Midler, Bette
500 S. Buena Vista, #1G2
Burbank, CA 91521
singer

Midnight Films Ltd.
6404 Hollywood Blvd., #S-316
Hollywood, CA 90028
Paul Spencer, Director of Operations
video production

Midnight Films Ltd./London
Ramilies House, 4th Fl., 1 Ramillies St.
London W1 U.K.
Michael Hamlyn
video production

Midnight Music Management
8722 1/2 W. Pico Blvd.
Los Angeles, CA 90035
Stuart Wax
artist management

Midnight Oil
c/o Sony
51 W. 52nd St.
New York, NY 10019
group

Miller & Associates Inc.
1036 Queens
Glenview, IL 60025
artist management

Miller, Steve
P.O. Box 4127
Mercer Island, WA 98040
musician

Milli Vanilli
8730 Sunset Blvd., PH W
Los Angeles, CA 90069
singers??????

Milnes, Sherrill Eustace
c/o Barrett
1776 Broadway, #584
New York, NY 10019
baritone

Milo, Aprile Elizabeth
Metropolitan Opera Assoc. Inc.
Lincoln Center
New York, NY 10023
opera singer

Milsap, Ronnie
12 Music Circle Sq.
Nashville, TN 37203
singer

Minnelli, Liza
PMK
1776 Broadway
New York, NY 10019
singer

Minor, Laura
4567 St. John Bluff Rd. S, Bldg. 2
Jacksonville, FL 32216
jazz trumpet artist management

Mirage Productions
333 N. 17th S.
Richmond, VA 23219
video production

Miramar Recordings
200 Second Ave. West
Seattle, WA 98119
Sean Gleason VP/GM
video production

Mission Impossible Management
19 All Saints Rd.
London W11 1HE U.K.
Tim Collins
artist management

Mitas Touch Video Production
399 E. 72 St., Suite 12K
New York, NY 10021
Andrew Peretz
video production

Mitchell, Joni (Roberta Joan Anderson)
c/o Peter Asher
644 N. Doheny Dr.
Los Angeles, CA 90069
singer

Mitchell, Leona Pearl
c/o Columbia Artists
165 W. 57th St.
New York, NY 10019
soprano

Mix, the Recording Industry Magazine
Act III Publishing
6400 Hollis St., #12
Emeryville, CA 94608

MMA/Marro-Matson
121 W. 19th St., 10th Fl.
New York, NY 10011
video production

Mob Music Management
The Granary Studley
Wilshire
Mo Norrington SN11 9LT London U.K.
artist management

Modern Enterprises
907 Pine, #701
Seattle, WA 98101
Terry D. Morgan
artist management

Modern Image Productions, Inc.
232 W. Willow
Chicago, IL 60614
video production

Mogul Entertainment Group
433 N. Camden Dr., #828
Beverly Hills, CA 90210
George Ghiz
artist management

Mohawk Trail Concerts
P.O. Box 843
Greenfield, MA 01302

Moir, Steve Company, The
3601 W. Olive Ave., #210
Burbank, CA 91505
producer/engineer/artist management

Mojo Management
701 E. 2nd St., #2
Boston, MA 02127
artist management

Mona Lisas and Mad Hatters
Rte. 1, Box 200
Todd, NC 28684
Elton John fan club

Monadnock Music Festival
P.O. Box 255
Peterborough, NH 03458

Monkees, Boyce and Hart Photo Fan Club, The
P.O. Box 411
Watertown, SD 57201

Monopoli Productions/Entertainment Inc.
1150 S. La Brea Ave.
Hollywood, CA 90019
John Gray, President
video production

Monroe, William Smith
c/o Buddy Lee Attractions
38 Music Sq., #300
Nashville, TN 37203
mandolin player, singer—originated
term "bluegrass"

Monterey Jazz Festival
P.O. Box JAZZ
Monterey, CA 93940

Montoya, Carlos Garcia
c/o Kolmar/Luth Entertainment Inc.
165 W. 46th St., #1202
New York, NY 10036
classical guitarist

Montster Management
7510 Sunset Blvd., #330
Hollywood, CA 90046
Monty Hudson
artists/songwriters/producers management

Moody Blues
151 El Camino
Beverly Hills, CA 90212
group

Moonlight & Magnolias
20215 Saticoy St.
Canoga Park, CA 91306
Jim Mancuso
artist management

Moore, Melba
First Global Mgmt.
Lips and Mouth Communications
1370 6th Ave., 15th Fl.
New York, NY 10019
singer

Moore, Stan Productions
117 E. Blake Court
Franklin, TN 37064
video production

Moravian Music Foundation
20 Cascade Ave.
Winston-Salem, NC 27127
C. Daniel Crews, Acting Director

Moress/Nanas/Shea Entertainment
Nashville
1209 16th Ave S
Nashville, TN 37212
Stan Moress
artist management

Moress/Nanas/Shea Entertainment
Los Angeles
12424 Wilshire Blvd., #840
Los Angeles, CA 90025

Morgado, Robert
Warner Communications, Inc.
75 Rockefeller Plaza
New York, NY 10019
chairman

Morgan Creek Music Group
1875 Century Park E., #600
Los Angeles, CA 90067
James G. Robinson, Chairman/CEO
record label

Morris Bliesener & Associates
4155 E. Jewell Ave., #412
Denver, CO 80222
Chuck Morris
artist management

Morris, James Peppler
c/o Colbert Artists Mgmt. Inc.
111 W. 57th St.
New York, NY 10019
bass-baritone

Morrison, Van
c/o Sony
51 W. 52nd St.
New York, NY 10019
musician

Moss, Ron Management
2635 Griffith Park Blvd.
Los Angeles, CA 90039
artist management

Mostly Mozart Festival
Avery Fisher Hall
140 W. 65th St.
New York, NY 10023

Motion City Films
900 S. Serrano
Los Angeles, CA 90006
video production

Motley Crue
345 North Maple Dr., #123
Beverly Hills, CA 90210
group

Motown Records
6255 Sunset Blvd., 17th Fl.
Los Angeles, CA 90028
Jheryl Busby, President/CEO
record label

Motown Records
New York
1350 Ave. of the Americas, 20th Fl.
New York, NY 10019

Mountain Thunder Management
900 Logan, #3
Denver, CO 80203
Dugg Duggan
artist management

Mr. Big Productions Inc.
3312 W. Belle Plaine
Chicago, IL 60618
video production

Mt. Desert Festival of Chamber Music
P.O. Box 862
Northeast Harbor, ME 04662

MTV Networks
1515 Broadway
New York, NY 10036
Thomas E. Freston, Chairman/CEO
music television cable network

Muldaur, Maria
P.O. Box 5535
Mill Valley, CA 94942
singer

Mulligan, Gerry
1416 N. LaBrea Ave.
Hollywood, CA 90028
jazz composer, arranger, musician,
songwriter

Munzer, Cynthia Brown
165 W. 57th St.
New York, NY 10019
mezzo-soprano

Murphy, Edward P.
National Music Publishers Assoc.
Harry Fox Agency
205 E. 42nd St.
New York, NY 10017
CEO, president music publishers

Murray, Anne
Balmur Ltd.
4950 Yonge St., #2400
Toronto, Ontario M2N 6K1 Canada
singer

Museum of Broadcasting, The
25 W. 52nd St.
New York, NY 10019
Dr. Robert M. Batscha, President

Musgrave, Thea
c/o Theodor Presser Co.
Presser Pl.
Bryn Mawr, PA 19010
composer, conductor

Music Academy of the West Summer Festival
1070 Fairway Rd.
Santa Barbara, CA 93108

Music Advisory Group
7421 Beverly Blvd., #11
Los Angeles, CA 90036
Stephen Smith
artist management

Music Alliance
c/o WNCN
1180 6th Ave.
New York, NY 10036
Cheryl Bell, Exec. Director
promotes increase in classical music
audience

Music at the Vineyards
P.O. Box 1852
Saratoga, CA 95070
music festival

Music Book Management, The
P.O. Box 110079
Nashville, TN 37222
Ray Chenowith
artist management

Music City News
50 Music Sq. W, #601
Nashville, TN 37203
country music magazine

Music Connection
6640 Sunset Blvd., #120
Hollywood, CA 90028
trade publication

Music Critics Association
7 Pine Court
Westfield, NJ 07090
Nancy Malitz, President

Music Factory Enterprises Inc.
500 E. Washington St., #300
Norristown, PA 19401
Jeffrey Calhoun
artist management

Music Festival of Rhode Island
P.O. Box 3279 Wayland Square
Providence, RI 02906

Music From Angel Fire
P.O. Box 502
Angel Fire, NM 87710
music festival

Music From Bear Valley
P.O. Box 5068
Bear Valley, CA 95223
music festival

Music Group, Inc.
3500 W. Olive Ave., #950
Burbank, CA 91505
Joe Isgro
artist management

Music in Ouray
P.O. Box 14
Ouray, CO 81427
music festival

Music in the Mountains
Rocky Ridge Music Center
465 Longs Peak Rd.
Estes Park, CO 80517
music festival

Music Mountain
Music Mountain Rd.
Falls Village, CT 06031
music festival

Music of the World
P.O. Box 3620
Chapel Hills, NC 27515
artist management

Music Performance Trust Funds
1501 Broadway, #202
New York, NY 10036
Martin A. Paulson, Trustee
promotes free music performances

Music Trades Magazine
80 West St., P.O. Box 432
Englewood, NJ 07631
magazine for music stores

Music Video Productions
2301 W. 20th St.
Los Angeles, CA 90018
Christopher McKinnon,
producer/director

Musica Nosta Et Vostra, National Corporation of America
445 E. 68th St., #12L
New York, NY 10021
Bruno George Ronty, PhD, President
and General Director
promotes foreign music exchange

Musician
33 Commercial St., #2
Gloucester, MA 01930
magazine for the serious pop musician

Musicians Foundation
200 W. 55th St.
New York, NY 10019
Brent Williams, Executive Director
represents interests and advances the
condition and social welfare of professional musicians and their families

Musicians National Hot Line Association
277 East 6100 South
Salt Lake City, UT 84107
Marvin C. Zitting, Executive Director
seeks to increase employment of
musicians

Musick, Gary Productions Inc.
2 Twin Elms Ct.
Nashville, TN 37210
video production

Musicworld
320 W. 57th St.
New York, NY 10019
News About BMI Music and Writers

Mutual Musicians Foundation
1823 Highland
Kansas City, MO 64108
seeks to preserve jazz heritage of
Kansas City

N

Jazz music is an appeal to the emotions by an attack to the nerves.
—ANONYMOUS

NABET
National Association of Broadcast
Employees & Technicians
7101 Wisconsin Ave., #800
Bethesda, MD 20814

Nabors, Jim
151 El Camino
Beverly Hills, CA 90212
singer

Nadler, Sheila June
165 W. 57th St.
New York, NY 10019
opera singer

Nammour Films Inc.
37 W. 28th St., 7th Fl.
New York, NY 10001
video production

Nancy Sinatra Fan Club
160 Apple Ct.
Luling, LA 70070

Nanoia, Frank Productions
1259 N. LaBrea Ave.
Los Angeles, CA 90038
tv/film artist management

Nash, Graham
c/o Atlantic Records
75 Rockefeller Pl.
New York, NY 10019
singer, composer

Nashville Network, The
2806 Opryland Dr.
Nashville, TN 37214
music television

**Nashville Songwriters Association,
International**
1025 16th Ave., S., #200
Nashville, TN 37212
Pat Huber, Executive Director

**National Academy of Popular
Music**
875 3rd Ave., 8th Fl.
New York, NY 10022
Christian Malone, Managing Director

National Academy of Songwriters
6381 Hollywood Blvd., #780
Hollywood, CA 90028
Daniel A. Kirkpatrick, Managing
Director

**National Association of Accompa-
nists and Coaches**
395 Riverside Dr., #13A
New York, NY 10025
Miriam Charney, President

**National Association of Com-
posers**
P.O. Box 49652, Barrington Station
Los Angeles, CA 90049
Marshall Bialosky, President

National Association of Fan Clubs
2730 Baltimore Ave.
Pueblo, CO 81003

National Association of Negro Musicians
P.O. Box S-011
237 E. 115th St.
Chicago, IL 60628
Ona B. Campbell, Executive Secretary

National Association of Pat Boone Fan Clubs
c/o Chris Bujnovsky
526 Boeing Ave.
Reading, PA 19601

National Band Association
P.O. Box 121292
Nashville, TN 37212
L. Howard Nicar, Jr., Secretary/Treasurer

National Captioning Institute
1443 Beachwood Dr.
Hollywood, CA 90026
close captioning for music videos

National Catholic Bandmasters' Association
P.O. Box 948
Notre Dame, IN 46556
Robert O'Brien, Secretary/Treasurer

National Federation of Music Clubs
1336 N. Delaware St.
Indianapolis, IN 46202
Patricia M. Midgley, Executive Secretary

National Flute Association
c/o Myrna Brown
805 Laguna
Denton, TX 76201

National Jazz Service Organization
409 7th NW
Lower Level
Washington, DC 20004
Willard Jenkins, Executive Director

National Music Council
P.O. Box 5551
Englewood, NJ 07631
chartered by U.S. Congress, a national forum, bestows American Eagle Award

National Old-Time Fiddlers' Association
c/o Wes Nivens
P.O. Box 1427
Truth or Consequences, NM 87901

National Opera Association
c/o Marajean Marvin
1866 N. College Rd.
Columbus, OH 43210

National Orchestral Association
475 Riverside Dr., #249
New York, NY 10115
Jennifer Bilfield, Executive Officer

National Repertory Orchestra
P.O. Box 38
Keystone, CO 80435

National Rick Nelson Fan Club
P.O. Box 370
Churchville, MD 21028

National Sheet Music Society
1597 Fair Park Ave.
Los Angeles, CA 90041
Marilyn Brees, Secretary
songwriters and sheet music collectors

National Society of Student Keyboardists
361 Pin Oak Lane
Westbury, NY 11590
Dr. Albert DeVito, President

National Traditional Music Associations
P.O. Box 438
Walnut, IA 51577
Robert Everhart, President
preservation and presentation of
acoustic music

Nationwide Entertainment Services
7770 Regents Rd., #113-905
San Diego, CA 92122
A.J. Sagman
artist management

Naughty by Nature
c/o Tommy Boy Records
1747 First Ave.
New York, NY 10128
group

Naylor, David & Associates Inc.
6535 Santa Monica Blvd.
Hollywood, CA 90038
Sam Aslanian, head of production
video production

Nederlander of California
6233 Hollywood Blvd.
Los Angeles, CA 90028
Stan Seiden, President
artist management

Nelson (Matt and Gunnar)
9130 Sunset Blvd.
Los Angeles, CA 90069
singing duo, third generation of musical Nelsons

Nelson, Willie
c/o Mark Rothbaum and Assoc.
P.O. Box 2689
Danbury, CT 06813
singer, songwriter

Nero, Peter
Gutman Murtha Assoc.
162 W. 56th St., #404
New York, NY 10019
pianist

Nesna Entertainment Inc.
959 W. Belmont
Chicago, IL 60657
Roger Jansen
artist management

Network Entertainment
1280 Winchester Pkwy., #245
Atlanta, GA 30080
Stephen Klein
artist management

Neville Brothers (Aaron, Art, Charles, Cyril)
A & M Records
1416 N. LaBrea Ave.
Los Angeles, CA 90028
group and solo artists

New England Bach Festival
Brattleboro Music Center
15 Walnut St.
Brattleboro, VT 05301

New Generation Pictures
7 W. 20th St., #2F
New York, NY 10011
video production

New Hampshire Music Festival
P.O. Box 147
Center Harbor, NH 03226

New Kids on the Block
P.O. Box 7001
Quincy, MA 02269
group

New Orleans Entertainment Agency
3530 Rue Delphine
New Orleans, LA 10131
Jim Maxwell
artist management

New Orleans Jazz and Heritage Festival
1205 N. Rampart St.
New Orleans, LA 70116

New Orleans Jazz Club
828 Royal St., #265
New Orleans, LA 70116
Marshall Ryals, President

New Orleans Management
5811 Tchoupitoulas St.
New Orleans, LA 70115
Greg Eveline
artist management

New Wilderness Foundation
611 Broadway, #817
New York, NY 10012
Charlie Morrow, President
promotes appreciation of innovative music

New York End Ltd., The
29 W. 65th St., #4A
New York, NY 10023
Peter Leak
alternative artist management

Newland, Larry J.
Harrisburg Symphony Orchestra
128 Locust St.
Harrisburg, PA 17101
orchestra conductor

Newley, Anthony
c/o R. Katz
9255 Sunset Blvd., #1115
Los Angeles, CA 90069
composer, singer

Newman, Randy
Renaissance Mgmt. Corp.
21241 Ventura Blvd., #251
Woodland Hills, CA 91364
singer, songwriter, musician

Newsline Fan Club
P.O. Box 1926
Sandy, UT 84091
Huey Lewis and the News fan club

Newton, Wayne
Flying Eagle Inc.
6000 S. Eastern Ave., #7B
Las Vegas, NV 89119
singer

Newton-John, Olivia
c/o Bill Sammeth
1888 Century Park E., 6th Fl.
Los Angeles, CA 90067
singer

NFL Films
330 Fellowship Rd.
Mount Laurel, NJ 08054
video production

Nicks, Stevie (Stephanie)
P.O. Box 6907
Alhambra, CA 91802
singer

Nightmare Management
2051 Third St.
San Francisco, CA 94107
artist management

Nilsson, Harry
CL Sims Corp.
11330 Ventura Blvd.
Studio City, CA 91604
singer, songwriter.

0-D South Records
P.O. Box 381, Station A
Vancouver, BC V6C 2N2 Canada
independent record label

900 Frames
140 E. 46th St., #3C
New York, NY 10017
music video production company

19 Management Ltd.
Unt. 32 Ramsomes Dock 35-37 Park-
gate Rd.
London SW11 U.K.
Simon Fuller
artist management

19th-Century Music
University of California Press
2120 Berkeley Way
Berkeley, CA 94704
magazine

Nirvana
9130 Sunset Blvd.
Los Angeles, CA 90069
group

Nixon, Marni
9000 Sunset Blvd., #1200
Los Angeles, CA 90069
everybody's film singing voice

Nixon/Katz Associates
9255 Sunset Blvd., #1115
Los Angeles, CA 90069
r&b artist management

Noh Hands Productions
1 Union Square W., #606
New York, NY 10003
video production

Noir Film
2101 Cloverfield Blvd., #201
Santa Monica, CA 90404
Stephen A. Blake, Owner/Director
video production

Noone, Peter
VH-1
1515 Broadway
New York, NY 10036
My Generation host, Herman of Her-
man's Hermits.

Nordic Fest
P.O. Box 364
Decorah, IA 52101
music festival

Norfolk Chamber Music Festival
Yale Summer School of Music and Art
96 Wall Street
New Haven, CT 06520

**Norma Zimmer National Fan
Club**
1604 E. Susquehanna St.
Allentown, PA 18103
Lawrence Welk "Champagne Lady"

Norman, Jessye
c/o Shaw Concerts
1995 Broadway
New York, NY 10023
soprano

**North American Band Directors
Coordinating Committee**
c/o Dr. Edgar B. Gangware
1225 Candlewood Hill
Northbrook, IL 60062

North American Brass Band Association
c/o Paul Droste
1310 Maize Road Court
Columbus, OH 43229

North American Management
3330 E. Tropicana, #E
Las Vegas, NV 89121
Robert Garganese
artist management

North American Saxophone Alliance
c/o Dale Underwood
13408 Piscataway
Ft. Washington, MD 20744

North American Singers Association
6236 N. Kildare Ave.
Chicago, IL 60646
Frank H. Pascher, Secretary
German-American men's and women's mixed choruses

North Star Productions
213 Cherokee Rd.
Nashville, TN 37205
video production

Northeastern Sangerbund of America
c/o George E. Winzer
17721 Mill Creek Drive
Derwood, MD 20855
German song singers

Northern Light Productions
2351 South Shore Center, Box 67
Alameda, CA 94501
Frank E. Barczak, producer
video production

Northern Rockies Folk Festival
Sun Valley Center for the Arts & Humanities
P.O. Box 656
Sun Valley, ID 83353

Norwegian Singers Association of America
Rte. 2, Box 137
Kenyon, MN 55946
Donald Berg, Corresponding Secretary

Norwest Communications Inc.
123 S. Hough St.
Barrington, IL 60010
Mark Karney, President
video production

Norwitz, Eric
Attorney at Law
3333 W. 2nd St., #52-214
Los Angeles, CA 90004
music attorney

Novastar
6430 Sunset Blvd., #1400
Los Angeles, CA 90028
Bob Sky, Partner
video production

Nucci, Leo
40 W. 57th St.
New York, NY 10019
baritone

Nunenmacher, Dan
822 Green St.
Glendale, CA 91205
free lance production manager/a.d. for concerts/videos

NVision Inc.
P.O. Box 1658
Nevada City, CA 95959
Bill Amos, Vice President
video production

*Opera is where a guy gets stabbed in the back,
and instead of bleeding he sings.*
— ANONYMOUS

O Pictures Inc.
5636 Melrose Ave.
Los Angeles, CA 90038
Sharon Oreck, Executive Producer
video production

O'Connell, Sean Films
26 Bon Oak Ct.
Reistertown, MD 21136
Sean O'Connell, Director
video production

O'Connor, Sinead
13 Red Lion Square, 10 Halsey
House
London WC1 U.K.
singer

O'Malley, Scott & Associates
P.O. Box 9188
Colorado Springs, CO 80932
artist management

Oak Ridge Boys
329 Rockland Rd.
Hendersonville, TN 37075
group

**Oak Ridge Boys International
Team Spirit**
329 Rockland Rd.
Hendersonville, TN 37075
fan club

Oasis Management
3015 E. Corrine
Phoenix, AZ 85032
Gloria Bujnowski
artist management

Oberman, Michael Management
3027 Rodman St. NW
Washington, DC 20008
artist management

Ocasek, Rick
9830 Wilshire Blvd.
Beverly Hills, CA 90212
rock vocalist, songwriter, producer,
guitarist

Official Country Music Directory
Entertainment Media Corp.
P.O. Box 2772
Palm Springs, CA 92263

**Official Electronic Keyboard Blue
Book**
Sights and Sound, Inc.
1220 Mound Ave.
Racine, WI 53404
valuation of used keyboards

**Official Gary Lewis and the Play-
boys Fan Club**
P.O. Box 16428
Rochester, NY 14616

OK Mozart International Festival
P.O. Box 2344
Bartlesville, OK 74005

Oken, Alan Organization, The
1840 Century Park E, 11th Fl.
Los Angeles, CA 90067
artist management

Oliveira, Elmar
1 Lincoln Plaza, 2nd Fl.
1900 Broadway
New York, NY 10023
violinist

Omega Productions
7027 Twin Hills Ave., #5
Dallas, TX 75231
Paul Christensen, President
video production

Omen International
337 Pitt Town
Marayla, NSW 2750 Australia
Ian Riddington
artist management

Omni Creative Artists
P.O. Box 1591
Cambridge, MA 02238
David Vaughn
artist management

Omni Talent Group Inc.
101 Wymore Rd., #539
Altamonte Springs, FL 32714
Albert Teebagy
artist management

On Track Video
124 W. 24th St.
New York, NY 10011
video production

One Eight One Productions
503 Broadway, 5th Fl.
New York, NY 10012
video production

One Heart Productions
46255 Afton Place
Hollywood, CA 90028
Tammara Wells, President
video production

100 Flowers
c/o Happy Squid Records
P.O. Box 94565
Pasadena, CA 91109
group

111 East Records
161 Hudson St., Fl. 5
New York, NY 10013
James Bratton
independent record label

148th St Block
Work It!
P.O. Box 180, Cooper Station
New York, NY 10276
group

101 Records
159 S. Highway 101
Solana Beach, CA 92075
Marc Wintriss
independent record label

1000 Home DJ's
c/o Megaforce Entertainment
210 Bridge Plaza Dr.
Manalapan, NJ 07726
group

1171 Production Group
303 South Sweetzer
Los Angeles, CA 90048
Grant Cihlar, Producer
Bruce Martin, Director
music video production company

1334 North Beechwood Drive Irregulars
c/o Sue Roach
1719 Gardenia, #2
Royal Oak, MI 48067
Monkees fan club

One Two Three Four
Strong Sounding Thought Press
1854 W. 84th Pl.
Los Angeles, CA 90047
socio-cultural & aesthetic criticism of popular music

Only Official Peggy Lee Fan Club and Archives
c/o Ray Richards Allen
133 W. 72nd St., #601
New York, NY 10023

Ono, Yoko
One W. 72nd St.
New York, NY 10023
singer, famous widow

Open Door Management
15327 Sunset Blvd., #365
Pacific Palisades, CA 90272
Bill Traut
artist management

Opera America
777 14th St., NW, #520
Washington, DC 20005
Marc A. Scorca, CEO
association of professional opera companies

Opera Digest
Opera Index
315 W. 23 St., #6F
New York, NY 10011
magazine

Oregon Bach Festival
University of Oregon, School of Music
961 E. 18th Ave.
Eugene, OR 97403

Organ Clearing House
P.O. Box 104
Harrisville, NH 03450
Alan M. Laufman, Executive Director
facilitates the relocation of used pipe organs

Organ Historical Society
P.O. Box 26811
Richmond, VA 23261
William T. VanPelt, Executive Director

Organ Literature Foundation
45 Norfolk Rd.
Braintree, MA 02184
Henry Karl Baker, President

Original Films
1632 Fifth St.
Santa Monica, CA 90401
video production

Original Projects Unlimited
1071 Washington St.
Denver, CO 80203
Lauri Day-Workman
artist management

Osborne, Jeffrey
c/o Arista
6 W. 57th St.
New York, NY 10019
singer

Osbourne, Ozzy
1801 Century Park West
Los Angeles, CA 90067
singer

Osby, Greg
c/o Blue Note Records
1750 Vine St.
Hollywood, CA 90028
hip hop

Oslin, K.T. (Kay Toinette)
c/o Stan Moress
21 Music Sq. E.
Nashville, TN 37203
singer

Osmond, Donny (Donald Clark)
151 El Camino
Beverly Hills, CA 90212
singer

Outlaw Films
130-132 New Kings Rd.
London SW6 4LZ U.K.
video production

Overseas Jazz Club
c/o Wilma Dobie
15 Autenrieth Rd.
Scarsdale, NY 10583
seeks to draw attention to jazz as an
original art form

Owen Electric Pictures
84 Wooster St., Room 503
New York, NY 10012
Michael Owen, Executive Producer
video production

Owens, Buck (Alvis Edgar, Jr.)
Buck Owens Productions
3223 N. Sillect Ave.
Bakersfield, CA 93308
singer, musician, songwriter, producer

Owl's Head
12050 Valley Heart Dr.
Studio City, CA 91604
video production

Ox Tung
850 E. 7th St.
Tucson, AZ 85719
Tung, Owner
rave/disco/alternative artist management

Ozawa, Seiji
Boston Symphony Orchestra
Symphony Hall
301 Massachusetts Ave.
Boston, MA 02115
conductor

P

Many rock singers have the kind of voice that belongs in a silent movie.

—ANONYMOUS

P C Quest (Drew Nichols, Kim Whipkey, Steve Petree, Chad Petree)
1133 Ave. of the Americas
New York, NY 10036
group

P M Dawn
14 East Fourth St.
New York, NY 10012
group

Pacific Northwest Festival
Seattle Opera
P.O. Box 9248
Seattle, WA 98109
music festival

Paisley Park Management
7801 Audubon Rd.
Chanhassen, MN 55317
artist management

Palm Beach Festival
249 Royal Palm Way, #503
Palm Beach, FL 33480
music festival

Palmer, Robert
2A Chelsea Manor
Blood Street
London, SW3, U.K.
singer

Palmer, Shelton Leigh & Co.
19 West 36th St., 11th Fl.
New York, NY 10018
Shelton Leigh Palmer, President/Creative Director
video production

Pan Productions
223 Water St.
Brooklyn, NY 11201
video production

Papa Bear Productions
413-810 W. Broadway
Vancouver, BC B5Z 4C9 Canada
Tony Papa, Director
video production

Paper + Pen/Dreamin' Out Loud Productions Inc.
P.O. Box 13004
Kansas City, MO 64199
Arthur "Poetry" Payne III
artist management

Paradise June Arts Festival
Paradise Area Arts Council
6686 Brook Way
Paradise, CA 95969
music festival

Parker, Alan William
9830 Wilshire Blvd.
Beverly Hills, CA 90212
music film director, writer

Parker, Colonel Tom
P.O. Box 220
Madison, TN 37118
Elvis mentor

Parker, Maceo
Verve Digital Records
825 5th Ave.
New York, NY 10019
jazz musician

Parton, Dolly
Crockett Road, Rt. #1
Brentwood, TN 37027
singer, composer

Party, The
P.O. Box 2510
Los Angeles, CA 90078
group

Pass, Joe
Pablo Records
2600 10th St.
Berkeley, CA 94710
jazz guitarist

Patsy Cline International Fan Club
P.O. Box 244
Dorchester, MA 02125

Patti Page Appreciation Society
8040 Seymour Rd.
Gaines, MI 48436
fan club

Paul Anka Fan Club
124 Terryville Rd.
Port Jefferson Station, NY 11776

Paul Masson Summer Series
Paul Masson Mountain Winery
P.O. Box 1852
Saratoga, CA 95070
music festival

Paul, Jackie Management
559 Wanamaker Rd.
Jenkintown, PA 19046
rap artist management

Paul, Rod Productions
1820 Briarwood Industrial Ct.
Atlanta, GA 30329
video production

Pavarotti, Luciano
941 Via Giardini
41040 Saliceta S. Guiliano
Modena, Italy
singer

Paxton, Tom
P.O. Box 2256
East Hampton, NY 11937
songwriter, entertainer

Payne, Bruce
45 E. Putnam Ave.
Greenwich, CT 06830
heavy metal artist management

Paynter, John Philip
Northwestern University
School of Music
Evanston, IL 60208
band conductor

Pearl Jam
P.O. Box 4450
New York, NY 10101
group

Pearl, Minnie (Sarah Ophelia Colley Cannon)
c/o J. Seale
Refugee Mgmt.
1025 16th Ave. S, #300
Nashville, TN 37212
comic singer

Peckham Productions
65 S. Broadway
Tarrytown, NY 10591
video production

Pecos Film Company
215 Central Ave. NW
Albuquerque, NM 87102
video production

Pedal Steel Guitar Association
P.O. Box 248
Floral Park, NY 11001
Bob Maickel, President

Peeples, Nia
822 S. Robertson Blvd., #200
Los Angeles, CA 90035
singer, Dance Party hostess

Pegasus Pictures Corp.
821 Cooke St.
Honolulu, HI 96813
video production

Penderecki, Krzysztof
Panstwowa Wyzsza
Szkola Muzyczna
61 Bahaterow Stalingradu 3
31-038 Cracow Poland
composer, conductor

Pendergrass, Teddy
Teddy Bear Enterprises
33 Rockhill Rd.
Bala-Cynwyd, PA 19004
musician

Peninsula Festival
P.O. Box 340
Door County
Ephraim, WI 54211
music festival

Pensacola Chamber Music Festival
Christ Church
P.O. Box 12683
Pensacola, FL 32574

People Magazine
Time-Warner Inc.
1675 Broadway
Rockefeller Center
New York, NY 10019

Percussive Arts Society
P.O. Box 25
Laton, OK 73502
Steven Beck, Manager

Perlman, Itzhak
40 W. 57th St.
New York, NY 10019
violinist

Perry, Gail S., Esq.
1727 1/4 N. Sycamore Ave.
Hollywood, CA 90028
music attorney

Pershing, Verne Productions
1800 N. Argyle Ave., #100A
Hollywood, CA 90028
video production

Peter Britt Festival
P.O. Box 1124
Medord, OR 97501
music festival

Peter Noone Just a Little Bit Better Promotion Club
P.O. Box 661
Oceanside, CA 92049
fan club

Peter, Paul and Mary
853 7th Ave.
New York, NY 10019
group

Peters, Roberta
40 W. 57th St.
New York, NY 10019
soprano

Petty, Tom
8730 Sunset Blvd., 6th Fl.
Los Angeles, CA 90069
rock guitarist, bandleader, composer

Phil Collins Information
c/o Brad Lentz
P.O. Box 12250
Overland Park, KS 66212
fan club

Phonolog
Trade Service Publications
10996 Torreyana Rd.
San Diego, CA 92121
catalog

Phusion
P.O. Box 91507
Portland, OR 97291
Mark Paul
artist management

Pia Zadora Fan Club
c/o Zadora Enterprises
Trump Tower
725 Fifth Ave.
New York, NY 10022

Pianists Foundation of America
P.O. Box 64115
Tucson, AZ 85740
Deborah Shisler, Executive Secretary

Picture Music International
20 Manchester Square
London W1A 1ES U.K.
Elizabeth Flowers
video production

Picture Vision
900 Broadway, #604
New York, NY 10003
video production

Pink Floyd
43 Portland Road
London, W11, U.K.
group

Planet Inc.
6311 Romaine St., #7235
Hollywood, CA 90038
Susan Silverman, Executive Producer
video production

Plant, Robert Anthony
c/o Atlantic Records
75 Rockefeller Plaza
New York, NY 10019
singer, composer

Plasma Films Inc.
1510 Nelson St., #310
Vancouver, BC V6G 1M1 Canada
Gary Blair Smith, Owner/Director
video production

Platinum Gold Productions
9200 Sunset Blvd., #1220
Los Angeles, CA 90069
Steve Cohen
artist management

Platters Fan Club, The
P.O. Box 39
Las Vegas, NV 89125

Platters, The
P.O. Box 39
Las Vegas, NV 89101
group

Playboy
680 N. Lakeshore Dr.
Chicago, Il 60611
Christine Hefner, Publisher
magazine

Playboy Jazz Festival
8560 Sunset Blvd.
Los Angeles, CA 90069

Pleasants, Henry
95 Roebuck House
Palace St.
London SW1E 5BE U.K.
music critic

PMC Pictures
9336 W. Washington Blvd.
Culver City, CA 90232
video production

Pointer Sisters
151 El Camino
Beverly Hills, CA 90212
group

Poison
1750 N. Vine St.
Hollywood, CA 90028
group

Police, The
194 Kensington Park Rd.
London, W11 2ES U.K.
defunct group

Polish Singers Alliance of America
180 2nd Ave.
New York, NY 10003
Barbara Blyskal, General Secretary

Polivnick, Paul
Alabama Symphony Orchestra
2001 Park Ave., #575
P.O. Box 2125
Birmingham, AL 35203
conductor

Pollaro Media Productions
400 W. Main St.
Denison, TX 75020
Stephanie Clift, Producer
video production

Pollstar
4838 N. Blackstone Ave., 2nd Fl.
Fresno, CA 93726
charts, box office results, artist
itineraries, etc.

PolyGram Label Group
Worldwide Plaza, 825 8th Ave.
New York, NY 10019
Rick Dobbis, President/CEO
record label, includes Polydor, Lon-
don, Smash, PolyGram Jazz, Victory,
Delicious Vinyl, Verve

PolyGram Label Group
Los Angeles
11150 Santa Monica Blvd., #1000
Los Angeles, CA 90025

PolyGram Records
901 18th Avenue South
Nashville, TN 37212
Paul Lucks, VP/GM
record label

**Pop, Iggy (James Newell Oster-
berg)**
c/o Floyd Peluce
449 S. Beverly Dr., #102
Beverly Hills, CA 90212
composer, singer, musician

Pop/Art Film Factory
513 Wilshire Blvd., #215
Santa Monica, CA 90401
Daniel Zirilli, CEO/Director
video production

Porter Productions
3759 Griffith View Dr.
Los Angeles, CA 90039
video production

Portfolio Artist's Network
120 W. 25th St., #2E
New York, NY 10001
video production

Post, Mike
7007 W. Olive Ave.
Burbank, CA 91506
composer

Potsdam Summer Festival of the Arts
Postdam College of SUNY
Potsdam, NY 13676
music festival

Power Star Management
6981 N. Park Dr. W, #618
Pennsauken, NJ 18109
Brian Kushner
artist management

Powerhouse Management
3053 McQueen St.
Montgomery, AL 36107
Martin N. Brasfield
artist management

Powerhouse Multi-Media
19347 Londelius St.
Northridge, CA 91324
Paul Stillman/Jeff Stillman, Partners
video production

Premiere
Murdoch Publications, Inc.
2 Park Ave., 4th Fl.
New York, NY 10016
Susan Lyne, Editor
entertainment magazine

Presley, Priscilla Beaulieu
151 El Camino
Beverly Hills, CA 90212
famous ex-wife

Previn, Andre
Harrison Parrot Ltd.
12 Penzance Place
London W11 4PA U.K.
composer, conductor

Price, Leontyne
1133 Broadway
New York, NY 10010
opera singer

Price, Ray
P.O. Box 1986
Mount Pleasant, TX 75456
singer

Pride, Charley
c/o Chardon Inc.
3198 Royal Ln., #204
Dallas, TX 75229
singer

Primalux Video
30 W. 26th St.
New York, NY 10010
video production

Primedia Inc.
1655 Peachtree St., 12th Fl.
Atlanta, GA 30309
Mark Johnson, President
video production

Prince (Prince Rogers Nelson)
3300 Warner Blvd.
Burbank, CA 91510
singer

Princeton Festival, The
160 W. 73rd St.
New York, NY 10023
music festival

Programe
17 Rue Lambert
Paris 75018 France
Bernard Batzen
artist management

Promo Palace
2627 D'Arbley St.
London W1Z 3FH U.K.
Paula Walker
video production

Propaganda Films
940 N. Mansfield Ave.
Los Angeles, CA 90038
video production

Public Broadcasting Service
(PBS)—Executive Headquarters
1320 Braddock Place
Alexandria, VA 22314
Bruce Christensen, President/CEO
heavy classical music programming

Public Enemy
c/o Columbia Records
2100 Colorado Blvd.
Santa Monica, CA 90404
group

Puente, Tito Anthony
c/o Ralph Mercado Mgmt.
1650 Broadway
New York, NY 10019
orchestra leader, composer, arranger

Pulsar Entertainment
121 Madison Ave., #8F
New York, NY 10016
video production

*After silence that which comes nearest to expressing
the inexpressible is music.*

—ALDOUS HUXLEY

Q Entertainment Corporation
725 W. Randolph
Chicago, IL 60606
Dave de Merlier
artist management

Q-Prime Management
729 7th Ave., 14th Fl.
New York, NY 10019
Cliff Burnstein
artist management

QPM Inc.
3315 Silverstone Dr.
Plano, TX 75023
Tommy Quon
artist management

Quantum Management
1210 N. Cherokee Ave., #211
Los Angeles, CA 90038
Roland Baker
artist management

Quinn, Martha
c/o MTV
1515 Broadway
New York, NY 10036
MTV hostess

R

*Whether angels play only Bach in praising God, I am not sure.
I am sure, however, that en famile they play Mozart.*
—KARL BARTH, QUOTED IN *THE NEW YORK TIMES* OBITUARY,
DEC. 11, 1968

R & R Music Management
P.O. Box 17266
Phoenix, AZ 95011
Randi Reed
artist management

R.E.M.
P.O. Box 8032
Athens, GA 30603
group

Ra, Sun (Le SonY'R Ra)
c/o Brad Simon
122 E. 57th St.
New York, NY 10001
jazz musician

Rabbitt, Eddie
c/o Moress, Nanas, Golden Entertainment
12424 Wilshire Blvd.
Los Angeles, CA 90025
singer, songwriter

Rad Productions Ltd.
8306 Wilshire Blvd., #972
Beverly Hills, CA 90211
Keith Kurlander, President
video production

Raffi (Cavoukian)
c/o Jensen Communications
120 S. Victory Blvd., #201
Burbank, CA 91502
singer

Ragtime Society
P.O. Box 520, Station A
Toronto, Ontario, Canada M5H 1
John Arpin, Treasurer

Railroad Productions
12021 Wilshire Blvd.
Los Angeles, CA 90025
Gary Calamar
alternative rock artist management

Raimondi Films
2121 Wisconsin Ave., NW
Washington, DC 20007
video production

Raitt, Bonnie
P.O. Box 626
Los Angeles, CA 90078
singer

Ralph, Stanley
Rebel Records
P.O. Box 3057
Roanoke, VA 24015
bluegrass musician

Rampal, Jean-Pierre Louis
15 Avenue Mozart
75016 Paris France
flutist

Randy Travis Fan Club
1604 16th Ave., S
Nashville, TN 37212

Rankin, Richard Photography
4649 Beverly Blvd., #101
Los Angeles, CA 90004
video production

Rap-A-Lot Productions
12337 Jones Rd., #L-221
Houston, TX 77070
video production

Rase, Bill Productions
955 Venture Ct.
Sacramento, CA 95825
video production

Rattle, Simon
c/o H. Holt
31 Sinclair Rd.
London W14 0NS U.K.
conductor

Ravinia Festival
1575 Oakwood Ave.
P.O. Box 896
Highland Park, IL 60035
music festival

Raw Entertainment
1230 Hill St.
Santa Monica, CA 90405
Robert Anderson
artist management

Raw Productions
34 Fransworth St.
Boston, MA 00210
Brian Bothwell, Director
video productions

Rawls, Lou
Philadelphia International Records
51 W. 52nd St.
New York, NY 10019
singer

Reba McEntire International Fan Club
P.O. Box 121996
Nashville, TN 37212

Rebel Management
P.O. Box 170545
San Francisco, CA 94117
Katrina Sirdofsky
artist management

Rebo High Definition Studio
530 W. 25th St.
New York, NY 10001
Steven Dupler
video production

Recording Industry Source-book
Ascona Communications, Inc.
3301 Barham Blvd., #300
Los Angeles, CA 90068
lists of music industry contacts

Red Hot Chili Peppers
75 Rockefeller Plaza, 20th Fl.
New York, NY 10010
group

Red Hots Entertainment
813 N. Cordova St.
Burbank, CA 91505
Chip Miller, Director/Producer
video production

Redding, Otis
c/o Atlantic
75 Rockefeller Plaza
New York, NY 10019
singer

Reddy, Helen
c/o Olson
2049 Century Park E, #1880
Los Angeles, CA 90067
singer

Redlands Bowl Summer Music Festival
P.O. Box 466
Redlands, CA 92373

Reed Organ Society
Musical Museum
Deansboro, NY 13328
Arthur H. Sanders, Executive Officer

Reed, Lou
38 E. 68th St.
New York, NY 10021
musician

Reel Image Films
19 Music Square West
Nashville, TN 37203
Don King, President
video production

Reid, L.A. (Antonio)
Kear Music, c/o Carter Tuner
9229 Sunset Blvd.
West Hollywood, CA 90069
musician, songwriter

Relativity Records
187-07 Henderson Ave.
Hollis, NY 11423
Barry Kobrin, President
record label

Relativity Records
Torrance
20525 Manhattan Place
Torrance, CA 90501

Remember That Song
5821 N. 67th Ave., #103-306
Glendale, AZ 85301
Lois Ann Cordrey, Editor
music history society

Renegade West Films
8222 Delongpre Ave., #10
West Hollywood, CA 90046
video production

Renge Films Inc.
8400 Delongpre Ave., #212
West Hollywood, CA 90069
video production

Reprise Records
3300 Warner Blvd.
Burbank, CA 91510
Mo Ostin, Chairman
record label

Retro Rock
44 E. 5th St.
Brooklyn, NY 11218
magazine

Reunion of Professional Entertainers
Box 4767
Nashville, TN 37216
Mac Wiseman, President
retirement organization

Rhino Records
2225 Colorado Ave.
Santa Monica, CA 90404
Richard Foos, President
record label

Rhodes, Samuel
Juilliard School of Music
Lincoln Center
New York, NY 10023
violist

Rhythm and Blues Rock and Roll Society
P.O. Box 1949
New Haven, CT 06510
William J. Nolan, Director

Ricciarelli, Katia
c/o John Coast Ltd.
Manfield House/ 376-9 Strand
London WC2 OLR U.K.
soprano

Rice, Tim
500 S. Buena Vista St.
Burbank, CA 91521
lyricist

Rich, Alan
L.A. Weekly
2140 Hyperion Ave.
Los Angeles, CA 90019
music critic

Rich, Charlie
6584 Poplar, #460
Memphis, TN 38138
singer

Richards, Keith
Raindrop Services
1776 Broadway
New York, NY 10019
musician

Richie, Lionel
P.O. Box 1862
Encino, CA 91426
singer, songwriter, producer

**Ricky Skaggs International
Fan Club**
P.O. Box 121799
Nashville, TN 37212

Rider Management
1333 Ventura Blvd., #206
Sherman Oaks, CA 91423
artist management

Righteous Brothers
5218 Almont St.
Los Angeles, CA 90032
duo

Riley, Jeannie C.
P.O. Box 454
Brentwood, TN 37027
singer

Rio Moving Pictures Worldwide
639 Broadway, P.O. Box 5
New York, NY 10012
Walter Dawkins
video production

Rising Son Records
P.O. Box 657
Housatonic, MA 01236
Sharon Palmer
artist management

Riverrun Entertainment
650 N. Bronson Ave.
Los Angeles, CA 90004
video production

Roach, Maxwell Lemuel
c/o PSI
810 7th Ave.
New York, NY 10019
jazz musician

Robertson, Stewart
Santa Fe Symphony Orchestra
P.O. Box 9692
Santa Fe, NM 84504
conductor

Robinson, Smokey
c/o Michael Roshkind
6244 Sunset Blvd., #18
Los Angeles, CA 90028
singer, composer

Rock & Roll Confidential
Box 1073
Maywood, NJ 07607
magazine

Rock 'N' Reel
14 Bulwar St.
Toronto, Ontario, Canada
Kari Skogland
video production

Rock and Roll Hall of Fame Foundation
c/o Suzan Evans
Atlantic Records
75 Rockefeller Plaza, 2nd Fl.
New York, NY 10019

Rock Legend
Dream Guys Inc.
Box 7042
New York, NY 10021
magazine

Rock Solid Productions
801 S. Main St.
Burbank, CA 91506
video production

Rocket and Rosenberg
222 E. 44th St.
New York, NY 10017
video production

Rockit Management
9000 Sunset Blvd., #707
Los Angeles, CA 90069
William Thomas
artist management

Rocklive/Modernrock
4545 Schenley Rd.
Baltimore, MD 21210
video production

Rockport Chamber Music Festival
P.O. Box 312
Rockport, MA 01966

Rockpress
P.O. Box 99090
San Diego, CA 92169
rock music book publishing company

Rockstyles by Ellyse
135 W. Dundee Rd.
Buffalo Grove, IL 60089
hairstylist

Rockville Management
8400 NE 2nd Ave., #336
Miami, FL 33138
Michael Hopkins
rap artist management

Rockwell, John Sargent
The New York Times
3 Rue Scribe
75009 Paris France
music critic

Rodeotime Music
3312 W. Belle Plaine
Chicago, IL 60618
video production

Rogers, Kenny
Box 100, Rt. #1
Colbert, GA 30628
singer

Rogers, Roy (Leonard Slye)
15650 Seneca Rd.
Victorville, CA 92392
singing cowboy on the comeback trail

Roland, Glenn Films
10711 Wellworth Ave.
Los Angeles, CA 90024
video production

Rolandi, Gianna
c/o Columbia Artists
165 W. 57th St.
New York, NY 10019
coloratura soprano

Rolling Stone
1290 Ave. of the Americas
New York, NY 10104
Jann S. Wenner, Editor and
Publisher
magazine

Rolling Stones Fan Club
c/o Bill German
P.O. Box 6152
New York, NY 10128

Rolling Stones, The
1776 Broadway, #507
New York, NY 10019
Grandaddies of rock and roll

Romantic Music Festival
Butler University
Jordan College of Fine Arts
4600 Sunset Ave.
Indianapolis, IN 46208

Roney, Wallace
Muse Records
160 W. 71st St.
New York, NY 10023
jazz musician

Ronnie Milsap Fan Club
P.O. Box 23109
Nashville, TN 37202

Ronnie Smith Fan Club
P.O. Box 334
Herkimer, NY 13350

Ronstadt, Linda
c/o Peter Asher
644 N. Doheny Dr.
West Hollywood, CA 90069
singer

Rose, Beatrice Schroeder
Houston Symphony
Jones Hall
Houston, TX 77002
harpist, educator

Rosebud Agency, The
P.O. Box 170429
San Francisco, CA 94117
Mike Kappus
artist management

Ross, Diana
RTC Mgmt.
P.O. Box 1683
New York, NY 10185
singer

**Rostropovich, Mstislav
Leopoldovich**
National Symphony Orchestra
John F. Kennedy Center for the Per-
forming Arts
Washington, DC 20566
musician

Roth, David Lee
c/o Warner Bros.
3300 Warner Blvd.
Burbank, CA 91510
singer

**Roxette (Marie Fredrikson, Per
Gessle)**
1800 North Vine St.
Hollywood, CA 90028
duo

Roxy, The
9009 Sunset Blvd.
Hollywood, CA 90069
club

Roy Clark International Fan Club
P.O. Box 470304
Tulsa, OK 74145

Roy Rogers—Dale Evans Collectors Association
P.O. Box 1166
Portsmouth, OH 45662
fan club

Rozla, Miklos
c/o Screen Composers Guild
2451 Nichols Canyon
Los Angeles, CA 90046
composer

RSA Productions
1040 N. Las Palmas Ave.
Hollywood, CA 90038
video production

Rubinstein, John Arthur
c/o TAA
1000 Santa Monica Blvd., #305
Los Angeles, CA 90067
composer

Rumsey Entertainment
6201 Sunset Blvd., #76
Hollywood, CA 90028
country artist management

Run D.M.C.
296 Elizabeth St.
New York, NY 10012
rappers

Rundgren, Todd
c/o Bearsville
Warner Records
3300 W. Warner Blvd.
Burbank, CA 91505
musician, record producer

Runlikehell Productions
2269 Chestnut St., #143
San Francisco, CA 94123
Mark Barbeau
alternative artist management

Rush Associated Labels (also Def-Jam)
652 Broadway, 3rd Fl.
New York, NY 10012
Russell Simmons, Chairman
record label

Rush Hour
6253 Hollywood Blvd.
Hollywood, CA 90028
video production

Russell, George Allen
c/o Concept
1770 Massachusetts Ave., #182
Cambridge, MA 02140
composer, musicologist

Rustron Music Productions
1156 Park Lane
West Palm Beach, FL 33417
Rusty Gordon
artist management

Ruthless Representation
21860 Burbank Blvd., #100
Woodland Hills, CA 91367
Jerry Heller
artist management

Our sweetest songs are those that tell of saddest thoughts.
—PERCY BYSSHE SHELLEY, *TO A SKYLARK*

Saco River Festival Association
Old Meeting House Rd.
P.O. Box 95
Kezar Falls, ME 04047
music festival

Sager, Carole Bayer
c/o Guttman & Pam
8500 Wilshire Blvd., #801
Beverly Hills, CA 90211
lyricist, singer

Salonen, Esa-Pekka
135 S. Grand Ave.
Los Angeles, CA 90012
artistic director, conductor

Salvador, Sal
315 W. 53rd St.
New York, NY 10019
jazz musician, guitarist, composer

Sammeth, Bill Organization, The
1888 Century Park E, 6th Fl
Los Angeles, CA 90067
artist manager

Samsh Artist Services
11-79 Old South Head Rd.
Bondi, New South Wales 2022 Australia
Brian Chaladil
artist management

Samuels, Stuart Productions
322 West 57th St., #36S
New York, NY 10019
video production

Samurai Productions
45 W. 45th St., 12th Fl.
New York, NY 10036
video production

San Luis Obispo Mozart Festival
P.O. Box 311
San Luis Obispo, CA 93406

Sanborn Perillo & Company
125 Cedar St., Suite 8-S
New York, NY 10006
John Sanborn
video production

Sanders, Pharoah
c/o T. Kurland Assoc.
173 Brighton Ave.
Allston, MA 02134
saxophonist, composer

Sanders, Steve
Oak Ridge Boys
329 Rockland Rd.
Hendersonville, TN 37075
musician

Santa Fe Chamber Music Festival
P.O. Box 853
Santa Fe, NM 87504

Santa Fe Chamber Music Festival in Seattle
93 Pike St., #310
Seattle, WA 98101

Santa Fe Opera, The
P.O. Box 2408
Santa Fe, NM 87504

Santana
P.O. Box 26671
San Francisco, CA 94126
group

Santana, Carlos
P.O. Box 881630
San Francisco, CA 94188
guitarist

Sarasota Music Festival
709 N. Tamiami Trail
Sarasota, FL 34236

Saratoga Performing Arts Center
Saratoga State Park
Saratoga Springs, NY 12866
music festival

Sasaki, Tatsuo
San Diego Symphony
1245 7th Ave.
San Diego, CA 92101
xylophonist

Sasson, Michel
Symphony Hall
Boston, MA 02115
conductor

Sawallisch, Wolfgang
Philadelphia Orchestra
1420 Locust St.
Philadelphia, PA 19102
conductor

Sawyer Brown Fan Club
4205 Hillsboro Rd., #208
Nashville, TN 37215

Scaggs, Boz (William Royce Scaggs)
CBS Records
1801 Century Park W
Los Angeles, CA 90067
musician

Scene East Productions
229 W. 97th St.
New York, NY 10025
video production

Scene Three Inc.
1813 8th Ave. South
Nashville, TN 37221
Eric George, Director of Marketing
video production

Schermerhorn, Kenneth Dewitt
Nashville Symphony Orchestra
208 23rd Ave. N
Nashville, TN 37203
conductor

Schickele, Peter
c/o Warkow
40 W. 57th St.
New York, NY 10019
composer

Schifrin, Lalo
Glendale Symphony Orchestra
401 Brand Blvd., #520
Glendale, CA 91203
composer

Schonberg, Harold Charles
160 Riverside Dr.
New York, NY 10024
music critic, author

Schroeder, Aaron Harold
200 W. 51st St., #706
New York, NY 10019
songwriter

Schuur, Diane Joan
c/o GRP
555 W. 57th St.
New York, NY 10019
jazz vocalist

Schwartz, Stephen Lawrence
Paramuse Assoc.
Ave. of the Americas
New York, NY 10019
composer, lyricist

Schwartzberg and Company
12700 Ventura Blvd., 4th Fl.
Studio City, CA 91604
video production

Scott Joplin Foundation of Sedalia
113 E. 4th St.
Sedalia, MO 65301
John Moore, Festival Coordinator

Scotti Bros. Records
2114 Pico Blvd.
Santa Monica, CA 90405
Myron Roth, President
record label

Scottish Harp Society of America
1243 Druid Pl., #1
Atlanta, GA 30307
Sandra Sparks, Executive Director

Scotto, Renata
Il Teatro la Scala
Via Filodrammatici 2
Milan Italy
soprano

Screen Composers of America
2451 Nichols Canyon
Los Angeles, CA 90046
Herschel Burke Gilbert, President

Seacrest Productions
2670 Del Mar Heights Rd., #292
Del Mar, CA 92014
Jack Miesel
video production

Seattle Chamber Music Festival
2618 Eastlake Ave. E.
Seattle, WA 98102

Seconds Magazine
Seconds, Inc.
24 Fifth Ave., #405
New York, NY 10011
magazine

Sedaka, Neil
888 7th Ave., #1905
New York, NY 10102
singer, songwriter

Sedares, James L.
Phoenix Symphony Orchestra
3707 N. 7th St., #107
Phoenix, AZ 85014
conductor

Seeger, Michael
P.O. Box 1592
Lexington, VA 24450
musician, singer, folklorist

Seeger, Peter
c/o Harold Leventhal
250 W. 57th St.
New York, NY 10107
songwriter

Seger, Bob
c/o Capitol
1750 Vine St.
Los Angeles, CA 90028
musician

Selig Productions Inc.
1243 College Ave., #1
Bronx, NY 10456
Tyrone C. Giles
rap/reggae artist management

Seminar on Contemporary Music for the Young
c/o Music School at Rivers
337 Winter St.
Weston, MA 02193

Senses Bureau Inc., The
P.O. Box 101107
San Antonio, TX 78212
Fred Weiss, President
video production

September Moon
Production Network
25925 Telegraph, #190
Southfield, MI 48034
video production

Seraphine, Danny Peter
c/o Warner Bros.
75 Rockefeller Plaza
New York, NY 10019
drummer

Sevenars Music Festival
S. Ireland St.
Worthington, MA 01098

78 Quarterly
P.O. Box 283
Key West, FL 33041
blues, jazz magazine

77 Records
77 Newbern Ave.
Medord, MA 02155
Rocco
independent record label

Severinsen, Doc (Carl H.)
c/o NBC Press Dept.
KNBC
3000 W. Alameda Ave.
Burbank, CA 91523
conductor, musician

Sewanee Summer Music Center
University of the South
Sewanee, TN 37375

Shadowland Music/Rialto Recordings
P.O. Box 46172
Los Angeles, CA 90046
Greg MacKellan, Mark D. Kaufmann—Producers
independent record label

Shaffer, Paul
CBS
Worldwide Pants, Inc.
1697 Broadway
New York, NY 10019
musician, The Late Show bandleader

Shark Entertainment
210 Westfield Ave.
Clark, NJ 07066
Ken Makow
artist manager

Shaw, Artie
c/o ASCAP
1 Lincoln Plaza
New York, NY 10023
musician

Shaw, Robert Lawson
Atlanta Symphony Orchestra
1280 Peachtree St. NE
Atlanta, GA 30309
conductor

Shearing, George Albert
c/o J. Shulman
103 Avenue Rd., #301
Toronto Ontario M5R 2G9 Canada
jazz pianist, composer

Sheldon, Gary
Columbus Symphony Orchestra
55 E. State St.
Columbus, OH 43215
conductor

Sherman, Robert B.
c/o Conner
9030 Harratt St.
West Hollywood, CA 00069
composer, lyricist

Shimada, Toshiyuki
Portland Symphony Orchestra
30 Myrtle St.
Portland, ME 04101
conductor

Shire, David
c/o Laventhol & Horwath
2049 Century Park E., #3700
Los Angeles, CA 90067
composer

Shoot Til U Drop
800 N. Moore St.
New York, NY 10014
video production

Shooting Star Pictures
245 Ramona
Palo Alto, CA 94302
Jonathan Heuer, Producer
video production

Shore, Dinah
151 El Camino
Beverly Hills, CA 90212
singer

Shore, Howard
Prince in NY Music Corp.
1619 Broadway, 9th Fl.
New York, NY 10019
film composer

Short, Bobby
Cafe Carlyle
Madison Ave. at 76th St.
New York, NY 10021
singer, pianist

Shorter, Wayne
c/o Blue Note Records
1750 Vine St.
Los Angeles, CA 90028
jazz musician

Shostakovich, Maxim Dmitriyevich
Columbia Artists
165 W. 57th St.
New York, NY 10019
conductor

Show Music
Goodspeed Opera House
Box 466
East Haddam, CT 06423
musical theatre magazine

Showtime Productions
120 N. Springfield St.
Bolivar, MO 65613
Charlie Ealy
artist management

Sills, Beverly
c/o Edgar Vincent
157 W. 57th St.
New York, NY 10019
opera company director, coloratura
soprano

Silver, Horace
Bridge Agency
8 S. Oxford St.
Brooklyn, NY 11217
blues composer, pianist

Silvereye Production Inc.
13942 Ventura Blvd., #255
Sherman Oaks, CA 91423
video production

Silvey/Co.
8306 Wilshire Blvd., #2300
Beverly Hills, CA 90211
Tina Silvey, Producer
video production

Simmons Management Group
5214 Western Blvd.
Raleigh, NC 27606
Harry Simmons
artist management

Simmons, Gene
c/o Polygram
825 8th Ave.
New York, NY 10019
musician

Simon, Brad Organization Inc.
122 E. 57th St.
New York, NY 10022
Brad Simon, President
artist's rep

Simon, Carly
135 Central Park W
New York, NY 10023
singer, composer

Simon, Paul
1619 Broadway, #500
New York, NY 10019
singer, songwriter

Sinard, Craig
420 N. Fifth St., #455
Minneapolis, MN 55401
video production

Sinatra Society of America
P.O. Box 269
Newtonville, NY 12128
fan club

Sinatra, Frank
1041 N. Formosa Ave.
Los Angeles, CA 90046
singer

Sir Douglas Quintet Fan Club
Box 7887
Corpus Christi, TX 78467

Sir Thomas Beecham Society
c/o Charles Niss
664 S. Irena Ave.
Redondo Beach, CA 90277
to preserve the memory of the composer

Sire Records
75 Rockefeller Plaza, 21st Fl.
New York, NY 10019
Sandy Alouete, Label Manager
record label

Sire Records
Burbank
3300 Warner Blvd.
Burbank, CA 91510

Sitka Summer Music Festival
P.O. Box 20-1988
Sitka, AK 99835

16 Carrots Production Services
16 Abingdon Sq.
New York, NY 10014
video production company

Skaggs, Ricky
54 Music Sq. E, #100
Nashville, TN 37203
musician

Skid Row
9229 Sunset Blvd., #710
Los Angeles, CA 90069
group

Skowronski, Vincent Paul
EB-SKO Productions
1726 1/2 Sherman Ave.
Evanston, IL 60201
concert violinist, classical record co.
exec.

Slatkin, Leonard Edward
St. Louis Symphony Orchestra
Powell Symphony Hall
718 N. Grand Blvd.
St. Louis, MO 63101
conductor

Slaughter Pig Productions
2500 Skyline Dr.
Signal Hill, CA 90806
Brian Gunter, Producer/Engineer
video production

Sleepy Town Productions
P.O. Box 4763
Topeka, KS 66604
Jacalyn Helms Mindell
artist management

Slick, Grace Wing
Starship
1319 Broadway
Sausalito, CA 94965
singer

Slim Whitman Appreciation Society of the U.S.
c/o Loren R. Knapp
1002 W. Thurber St.
Tucson, AZ 85705
fan club

Smith Co., The
12321 Riverside Dr.
N. Hollywood, CA 91607
Paul Smith
artist management

Smith, Anson Management
3 Bethesda Metro Center, #505
Bethesda, MD 20814
artist management

Smith, Jimmy
c/o Abby Hoffer
312 E. 48th St.
New York, NY 10017
jazz organist

Smothers Brothers (Dick and Tom)
8489 W. Third St., #1020
Los Angeles, CA 90048
comic musicians

Snow
c/o East West
75 Rockefeller Plaza
New York, NY 10019
rappers

Snowbird Institute String Chamber Music Festival
Snowbird Institute
Snowbird, UT 84092

Society for Asian Music
Cornell University
Department of Asian Studies
388 Rockefeller Hall
Ithaca, NY 14853
Marty Hatch, Treasurer

Society for Electro-Acoustic Music in the U.S.
2550 Beverly Blvd.
Los Angeles, CA 90057
Scott A. Wyatt, President

Society for Ethnomusicology
Morrison Hall, #005
Indiana University
Bloomington, IN 47405
Shelly Kennedy, Administrative Secretary
music as an aspect of culture

Society for Strings
Meadowmount School
RFD 2, Box 2230
Westport, NY 12993
Mrs. Ivan Galamian, President

Society for the Preservation and Advancement of the Harmonica
P.O. Box 865
Troy, MI 48099
Gordon M. Mitchell, President

Society for the Preservation and Encouragement of Barber Shop Quartet Singing in America
6315 Third Ave.
Kenosha, WI 53143
Joe Liles, Executive Director

Society for the Preservation of Film Music
P.O. Box 93536
Hollywood, CA 90093
Jeannie Pool, Executive Director

Solo Management
1965 Sheridan Rd., #202
Evanston, IL 60208
artist management

Solti, Sir Georg
Chicago Symphony Orchestra
220 S. Michigan Ave.
Chicago, IL 60604
conductor

Sondheim, Stephen Joshua
c/o F. Roberts
65 E. 55th St., #702
New York, NY 10022
composer

Songwriter's Market
Writer's Digest Books
1507 Dana Ave.
Cincinnati, OH 45207
lists publisher, record companies, producers, etc.

Songwriter's Musepaper
Music & Arts Foundations
Box 93759
Hollywood, CA 90093
songwriter publication which includes showcase listings

Songwriters and Lyricists Club
c/o Robert Makinson
P.O. Box 023304
Brooklyn, NY 11202

Sonneck Society
P.O. Box 476
Canton, MA 02021
Kate Keller, Executive Officer
studies all aspects of American music, named after Oscar Sonneck, historian, librarian

Sons of the Pioneers
12403 W. Green Mountain
Lakewood, CO 80228
group

Sony Classical
1285 Ave. of the Americas
New York, NY 10019
Gunther Breest, President
record label

Sony Music Nashville (also Columbia Nashville, Epic Nashville)
34 Music Square E
Nashville, TN 37203
Roy Wunsch, President
record label

Sorkin, Don Productions
2717 Motor Ave.
Los Angeles, CA 90064
artist management

Sound Affair Recording Ltd.
2727-G Croddy Way
Santa Ana, CA 92704
Ron Leeper, Owner
video production

Sound and Vision
30 Horatio St.
New York, NY 10014
Tima Surmelioglu
video production

Soundings of the Planet
2501 College St.
Bellingham, WA 98225
Dean Evenson, Owner
video production

Soundtrack City
187 Lafayette St., 5th Fl.
New York, NY 10013
video production

Source, The
Source Publications, Inc.
594 Broadway
New York, NY 10012
rap magazine

South Mountain Concerts
P.O. Box 23
Pittsfield, MA 01202

Southeastern Composers' League
c/o Don Freund
Memphis State University
Department of Music
Memphis, TN 38152
Jerry Sieg, President

Southern Appalachian Dulcimer Association
2700 Oak Shadow Terrace
Brimingham, AL 35215
A.J. Hayes, President

Southern Pacific International Fan Club
P.O. Box 362
Milwaukee, WI 53201

Southside Productions Inc.
22225 SW 112th Place
Miami, FL 33170
Larry Walker
r&b/gospel artist management

Southwest Productions
812 Gold SW
Albuquerque, NM 87102
video production

Special Friends of Dottie West
P.O. Box 61
Harrisburg, PA 17108
fan club

Spector, Phil
Warner-Spector Records Inc.
686 S. Arroyo Pkwy.
Pasadena, CA 91105
record co. exec.

Spellbound Pictures
6161 Santa Monica Blvd., #301
Hollywood, CA 90038
video production

Spike Jones International Fan Club
129 E. Colorado Blvd., #508
Monrovia, CA 91016

Spin
Spin Publications
6 W. 18th St.
New York, NY 10011
magazine

Splatter Effect
Box 2
Bound Brook, NJ 08805
magazine

Spoleto Festival U.S.A.
Box 157
Charleston, SC 29402
music festival

Spotlight Productions
10920 Indian Trail, #204
Dallas, TX 75229
video production

Springfield, Rick
9200 Sunset Blvd., PH15
Los Angeles, CA 90069
singer

Springsteen, Bruce
c/o Premier Talent Agency
3 E. 54th St.
New York, NY 10022
the boss

Stafford, Jo (Elizabeth)
Corinthian Records
P.O. Box 6296
Beverly Hills, CA 90212
singer

Stage Presence
170 E. 83rd St., #3G
New York, NY 10028
clothing/hair/makeup

Stansfield, Lisa
c/o Arista
6 W. 57th St.
New York, NY 10019
singer

Stapp, Olivia Brewer
c/o Artist Mgmt. Inc.
165 W. 57th St.
New York, NY 10019
opera singer

Star Direction Inc.
9255 Sunset Blvd., #610
Los Angeles, CA 90069
Shelly Berger
artist management

Starkravin' Management
8491 Sunset Blvd., #376
W. Hollywood, CA 90069
Ben McLane
artist management

Starlight Festival Inc.
32 Howard St.
New Haven, CT 06519
music festival

Starr, Ringo (Richard Starkey)
2 Glynde Mews
London SW3 1SB U.K.
musician

State Productions Ltd.
63 Great Portland St.
London W1N 5DH U.K.
Richard Bell
video production

Statler Brothers
P.O. Box 2703
Staunton, VA 24401
group

Stefanino Productions
9255 Sunset Blvd., #610
Los Angeles, CA 90069
Nancy Leiviska, Director
rockumentaries

Sterban, Richard Anthony
329 Rockland Rd.
Hendersonville, TN 37075
musician

Stern Grove Festival
1160 Battery St., #400
San Francisco, CA 94111
music festival

Stern, Howard
K-ROCK-FM (WXRK)
600 Madison Ave.
New York, NY 10022
DJ

Stern, Isaac
40 W. 57th St.
New York, NY 10019
violinist

Steven Adams Productions Ltd.
77A Landon Rd.
London SW9 9RT U.K.
video production company

Stewart, Rod
c/o Warner Bros.
3300 Warner Blvd.
Burbank, CA 91510
singer

Stiefel and Company
3-2 Eighth Ave., 15th Fl.
New York, NY 10001
video production

Stiletto Management
6640 Sunset Blvd., #200
Hollywood, CA 90028
Garry Kief
artist management

Sting (Gordon Matthew Sumner)
The Bugle House
21 A Noel St.
London W1 U.K.
singer

Stolzman, Richard Leslie
201 W. 54th St., #4C
New York, NY 10019
clarinettist

Stormfront Management
2020 Pennsylvania NW, #240
Washington, DC 20006
Norm Veenstra
artist management

Strait, George
c/o Erv Woolsey
1000 18th Ave. S
Nashville, TN 37212
singer

Stratas, Teresa (Anastasia Strataki)
Metropolitan Opera Company
Lincoln Center Plaza
New York, NY 10023
opera singer

Strato Films
4859 College View Ave.
Los Angeles, CA 90069
video production

Strauss, Herb Productions, Inc.
30 Park Ave.
New York, NY 10016
video production

Straw, Syd
Monterey Peninsula Artists
P.O. Box 7308
Carmel, CA 93921
singer

Stray Cats
113 Wardour Street
London, W1, U.K.
group

Street Knowledge Productions
6809 Victoria Ave.
Los Angeles, CA 90043
Patricia Chabonnet
rap/urban artist management

Streisand, Barbra (Barbara Joan)
9830 Wilshire Blvd.
Beverly Hills, CA 90212
singer

Studio Productions Inc.
4610 Charlotte Ave.
Nashville, TN 37209
Heather Hawthorne, Production
Coordinator
video production

Stulberg, Neal Howard
New Mexico Symphony Orchestra
P.O. Box 769
Albuquerque, NM 87103
conductor

Styne, Jule
237 W. 51st St.
New York, NY 10019
composer, producer

Sub-Pop
P.O. Box 2391
Olympia, WA 98507
magazine

Sugarman, Danny Management
449 S. Beverly Dr., #212
Beverly Hills, CA 90212
artist management

Summer Festival of Performing Arts
c/o City Celebration Inc.
Fort Mason, Bldg. A
San Francisco, CA 94123
music festival

Summer, Donna (LaDonna Adrian Gaines)
2401 Main St.
Santa Monica, CA 90405
singer, songwriter

Summerfest
La Jolla Chamber Music Society
P.O. Box 2168
La Jolla, CA 92038

Summerfest—PA
Fox Chapel Episcopal Church
P.O. Box 23181
Pittsburgh, PA 15222
music festival

Sun Valley Music Festival
Sun Valley Center for the Arts &
Humanities
P.O. Box 656
Sun Valley, ID 83353

Sunshine Communications
P.O. Box 1711
Tempe, AZ 85280
video production

Sutherland, Dame Joan
c/o Colbert Artists Mgmt.
111 W. 57th St.
New York, NY 10019
retired soprano

Swados, Elizabeth
40 W. 57th St.
New York, NY 10019
composer

Swannanoa Chamber Festival
P.O. Box 9002, Warren Wilson College
lege
Swannanoa, NC 28778
music festival

Sweet Adelines International
P.O. Box 470168
Tulsa, OK 74147
Sharon Green, Executive Director
association of womens's barbershop
quartets

Symphony on the Prairie
Indianapolis Symphony Orchestra
45 Monument Circle
Indianapolis, IN 46204

Happiness is learning that your daughter's boyfriend has had his electric guitar repossessed by the finance company.

—ANONYMOUS

T.L.P.
P.O. Box 56757
New Orleans, LA 70156
video production

Take Out Management
15125 Ventura Blvd., PH 200
Sherman Oaks, CA 91403
Howard Rosen
artist management

Takima Production
201 Clinton Ave.
Brooklyn, NY 11205
video production

Talking Heads
1775 Broadway, #700
New York, NY 10019
group

Talking Taco Records
5402 Timber Trail
San Antonio, TX 78228
Ben Travera King
independent record label

Talladega College Arts Festival
Talladega College
W. Battle Street
Talladega, AL 35160
music festival

Talmi, Yoav
P.O. Box 1384
Kfar Saba 44113 Israel
conductor

Tamburitza Association of America
2 Gandy Dr.
St. Louis, MO 63146
Alex Machaskee, President
guitar/mandolin society

Tammy Wynette International Fan Club
P.O. Box 753
Richboro, PA 18954

Tanglewood/Tanglewood Music Center
Boston Symphony Orchestra
Symphony Hall
301 Massachusetts Ave.
Boston, MA 02115

Tanya Tucker Fan Club
5200 Maryland Way, #103
Brentwood, TN 37027

Taos School of Music Chamber Music Festival
P.O. Box 1879
Taos, NM 87571

Tarock Music
P.O. Box 441, Village Station
New York, NY 10014
Theresa Marchione
independent record label

Task at Hand Productions
10850 Wilshire Blvd., 4th Fl.
Los Angeles, CA 90024
video production

Taylor, Cecil Percival
PSI—Soul Note Records
810 7th Ave.
New York, NY 10019
jazz pianist, composer

Taylor, James
c/o Peter Asher Mgmt.
644 N. Doheny Dr.
West Hollywood, CA 90069
musician

Te Kanawa, Kiri
Harrison/Parrott Ltd.
12 Penzance Place
London W11 4PA U.K.
opera and concert singer

Tears for Fears
50 New Bond Street
London, W1, U.K.
group

Tebaldi, Renata
c/o SA Gorlinsky Ltd.
33 Dover St.
London W1X 4NJ U.K.
opera singer

Teeman/Sleppin
147 W. 26th St.
New York, NY 10001
Stu Sleppin/Bob Teeman
video production

Teen Beat Magazine
215 Lexington Ave.
New York, NY 10016
Karen L. Williams, Editor
magazine

Teen Machine
Sterling's Magazines
355 Lexington Ave.
New York, NY 10017
Marie Therese Morreale, Editor
magazine

Telarc International
23307 Commerce Park Dr.
Cleveland, OH 44122
independent record label

Telegenics
Music Video Network
568 Broadway, Suite 502
New York, NY 10012
Christopher Russo, President
video production

Teller, Alvin Norman
MCA Music Entertainment Group
70 Universal City Plaza
Universal City, CA 91608
man

Telluride Chamber Music Festival
c/o Telluride Chamber Music Association
P.O. Box 115
Telluride, CO 81434

Telluride Jazz Festival, Inc.
P.O. Box 505
Telluride, CO 81435

Tennessee Production Center Inc.
400 Ensley Dr.
Knoxville, TN 37920
video production

Tennstedt, Klaus
The London Philharmonic
35 Doughty St.
London WC1 U.K.
conductor

10,000 Maniacs
9830 Wilshire Blvd.
Beverly Hills, CA 90212
group

Teresa Brewer Fan Club
c/o Bill Monroe
584 Prospect St.
New Haven, CT 06511

Terminal Records
P.O. Box 7927
Jackson, MS 39204
Rick Garner, President
independent record label

Terra Nova Records
P.O. Box 455
Sunland, CA 91041
Boris Menart, President
independent record label

Tesh, John
5555 Melrose Ave.
Los Angeles, CA 90038
musician

Tex Ritter Fan Club
c/o Sharon L. Sweeting
15326 73rd Ave. SE
Snohomish, WA 98290

Theatrix Moving Pictures
P.O. Box 61161
Seattle, WA 98121
Scott von Freiberg, Owner/Producer
video production

They Might Be Giants Information Club
P.O. Box 110553 Williamsburgh Station
Brooklyn, NY 11211
fan club

Third Ave. Productions
2720 Third Ave.
Seattle, WA 98121
video production

Third Mind
225 Lafayette St., #407
New York, NY 10012
Gary Levermore, Label Manager
independent record label

13 Engines
Collins Mgmt.
5 Bigelow St.
Cambridge, MA 02139
group

13 Stiches
Rustron Music Mgmt.
1156 Park Lane
W. Palm Beach, FL 33417
group

37 Records
7560 Garden Grove Blvd.
Westminster, CA 92683
Steve McClintock
independent record label

Thomas, B.J. (Billy Joe)
International Artists Mgmt.
P.O. Box 12061
Nashville, TN 37212
singer

Thomas, Jay
10351 Santa Monica Blvd., #211
Los Angeles, CA 90025
DJ

Thomas, Jess
P.O. Box 662
Belvedere, Tiburon, CA 94920
tenor

Thomas, Michael Tilson
000 7th Ave., 07th Fl.
New York, NY 10106
conductor

Thompson, Bill Management
2051 3rd St.
San Francisco, CA 94107
artist management

Three Rivers Arts Festival
207 Sweetbriar St.
Pittsburgh, PA 15211

Thunder and Lightning Productions
P.O. Box 392
New York, NY 10276
video production

Tillis, Mel
Prappas Co
9201 Wilshire Blvd.
Beverly Hills, CA 90210
singer

Time Warner Inc.
75 Rockefeller Plaza
New York, NY 10019
largest media and entertainment
company in the world

TLC
6 W. 57th St.
New York, NY 10019
group

Tom Petty and The Heartbreakers
1755 Broadway, 8th Fl.
New York, NY 10019
group

Top Rock Development
9000 Sunset Blvd., #901
Los Angeles, CA 90069
Doug Thaler
artist management

Toto
P.O. Box 7308
Carmel, CA 93921
group

Townshend, Peter
Entertainment Corporation America
99 Park Ave., 16th flr.
New York, NY 10016
musician, composer, singer

Trans Atlantic Productions
51 Deerfield Rd
Portland, ME 04101
Fraser Jones
artist management

Traveling Wilburys
c/o Warner Bros.
3300 Warner Blvd.
Burbank, CA 91510
"star" group

Travis, Randy
P.O. Box 121712
Nashville, TN 37212
singer

Tree, Michael
c/o Harry Beall Mgmt. Inc.
P.O. Box 30
Tenafly, NJ 07670
violinist

Tri-M Music Honor Society
c/o MENC
1902 Association Dr.
Reston, VA 22091
Sandra Fridy, Contact
honor society for music students in
junior and senior high

Trigger Happy Films Ltd.
Babley Wharhse. Kings Cross FD
Yorkway
London NW10BB U.K.
video production

Triple X Management
P.O. Box 1010
Hollywood, CA 90078
Charley Brown
alternative/hard rock artist manage-
ment

Troy Hess Fan Club
11623 Old Telegraph Rd.
Houston, TX 77067

Troyer Music Group
33200 Bainbridge Rd., #32
Cleveland, OH 44139
Lisa Dauwalder
artist management

Tubeworks Video Productions
1626 N. Wilcox Ave., #487
Hollywood, CA 90028
Arthur Pritz, Production Director
video production

**Tubists Universal Brotherhood
Association**
c/o Scott Watson
University of Kansas
Department of Music
Lawrence, KS 66045

Tucker Management
1420 NW Gilman Blvd., #2314
Issaquah, WA 98027
Bill Tucker
artist management

Tucker, Tanya
P.O. Box 15245
Nashville, TN 37215
singer

Tucson Festivals
Tucson Festival Society, Inc.
425 W. Paseo Redondo, #2
Tucson, AZ 85701
music festival

Tureck, Rosalind
c/o Columbia Artists Mgmt.
165 W. 57th St.
New York, NY 10019
harpsichordist

Turner, Tina (Anna Mae Bullock)
c/o Roger Davis Mgmt.
3575 Cahuenga Blvd., W
Los Angeles, CA 90068
singer

21/20 Records
175 5th Ave., #2253
New York, NY 10010
Murray Halpern
independent record label

21st Circuitry Records
396 Waller
San Francisco, CA 94117
Don Blanchard
independent record label

23 West Entertainment
71 W. 23rd St., #1161
New York, NY 10010
Bob Gordon
artist management

25 G's Max
1655 Cherokee, #200
Hollywood, CA 90028
music video production company

29th Street Saxophone Quartet
c/o Antilles Records
825 8th Ave., 26th Fl.
New York, NY 10019
group

Twitty, Conway Entertainment
1 Music Village Blvd.
Hendersonville, TN 37075
mgmt. group for late singer

2AZZ1
P.O. Box 2512
Toluca Lake, CA 91610
duo

2 Die 4
c/o Morgan Creek
1875 Century Park E., #600
Los Angeles, CA 90067
group

2 Live Crew
c/o Luke Records
8400 N.E. 2nd Ave.
Liberty City, FL 33138
group

2 Much Fun Productions
14803 Otsego Street
Sherman Oaks, CA 91403
Eddie Barber
music video production company

There is one good thing about today's popular music. If the acoustics are bad you don't know it.

—ANONYMOUS

U.S. Scottish Fiddling Revival
1938 Rose Villa St.
Pasadena, CA 91107
Jan Tappan, Vice-President

U2
4 Windmill Lane
Dublin 4, Ireland
group

Uggams, Leslie
151 El Camino
Beverly Hills, CA 90212
singer

Ugly Joe Kid
825 Eighth Ave.
New York, NY 10019
group

UN Productions Inc.
84 Kennedy St.
Hackensack, NJ 07601
video production

Underdog Films Inc.
1396 S. Orange Dr., Suite 2
Los Angeles, CA 90019
Linda Martinez, Head of Music Production
video production

Underdog Management
7705 Hollywood Blvd.
W. Hollywood, CA 90046
Rory Emerald
artist management

Unherd of Productions
44 E. 32nd St., 4th Fl.
New York, NY 10001
Jay Dorfman
video production

Unit, The
3 Bromley Place
London W1P 5HB U.K.
Ballie Walsh
video production

United in Group Harmony Association
P.O. Box 185
Clifton, NJ 07011
Ronald Italiano, President and Founder
rhythm and blues, doo-wop vocal group harmony

United Serpents
P.O. Box 8915
Columbia, SC 29202
Craig Kridel, President
serpent (forerunner of tuba) players

Unitel Video
515 W. 57th Street
New York, NY 10019
Joe Di Buono, VP
video production

Universal Recording
32 W. Randolph St., 14th & 15th Fl.
Chicago, IL 60601
David Kalish, Owner
video production

University of Notre Dame
Collegiate Jazz Festival
P.O. Box 115
Notre Dame, IN 46556

Unmanageable Talent
Castle Farm, 1 Natwick Rd.
W. Warwick, RI 02893
Jack Reich
artist management

US 95
6345 Fountain Ave.
Los Angeles, CA 90028
video production

Utah Arts Festival
168 W. 500 N.
Salt Lake City, UT 84103
music festival

A scientist claims that rock music is beneficial in some cases of deafness. But, then, deafness is also beneficial in some cases of rock music.

—Anonymous

Vadis International
P.O. Box 578305
Chicago, IL 60657
Hilton Weinberg
artist management

Valli, Frankie
8942 Wilshire Blvd.
Beverly Hills, CA 90211
singer

Van Ackeren Co., The
300 Fairview Ave. N
Seattle, WA 98109
video production

Van Halen, Eddie
Premier Talent Agency
3 E. 54th St.
New York, NY 10022
guitarist

Van Shelton, Ricky
c/o Michael Campbell
P.O. Box 121754
Nashville, TN 37212
singer, songwriter

Vanderberk, Dirk Photography
356 E. 13th St., #7
New York, NY 10021
video production

Vandross, Luther
c/o Epic Records
51 W. 52nd St.
New York, NY 10019
singer

Vaness, Carol
c/o H. Breslin
119 W. 57th St.
New York, NY 10019
soprano

Vanguard Films
135 E. 65th St.
New York, NY 10021
John H. Williams, President
video production

Vanguard Management
1524 N. Clairborne
New Orleans, LA 70116
Eric Cager
artist management

Vanilla Ice
8730 Sunset Blvd., 5th Fl. W
Los Angeles, CA 90069
rapper

Vanity
151 El Camino
Beverly Hills, CA 90212
singer

Variety
475 Park Ave. S
New York, NY 10016
Peter Bart, Editor
weekly trade paper

Vault Management Inc.
9157 Sunset Blvd., #310
Los Angeles, CA 90069
Greg Lewerke
artist management

Vector Management
P.O. Box 128037
Nashville, TN 37212
Ken Levitan
artist management

Vermont Mozart Festival
P.O. Box 512
Burlington, VT 05402

Viacom Inc.
1515 Broadway
New York, NY 10036
Sumner M. Redstone, Chairman
MTV and VH-1 parent company

Viagraph Production
922 1/2 S. Curson Ave.
Los Angeles, CA 90036
video production

Vibe
Time/Warner Inc.
1271 Ave. of the Americas
Rockefeller Center
New York, NY 10020
hip hop magazine

Victoria International Festival
103-3737 Oak Street
Vancouver, British Columbia V6H
1M4 Canada
music festival

Vide-U Productions
1034 Shenandoah St., #6
Los Angeles, CA 90049
Bradley Friedman, President
video production

Video Hits 1 (VH-1)
MTV Networks
1515 Broadway
New York, NY 10036
Edward A. Bennett, President
music video network geared for adults

Video Music Int.
11 Music Square E., #506
Nashville, TN 37203
video production

Video Spotlight
101 Continental Ave.
Belleville, NJ 07109
Al Cocchi, President/Exec. Producer
video production

Vikki's Special People
155 E. 92nd St., #117
New York, NY 10128
Vikki Carr fan club

Villa-Lobos Music Society
153 E. 92nd St., #4R
New York, NY 10128
Alfred Heller, President
renew and preserve interest in Brazil-
ian composer Heitor Villa-Lobos

Vinton, Bobby (Stanley Robert)
Rexford Productions
9255 Sunset Blvd., #706
Los Angeles, CA 90069
singer

Vinton, Will Productions, Inc.
1400 NW 22nd Ave.
Portland, OR 97210
video production

Viola D'Amore Society of America
39-23 47th St.
Sunnyside, NY 11104
Dr. Myron Rosenblum, Co-Director
promotes viola d'amore playing

Viola Da Gamba Society of America
c/o John A. Whisler
1308 Jackson Ave.
Charleston, IL 61920
bass of the viola family

Violin Society of America
85-07 Abingdon Rd.
Kew Gardens, NY 11415
Hans E. Tausig, President

Violoncello Society
340 W. 55th St., 5-D
New York, NY 10019
Bernard Greenhouse, President
amateur and professional cellists

Virgin Records
338 N. Foothill Rd.
Beverly Hills, CA 90210
Jordan Harris, Co-Managing Director
record label, also Charisma, Point
Blank

Virgin Records
New York
1790 Broadway, 20th Fl.
New York, NY 10019

Visages
8748 Holloway
West Hollywood, CA 90069
makeup/hairstylist rep

Voice of Youth Video
1700 E. Garry Ave., #229
Santa Ana, CA 92705
Michael Peleaux, Director Video Services
video production

Von Dohnanyi, Christoph
Cleveland Orchestra
11001 Euclid Ave.
Cleveland, OH 44106
conductor

Von Rhein, John Rochard
Chicago Tribune
P.O. Box 25340
Chicago, IL 60625
music critic

Von Stade, Frederica
165 W. 57th St.
New York, NY 10019
mezzo-soprano

Voodoo Child
P.O. Box 374
Des Plaines, IL 60016
Jimi Hendrix magazine

The rock music field is uncertain. A singing group can be only ordinary one day and retired millionaires the next day.

—Anonymous

W.M. Productions
1505 Mohle Dr.
Austin, TX 78703
video production

Waggoner, Porter
World Class Talent
1522 Demonbreun St.
Nashville, TN 37203
singer, composer

Wagner Society of New York
P.O. Box 949, Ansonia Station
New York, NY 10023
Nathalie Wagner, President
society of Richard Wagner enthusiasts

Waits, Tom (Thomas Alan)
c/o E. Smith
11 Eucalyptus Ln.
San Rafael, CA 94901
singer, composer

Wakeman, Rick
Bejanor Ltd.
Bejanor House
2 Bridge St.
Peel, Isle of Man, U.K.
composer, musician

Walker, Sandra
c/o Columbia Artists Mgmt.
165 W. 57th St.
New York, NY 10019
mezzo-soprano

Wallach, Peter Enterprises
17 W. 17th St.
New York, NY 10011
video production

Wallin, Daniel Guy
c/o IATSE local 659
11331 Ventura Blvd., #201
Studio City, CA 91604
music scoring engineer

Walter Dog Pictures
P.O. Box 132
Boston, MA 02123
Lauren Passarelli, Owner
video production

Walz, Ken Productions
150 Fifth Ave., #210
New York, NY 10011
video production

Wampuum
2016 Henley
Glenview, IL 60025
Paul Enzinger
folk artist management

Warfield, William Caesar
University of Illinois Department of
Music
2136 Music
Urbana, IL 61801
singer, educator

Warner Bros. Records
3300 Warner Blvd.
Burbank, CA 91510
Mo Ostin, Chairman
record label, also Reprise, Sire, Cold
Chillin', Paisley Park, Quest, Slash

Warner Bros. Records
New York
75 Rockefeller Plaza
New York, NY 10019

Warner/Alliance Records
24 Music Square E
Nashville, TN 37203
Neil Joseph, VP/GM
record label

Warner/Reprise Records
1815 Division St.
Nashville, TN 37203
Jim Ed Norman, President
record label

Warwick, Dionne
December Twelve
144 S. Beverly Dr., #503
Beverly Hills, CA 90212
singer

Washington, Grover Jr.
c/o Zane Mgmt.
Broad and Walnut Sts.
Philadelphia, PA 19102
musician, producer, composer,
arranger

Watanabe, Yoko
40 W. 57th St.
New York, NY 10019
soprano

Waterloo Music Festival
Village of Waterloo
Stanhope, NJ 07874

Waterville Valley Festival of the Arts
Waterville Valley, NJ 03215
music festival

Watley, Jody
8439 Sunset Blvd., #103
Los Angeles, CA 90069
singer

Watrous, William Russell
Welk Records
1299 Ocean Ave., #800
Santa Monica, CA 90401
composer, trombonist

Watson, Doc (Arthel Lane Watson)
Folklore Productions
1671 Appian Way
Santa Monica, CA 90401
vocalist, guitarist, banjoist

Watts, Andre
IMG
22 E. 71st St.
New York, NY 10021
concert pianist

Waveform International Inc.
One Cumberland Pl., #304
Bangor, ME 04401
Janet Cucinotti, President
independent record label

Wax Tax! Records Inc.
1659 N. Damen Ave.
Chicago, IL 60610
Kai Dohm
independent record label

Waxing Poetics Inc.
P.O. Box 11627
Norfolk, VA 23517
Carol Taylor
artist manager

Wayne, Tony Inc.
300 E. 33rd St., #5M
New York, NY 10016
video production

We Bite America
P.O. Box 10172
Chicago, IL 60610
Kai Dohm
independent record label

Wealth and Hellfare Music
P.O. Box 6061-225
Sherman Oaks, CA 91423
John Boegehold, President
independent record label

Weisner, Ron Entertainment
9200 Sunset Blvd., PH
Los Angeles, CA 90069
artist management

Wel-Dun International Management
1415 3rd St. Promenade, #301
Santa Monica, CA 90401
Dennis Dunstan
artist management

Welk Music Group
1299 Ocean Ave., #800
Santa Monica, CA 90401
Kent Crawford, VP
independent record label

Welsh Harp Society of North America
649 E. 39th St., #2-E
Kansas City, MO 64111
David R. Watson, Registered Agent

Wenner, Jann Simon
Straight Arrow Publications, Inc.
1290 Ave. of the Americas
New York, NY 10104
editor, publisher, exec. V.P. Rock &
Roll Hall of Fame

West Records
P.O. Box 8875
Universal City, CA 91608
Boots Clements
independent record label

Westcom Productions
1925 Barley Hill Rd.
Eugene, OR 97405
video production

Weston, Randy
P.O. Box 749
Maplewood, NJ 07040
jazz pianist, composer

Westwood Entertainment Group
1115 Iman Ave., #330
Edison, NJ 08820
Victor Kaplij, President
independent record label

Westworld
P.O. Box 43787
Tucson, ZA 85733
Bill Sassenberger, Owner
independent record label

Whiskey-a-Go-Go
8901 Sunset Blvd.
W. Hollywood, CA 90069
club

White Records
P.O. Box 146537
Chicago, IL 60614
David Pistrui
independent record label

White, Duncan
P.O. Box 1183
Carmel, IN 46032
artist management

Who, The
48 Harley House
Marylebone Rd.
London, NW1 U.K.
group

Wide Angle Records
2533 Nicollet Ave. S
Mineapolis, MN 55404
Jerome Sylvers, Owner
independent record label

Widely Distributed
142 W. Touhy
Chicago, IL 60626
Jack Frank
independent record label

Wild Pitch Records Ltd.
291 W. 29th St., 8th Fl.
New York, NY 10001
Stuart Fine
independent record label

Wild West Records
7201 Melrose Ave., #D
Los Angeles, CA 90046
Morris Taft, Jr., President
independent record label

Wilde Silas
P.O. Box 512
Katy, TX 77492
video production

Willem Mengelberg Society
6954 Crocus Ct., #2
Greendale, WI 53129
Ronald Klett, Director
society to study works of Dutch conductor

Williams, Andy
151 El Camino
Beverly Hills, CA 90212
singer

Williams, Hank Jr.
P.O. Box 850
Paris, TN 38242
singer, songwriter

Williams, Joe
c/o Berkeley Agency
2490 Channing Way, #406
Berkeley, CA 94704
jazz and blues singer

Williams, John
151 El Camino
Beverly Hills, CA 90212
conductor, composer

Williams, Lawrence
8715 W. 3rd St.
Los Angeles, CA 90048
songwriter

Williams, Paul
Lazy Creek Productions
4570 Encino Ave.
Encino, CA 91316
composer, singer

Williams, Tony
Manhattan Records
1370 Ave. of the Americas
New York, NY 10019
jazz drummer

Williams, Vanessa
Rt. #100
Millwood, NY 10546
singer

Willow Music, Inc.
1221 Anderson Dr., #11
San Rafael, CA 94901
Susan Sitterle, President
independent record label

Wilshire Artists
100 Wilshire Blvd., #550
Santa Monica, CA 90401
Daniel Leeway
artist management

**Wilson Phillips (Chynna Phillips,
Carnie Wilson, Wendy Wilson)**
1290 Ave. of the Americas
New York, NY 10104
group, temporarily disbanded

Wilson, Ann
219 1st Ave. N, #333
Seattle, WA 98109
singer

Wilson, Brian
151 El Camino
Beverly Hills, CA 90212
composer, singer, record producer

Wilson, Nancy
c/o John Levy
5455 Wilshire Blvd., #2208
Los Angeles, CA 90036
singer

**Windham Hill/High Street
Records**
3500 W. Olive Ave., 1430
Burbank, CA 91505
independent record label

Windswept Pacific
9320 Wilshire Blvd., #200
Beverly Hills, CA 90212
John Anderson
independent record label

Wingate Records
P.O. Box 10895
Pleasanton, CA 94588
P.A. Hanna
independent record label

Winter Park Bach Festival
Rollins College, Box 2763
Winter Park, FL 32789

Winwood, Steve
151 El Camino
Beverly Hills, CA 90212
musician, composer

Wise/Elite Filmworks
10153 1/2 Riverside Dr., #236
Toluca Lake, CA 91602
video production

Wolf Trap Farm Park for the Performing Arts
1624 Trap Rd.
Vienna, VA 22180
music festival

Wolfman Jack
Rt. 1, Box 56
Belvidere, NC 27919
perennial DJ

Wonder, Stevie (Steveland Morris)
4616 W. Magnolia Blvd.
Burbank, CA 91505
singer, musician, composer

Wood 'n' Strings
1513 Baker Rd.
Burleson, TX 76028
Russell Cook
independent record label

Wood, Ronald
c/o Columbia Records
CBS Records
51 W. 52nd St.
New York, NY 10019
musician

Woodenship Records
P.O. Box 1624
Burbank, CA 91507
Mark Romano
independent record label

Woods, Phil
P.O. Box 278
Delaware Water Gap, PA 18327
jazz composer, musician

Woolsey, Irv Co.
1000 18th Ave. S
Nashville, TN 37212
artist management

Wooton, Robbie
35a Barrow St.
Dublin 4 Ireland
artist management

Word Records
5221 N. O'Connor Blvd., #1000
Irving, TX 75039
Roland Lundy, President
record label

Word Records
Nashville
3319 W. End Ave., #200
Nashville, TN 37203

World Disc Productions Inc.
915 Spring St.
Friday Harbor, WA 98250
Michael Coyne, Sales Manager
independent record label

World Folk Music Association
P.O. Box 40553
Washington, DC 20016
Richard A. Cerri, President

World Movement Records
8306 Wilshire Blvd., #51
Beverly Hills, CA 90211
Lamont Patterson, Owner
independent record label

World of Michael Jackson
P.O. Box 1804
Encino, CA 91426
fan club

Wuorinen, Charles
c/o H. Stokar
870 W. End Ave.
New York, NY 10025
composer

Wyman, Bill
Ripple Records Ltd.
c/o Panacea Entertainment
2705 Glendower Ave.
Los Angeles, CA 90027
musician

Wynnette, Tammy
c/o Epic/CBS Records Inc.
51 W. 52nd St.
New York, NY 10019
singer

Wynnona
3907 Alameda Ave., 2nd Fl.
Burbank, CA 91505
singer

Wyoming Summer Music Festival
University of Wyoming
Department of Music
Laramie, WY 82071

An unsung hero is a guy who knows he can't sing and doesn't.
—A<small>NONYMOUS</small>

X-clusive Records Inc.
1162 NE 167th St. N
Miami Beach, FL 33162
independent record label

Xemu Records Inc.
36 E. 10th St., 2 East
New York, NY 10003
Dr. Claw, CEO
independent record label

Xena Media
P.O. Box 78
Arlington, MA 02174
Chryste Hall
artist management

XL Talent
27-A Pembridge Villas, #7
London W11 3EP U.K.
artist management

Xopix
501 N. Hwy. 35
Austin, TX 78702
video production

Y

A person is in a tough predicament when he has to face the music
with his nose to the grindstone and his back to the wall.

—Anonymous

Yachats Music Festival
Yachats, OR 97498

Yankovic, "Weird" Al
8842 Hollywood Blvd.
Los Angeles, CA 90069
composer, singer

Yellow Barn Music Festival, The
RD 2, Box 371
Putney, VT 05346

Yetnikoff, Walter
Trump Tower
721 5th Ave.
New York, NY 10022
music executive

Yoakum, Dwight
c/o Reprise
3300 Warner Blvd.
Burbank, CA 91510
singer

Young Concert Artists
250 W. 57th St., #921
New York, NY 10019
Susan Wadsworth, Director

Young, Jamie
Ziffren, Brittenham & Branca
2121 Ave. of the Stars, 32nd Fl.
Los Angeles, CA 90067
music attorney

Young, Neil
c/o Geffen Records
9126 Sunset Blvd.
W. Hollywood, CA 90069
songwriter, musician

Yuhas, Robert Production
307 E. 44th St.
New York, NY 10017
video production

Even if rock 'n' roll music died tomorrow, it would take several weeks for the sound to fade away.

—ANONYMOUS

Zanzibar Records
2021 Noble St.
Pittsburgh, PA 15218
Ernie Kaschauer, President
independent record label

Zappas (Moon Unit, Dweezil)
P.O. Box 5265
N. Hollywood, CA 91616
musicians

Zawinul, Josef
c/o Atlantic Jazz Records
75 Rockefeller Plaza
New York, NY 10019
jazz composer, bandleader

Zelos
535 Pacific Ave.
San Francisco, CA 94133
Geoff Workman
artist management

Zenobia Agency
130 S. Highland Ave.
Los Angeles, CA 90036
hairstylist/makeup rep

Zevon, Warren
c/o Virgin Records
9247 Alden Dr.
Beverly Hills, CA 90210
singer, songwriter

Zimmerman, Gerhardt
North Carolina Symphony Orchestra
Memorial Auditorium
P.O. Box 28026
Raleigh, NC 27611
conductor

Zink Communications
245 W. 19th St.
New York, NY 10011
video production

Zinman, David Joel
Baltimore Symphony Orchestra
1212 Cathedral St.
Baltimore, MD 21201
conductor

Zomba Group
916 19th Ave. S
Nashville, TN 37212
artist management

Zone Records
1923 49th NW
Canton, OH 44709
John Lepep
independent record label

Zoo Entertainment
6363 Sunset Blvd.
Los Angeles, CA 90028
Lou Maglia, President
record label

Zoo Entertainment
New York
1133 Ave. of the Americas
New York, NY 10036

Zoom Express
568 Broadway, #1104
New York, NY 10012
video production

Zoot Sandstone
501 N. 36th St., #157
Seattle, WA 98103
artist management

Zulieka Records
11684 Ventura Blvd. #967
Studio City, CA 91604
Victor Von Wright, Exec. Prod.
independent record label

ZZ Top
P.O. Box 19744
Houston, TX 77024
group

ZZ Top International Fan Club
P.O. Box 19744
Houston, TX 77224

RECORD LABELS

A&M
1416 N. La Brea Ave.
Los Angeles, CA 90028
Also:
595 Madison Ave.
New York, NY 10022

Allegiance
7525 Fountain Ave.
Hollywood, CA 90046

Alligator
P.O. Box 60234
Chicago, IL 60660

Amherst
1800 Main St.
Buffalo, NY 14208

Angel
1750 N. Vine St.
Hollywood, CA 90028

Arhoolie
10341 San Pablo Ave.
El Cerrito, CA 94530

Arista
6 W. 57th St.
New York, NY 10019

Also:
8370 Wilshire Blvd.
Los Angeles, CA 90211

218 Harding Pl.
Nashville, TN 37205

ATCO
75 Rockefeller Plaza
New York, NY 10019

Atlantic
75 Rockefeller Plaza
New York, NY 10019
Also:
9229 Sunset Blvd. (#710)
Los Angeles, CA 90069

Beserkley
2054 University Ave.
Berkeley, CA 94704

Blue Note
1370 Ave. of the Americas
New York, NY 10019

CBS
51 W. 52nd St.
New York, NY 10019
Also:

1801 Century Park W.
Los Angeles, CA 90067

34 Music Square E.
Nashville, TN 37203

Capitol
1750 N. Vine St.
Hollywood, CA 90028
Also:
1370 Ave. of the Americas
New York, NY 10019

1111 16th Ave. S.
Nashville, TN 37212

Chrysalis
645 Madison Ave.
New York, NY 10022
Also:
9255 Sunset Blvd.
Los Angeles, CA 90069

Cinema
P.O. Box 775
Bryn Mawr, PA 19010

Compleat
21 Music Square E.
Nashville, TN 37203
Also:
810 Seventh Ave.
New York, NY 10019

Concord Jazz
2888 Willow Pass Rd.
Concord, CA 94522

Curb
111 N. Hollywood Way
Burbank, CA 91505

Def American
9157 Sunset Blvd.
Los Angeles, CA 90069

Def Jam
298 Elizabeth St.
New York, NY 10012

Elektra/Asylum/Nonesuch
75 Rockefeller Plaza
New York, NY 10019
Also:
9229 Sunset Blvd
Los Angeles, CA 90069

1710 Grand Ave.
Nashville, TN 37212

EMI-Manhattan
1370 Ave. of the Americas
New York, NY 10019

Enigma
1750 E. Holly Ave.
El Segundo, CA 90245

Epic/Portrait/CBS Associated
51 W. 52nd St.
New York, NY 10019
Also:
1801 Century Park W.
Los Angeles, CA 90067

34 Music Square E.
Nashville, TN 37203

Fantasy
Tenth & Parker Sts.
Berkeley, CA 94710

Flying Fish
1304 W. Schubert Ave.
Chicago, IL 60614

Folkways
632 Broadway
New York, NY 10012

GRP
555 W. 57th St. (#1228)
New York, NY 10019

Geffen
9130 Sunset Blvd.
Los Angeles, CA 90069
Also:
75 Rockefeller Plaza
New York, NY 10019

I.R.S.
100 Universal City Plaza
(Bldg. 422)
Universal City, CA 91608
Also:
1755 Broadway
New York, NY 10019

Island
14 E. 4th St. (4th Floor)
New York, NY 10012
Also:
6525 Sunset Blvd.
(2nd Floor)
Los Angeles, CA 90028

Jem
3619 Kennedy Rd.
South Plainfield, NJ 07080
Also:
18629 Topham St.
Reseda, CA 91335

JiveZomba House
1348 Lexington Ave.
New York, NY 10128

Kicking Mule
P.O. Box 158
Alderpoint, CA 95411

K-Tel
15535 Medina Rd.
Plymouth, MN 55447

London
c/o MCA Records
70 Universal City Plaza
Universal City, CA 91608
Also:
P.O. Box 2LB 15
St. George St.
London W1A 2LB, England

MCA
70 Universal City Plaza
Universal City, CA 91608
Also:
1755 Broadway
New York, NY 10019

1514 South St.
Nashville, TN 37212

MTM
21 Music Square E.
Nashville, TN 37203

Metal Blade
18653 Ventura Blvd. (#311)
Tarzana, CA 91356

Motown
6255 Sunset Blvd.
Los Angeles, CA 90028
Also:
157 W. 57th St. (#1400)
New York, NY 10019

Nettwerk
1755 Robson St.
Vancouver, BC V6G 1C9, Canada

Nonesuch
75 Rockefeller Plaza
New York, NY 10019

Olivia
4400 Market St.
Oakland, CA 94608

Pablo
451 N. Canon Dr.
Beverly Hills, CA 90201

Pasha
5615 Melrose Ave.
Los Angeles, CA 90038

Passport
3619E Kennedy Rd.
South Plainfield, NJ 07080

Philadelphia International
309 S. Broad St.
Philadelphia, PA 19017

Planet
5505 Melrose Ave.
Los Angeles, CA 90038

Polygram
810 Seventh Ave.
New York, NY 10019
Also:
3800 Alameda Ave. (#1500)
Burbank, CA 91505

10 Music Square S.
Nashville, TN 37203

Private Music
220 E. 23rd St.
New York, NY 10010

Profile
740 Broadway
New York, NY 10003

Qwest
3300 Warner Blvd.
Burbank, CA 91510

RCA
1133 Ave. of the Americas
New York, NY 10036
Also:
6363 Sunset Blvd.
Los Angeles, CA 90028

30 Music Square W.
Nashville, TN 37203

Relativity/Combat
187-07 Henderson Ave.
Hollis, NY 11423

Reprise
3300 Warner Blvd.
Burbank, CA 91510
Also:
75 Rockefeller Plaza (20th Floor)
New York, NY 10019

Rhino
2225 Colorado Ave.
Santa Monica, CA 90404

Rooster Blues
102 S. Lemar Blvd.
Oxford, MS 38655

Rounder
1 Camp St.
Cambridge, MA 02140

Scotti Brothers
2114 Pico Blvd.
Santa Monica, CA 90405

Shanachie
Dalebrook Park
Hohokus, NJ 19144

Sire
75 Rockefeller Plaza
New York, NY 10019

Slash
P.O. Box 48888
Los Angeles, CA 90048

Solar
1635 N. Cahuenga Blvd.
Los Angeles, CA 90028

Tommy Boy
1747 First Ave.
New York, NY 10128

Virgin
Kensall House
533/579 Harrow Rd.
London W10 4RH, England
Also:
9247 Alden Dr.
Beverly Hills, CA 90210

30 W. 23rd St. (11th Floor)
New York, NY 10010

Warner Bros.
3300 Warner Blvd.
Burbank, CA 91510
Also:
75 Rockefeller Plaza (20th Floor)
New York, NY 10019

1815 Division St.
Nashville, TN 37212

Windham Hill
247 High St.
Palo Alto, CA 94305

Word
P.O. Box 1790
Waco, TX 76796
Also:
Northbridge Rd.
Berkhamster, Hertfordshire, England

MUSIC BUSINESS GLOSSARY

A&R Director. Record company executive in charge of the Artists and Repertoire Department who deals with new artists and songs, and oversees coordinating the best material with a particular artist.

A/C. Adult contemporary.

ACM. Academy of Country Music.

Advance. Money paid to the songwriter or recording artist before regular royalty payments begin. Sometimes called ""upfront" money, advances are deducted from royalties.

AFM. American Federation of Musicians. A union for musicians and arrangers.

AFTRA. American Federation of Television and Radio Artists.

AIMP. Association of Independent Music Publishers.

Airplay. The radio broadcast of a recording.

Aor. Album-oriented rock.

Arrangement. Adapting a composition for a performance or recording, with consideration for the melody, harmony, instrumentation, tempo, style, etc.

ASCAP. American Society of Composers, Authors, and Publishers. A performing rights organization.

A-side. Side one of a single, promoted by the record company to become a hit.

Assignment. Transfer of rights to a song from writer to publisher.

Audiovisual. Presentations using audio backup for visual material.

Bed. Prerecorded music used as background material in commercials.

Beta. <1/2> inch videocassette format.

BMA. Black Music Association.

BMI. Broadcast Music, Inc. A performing rights organization.

B-side. Side two, or flip side, of a single promoted by a record company. Sometimes the B-side contains the same song as the A-side so there will be no confusion as to which song should receive airplay.

Booking Agent. Solicits work and schedules performances for entertainers.

Business Manager. Person who handles financial aspects of artistic careers.

B/W. Backed with.

C&W. Country and Western.

CAPAC. Composers, Authors, and Publishers of Canada Ltd.

CARAS. Canadian Academy of Recording Arts and Sciences.

Catalog. The collected songs of one writer, or songs handled by one publisher.

CD. Compact Disc.

Chart. The written arrangement of a song.

Charts. Weekly trade magazines' lists of the bestselling records.

CHR. Contemporary Hit Radio.

CIRPA. Canadian Independent Record Producers Association.

CMRRA. Canadian Musical Reproduction Rights Association.

CMA. Country Music Association.

CMPA. Church Music Publishers Association.

Collaborator. Person who works with another in a creative situation.

Compact Disc. A small disc (about 4.7 inches in diameter) that is read by a laser beam in a CD player. On the disc, digitized music is stored as microscopic pits in an aluminum base.

Co-publish. Two or more parties own publishing rights to the same song.

Copyright. Legal protection given authors and composers for original work.

Cover Record. A new version of a previously recorded song.

CPM. Conference of Personal Managers.

CRIA. Canadian Recording Industry Association.

Crossover. A song that becomes popular in two or more musical styles (e.g., country and pop).

Cut. Any finished recording; a selection from an LP; or to record.

Demo. A recording of a song submitted as a demonstration of a writer's or artist's skills.

Disc. A record.

Distributor. Sole marketing agent of a record in a particular area.

Donut. Jingle with singing at the beginning and end and only instrumental background in the middle.

Engineer. A specially trained individual who operates all studio recording equipment.

Ep. Extended play record (usually 12 inch) containing more selections than a standard single, but fewer than standard LP.

Evergreen. Any song that remains popular year after year.

Exploit. To seek legitimate uses of a song for income.

Folio. A softcover collection of printed music prepared for sale.

GMA. Gospel Music Association.

Harry Fox Agency. Organization that collects mechanical royalties.

Hit. A song or record that achieves Top 40 status.

Hook. A memorable "catch" phrase or melody line which is repeated in a song.

IMU. International Music Union.

ips. Inches per second. A speed designation for tape recording.

IRC. International Reply Coupon, available at most post offices and necessary for the return of materials sent out of the country.

Jingle. Usually a short verse set to music, designed as a commercial message.

Label. Record company, or the "brand" name of the record it produces.

LASS. Los Angeles Songwriters Showcase.

Lead Sheet. Written version (melody, chord symbols and lyrics) of a song.

Leader. Plastic (non-recordable) section of a tape at the beginning and between songs for ease in selection.

Lp. Designation for long-playing record played at 33 1/3 rpm or a cassette containing the same material as its album counterpart.

Lyric Sheet. A typed or written copy of a song's lyrics.

Market. A potential song or music buyer; also a demographic division of the record-buying public.

Master. Edited and mixed tape used in the production of records; a very high-quality recording; the best or original copy of a recording from which copies are made.

Mechanical Right. The right to profit from the physical reproduction of a song.

Mechanical Royalty. Money earned from record and tape sales.

MIEA. Music Industry Educators' Association.

Mix. To blend a multi-track recording into the desired balance of sound.

Mor. Middle of the road.

MS. Manuscript.

Music Jobber. A wholesale distributor of printed music.

Music Publisher. A company that evaluates songs for commercial potential, finds artists to record them, finds other uses such as TV or film for the songs, collects income generated by the songs, and protects copyrights from infringement.

NAIRD. National Association of Independent Record Distributors.

NARAS. National Academy of Recording Arts and Sciences.

NARM. National Association of Record Merchandisers.

NAS. National Academy of Songwriters, formerly Songwriters Resources and Services (SRS).

Needle-Drop. Use of a prerecorded cut from a stock house in an audiovisual soundtrack.

NMPA. National Music Publishers Association.

NSAI. Nashville Songwriters Association International.

One-Stop. A wholesale distributor of records (and sometimes videocassettes, blank tapes, and record accessories), representing several manufacturers to record stores, retailers, and jukebox operators.

Payola. Dishonest payment to a broadcaster in exchange for airplay.

Performing Rights. A specific copyright granted by U.S. copyright law to protect a composition from being publicly performed without the owner's permission.

Performing Rights Organization. An organization that collects income from the public performance of songs written by its members, and proportionally distributes this income to the individual copyright holder based on the number of performances of each song.

Personal Manager. A person who represents artists, in numerous and varying ways, to develop and enhance their careers. Personal managers may negotiate contracts, hire and dismiss other agencies and personnel relating to the artist's career, screen offers and consult with prospective employers, review possible material, help with artist promotion, and perform miscellaneous services.

Piracy. The unauthorized reproduction and sale of printed or recorded music.

Pitch. To attempt to sell a song by audition; the sales talk.

Playlist. List of songs that a radio station will play.

Plug. A favorable mention, broadcast, or performance of a song; to pitch a song.

Points. A negotiable percentage paid to producers and artists for records sold.

Press. To manufacture a record.

PROCAN. Performing Rights Organization of Canada Ltd.

Producer. Person who supervises every aspect of recording a song.

Product. Records, CD's, and tapes for sale.

Production Company. Company that specializes in producing jingle packages for advertising agencies. May also refer to companies that specialize in audiovisual programs.

Professional Manager. Member of a music publisher's staff who screens submitted material and tries to get the company's catalog of songs recorded.

Program Director. Radio station employee who screens records and develops a playlist of songs that the station will broadcast.

PRS. Performing Rights Society of England.

PSA. Public Service Announcement; a free broadcast "advertisement" for a non-profit service organization.

Public Domain. Any composition with an expired, lapsed, or invalid copyright.

Publish. To reproduce music in a saleable form and distribute to the public by sale or other transfer (e.g. rent, lease, or lend) of ownership.

Purchase License. Fee paid for music used from a stock music library.

Query. A letter of inquiry to a potential song buyer soliciting his interest.

R&B. Rhythm and Blues.

Rack Jobber. A wholesaler of records, tapes, and accessories to retailers and mass-merchandisers not primarily in the record business (e.g. department stores).

Rate. The percentage of royalty as specified by contract.

Release. Any record issued by a record company.

Residuals. In advertising or television, payments to singers and musicians for subsequent use of music.

Rhythm Machine. An electronic device that provides various tempos for use as background rhythm for other instruments or vocalists.

RIAA. Recording Industry Association of America.

Royalty. Percentage of money earned from the sale of records or use of a song.

SAE. Self-addressed envelope (with no postage attached).

SASE. Self-addressed, stamped envelope.

Scratch Track. Rough working tape demonstrating an idea for a commercial.

Self-Contained. A band or recording act that writes all their own material.

SESAC. A performing rights organization.

SFX. Sound effects.

Shop. To pitch songs to a number of companies or publishers.

Showcase. A presentation of new artists or songs.

Single. 45 rpm record with only one song per side. A 12 inch single refers to a long version of a song on a 12 inch disc, usually used for dance music.

Solicited. Songs or materials that have been requested.

Song Shark. Person who deals with songwriters deceptively for his own profit.

The Songwriters Guild of America. Organization for songwriters, formerly called AGAC.

Soundtrack. The audio portion, including music and narration, of a film, videotape, or audiovisual program.

Split Publishing. To divide publishing rights between two or more publishers.

Staff Writer. A salaried songwriter who writes exclusively for one publishing firm.

Standard. A song popular year after year; an evergreen.

Statutory Royalty Rate. The minimum payment for mechanical rights guaranteed by law that a record company must pay the songwriter and his publisher for each record or tape sold.

Stiff. The first recording of a song that fails commercially.

Subpublishing. Certain rights granted by a U.S. publisher to a foreign publisher in exchange for promoting the U.S. catalog in his territory.

Sweeten. To add new parts to existing recorded tracks to enhance the sound of a master recording.

Synchronization. Technique of timing a musical soundtrack to action on film or video.

Synchronization Rights. Rights to use a composition in time-relation to action on film or video.

Take. Either an attempt to record a vocal or instrumental part, or an acceptable recording of a performance.

Track. Divisions of a recording tape (e.g., 24-track tape) that can be individually recorded in the studio, then mixed into a finished master.

Trades. Publications that cover the music industry.

U/C. Urban Contemporary.

U-Matic. <3/4> inch professional videocassette format.

Unsolicited. Songs or materials that were not requested and are not expected.

Veejay. Music-video program host.

VHS. <1/2> inch videocassette format.

Videocassette. Tape manufactured for video cassette recorder (VCR) that records and reproduces audiovisual programs.

Work. To pitch or shop a song.

BIRTHDAY LIST

Abdul, Paula	6/18/62	Connick, Harry Jr.	9/11/67
Alpert, Herb	3/31	Cooper, Alice	2/4/49
Andrews, Julie	10/1/35	Crosby, David	8/14/41
Anka, Paul	7/30	Cyrus, Billy Ray	8/25/61
Ann-Margret	4/28/41	Daltry, Roger	3/1/45
Atkins, Chet	6/21/24	Darren, James	6/9/36
Avalon, Frankie	9/18/39	Denver, John	12/31/43
Baez, Joan	1/9/41	Diamond, Neil	1/24/41
Belafonte, Harry	3/1/27	Dolenz, Micky	3/19/45
Bennett, Tony	8/3	Domino, Fats	2/26/28
Berry, Chuck	10/18/26	Dylan, Bob	5/24/41
Blades, Ruben	7/16/48	Easton, Sheena	4/27/59
Bolton, Michael	2/26	Estefan, Gloria	9/1/57
BonJovi, Jon	5/9	Evans, Dale	10/31/12
Boone, Pat	6/1/34	Feinstein, Michael	9/7/56
Bowie, David	1/8/48	Feliciano, Jose	9/10/45
Brown, James	5/3/28	Fitzgerald, Ella	4/24/18
Campbell, Glen	4/22/36	Franklin, Aretha	3/25/42
Carey, Mariah	3/26	Harrison, George	2/25/43
Carr, Vikki	7/19/41	Gabriel, Peter	2/13/50
Cash, Johnny	2/16/32	Garcia, Jerry	8/1/42
Cash, June Carter	6/22/29	Garfunkel, Art	11/5/41
Cassidy, David	4/12/50	Garrett, Leif	11/6/61
Cassidy, Shaun	9/27/48	Gatlin, Larry	5/2/48
Charles, Ray	9/23/32	Gibb, Barry	9/1
Cher	5/20/46	Gibson, Debbie	8/21/70
Clapton, Eric	3/30/45	Gore, Leslie	5/1
Clark, Dick	11/30/29	Grant, Amy	11/25/60
Clark, Roy	8/16	Grey, Joel	4/11/32
Cocker, Joe	5/20/42	Griffin, Merv	7/6/25
Cole, Natalie	2/8	Guthrie, Arlo	7/10/47
Collins, Phil	1/30	Hall, Daryl	10/11/49
Como, Perry	5/18	Hamlisch, Marvin	6/21/44

Harrison, George	2/24	Mellencamp, John Cougar	10/7/51
Henderson, Florence	2/14	Michael, George	6/25/63
Ho, Don	9/13/30	Midler, Bette	12/1/45
Horne, Lena	6/30/17	Minnelli, Liza	3/12/46
Humperdinck, Engelbert	5/2/36	Moore, Melba	10/27/45
Ice-T	2/14	Nabors, John	6/11/33
Idol, Billy	11/30/55	Nelson, Guunar & Mathew	9/20/67
Iglesias, Julio	9/23/43	Nelson, Willie	4/30/33
Ives, Burl	6/14/09	Nesmith, Michael	12/30/44
Jackson, Janet	5/16/66	Newley, Anthony	9/21/31
Jackson, Michael	8/29/58	Newton, Wayne	4/3/42
Jagger, Mick	7/26/44	Newton-John, Olivia	9/26/47
Joel, Billy	5/9/49	Nicks, Stevie	5/26/48
John, Elton	3/25/47	O'Connor, Sinead	12/8/66
Jones, Davey	12/30/45	Oates, John	4/7/49
Jones, Shirley	3/31	Ono, Yoko	2/18/33
Jones, Quincy	3/14/33	Osborne, Ozzy	12/3/48
Jones, Tom	6/7/40	Oslin, K.T.	5/15
Khan, Chaka	3/23/53	Osmond, Donny	12/9/57
King, B.B.	10/16/25	Palmer, Robert	1/19
King, Carole	2/9/42	Parton, Dolly	1/3/46
Knight, Gladys	5/28/44	Pavarotti, Luciano	10/12/35
Kotero, Appolonia	8/2/59	Pearl, Minnie	10/25
Kristofferson, Kris	6/22/36	Pendergrass, Teddy	3/26
Lennox, Annie	12/25	Phillips, Chynna	2/12
Levine, Michael	4/17/54	Plant, Robert	8/20/48
Lewis, Huey	7/5/50	Previn, Andre	4/6/29
Lewis, Jerry Lee	9/29/35	Prince	6/7/58
Little Richard	12/5/31	Raitt, Bonnie	11/8/49
LL Cool J	1/14	Reddy, Helen	10/25/41
Loggins, Kenny	1/7	Richie, Lionel	6/20/49
Lynn, Loretta	4/14	Robinson, Smokey	2/19/40
Ma, Yo Yo	10/7/55	Rogers, Kenny	8/21/41
Madonna	8/16/58	Rogers, Roy	11/15/12
Mangione, Chuck	11/29/40	Ross, Diana	3/26/44
Mandrell, Barbara	12/25	Santana, Carlos	7/20/47
Mancini, Henry	4/16	Shaw, Artie	5/23
Manilow, Barry	6/17	Shore, Dinah	3/1/17
Marsalis, Branford	8/26/60	Slick, Grace	10/30/39
Martin, Dean	6/18/17	Simon, Carly	6/25/45
Mathis, Johnny	9/10/35	Simon, Paul	10/13/41
Mattea, Kathy	6/21	Sinatra, Frank	12/12/15
McCartney, Paul	6/18/42	Smith, Will	9/25/68
McFerrin, Bobby	3/11/50	Smothers, Dick	11/20/39
McKuen, Rod	4/29/33	Smothers, Tommy	2/2/37

Spector, Phil	12/26/36	Valli, Frankie	5/3
Springfield, Rick	8/23/49	Vanilla Ice	10/31/68
Springsteen, Bruce	9/23/49	Vinton, Bobby	4/16/41
Starr, Ringo	7/7/40	Waits, Tom	12/7/48
Stern, Isaac	7/21/20	Warwick, Dionne	12/12/41
Stewart, Rod	1/10/45	Watley, Jody	1/30
Sting	10/2/51	Williams, Andy	12/3
Streisand, Barbra	4/24/42	Williams, Paul	9/19/40
Taylor, James	3/12	Williams, Vanessa	3/18/63
Tork, Peter	2/13/42	Wilson, Brian	6/20/42
Townshend, Peter	5/19/45	Wilson, Carnie	4/29
Tillis, Mel	8/8	Wilson, Wendy	10/16/69
Travis, Randy	5/4/59	Wonder, Stevie	5/3/50
Tucker, Tanya	10/10	Wynette, Tammy	5/5
Turner, Tina	11/26/39	Young, Neil	11/12/46